# Welfare for the Unemployed in Britain and Germany

For Toby

# Welfare for the Unemployed in Britain and Germany

Who Benefits?

Frances McGinnity

*Max Planck Institute for Human Development, Berlin, Germany*

**Edward Elgar**
Cheltenham, UK • Northampton, MA, USA

Published by
Edward Elgar Publishing Limited
Glensanda House
Montpellier Parade
Cheltenham
Glos GL50 1UA
UK

Edward Elgar Publishing, Inc.
136 West Street
Suite 202
Northampton
Massachusetts 01060
USA

A catalogue record for this book
is available from the British Library

**Library of Congress Cataloguing in Publication Data**
McGinnity, Frances.
    Welfare for the unemployed in Britain and Germany : who benefits / Frances McGinnity
        p.  cm.
    Based on the author's thesis (doctoral)—Oxford University, 2001.
    Includes bibliographical references and index.
    1. Insurance, Unemployment—Great Britain. 2. Insurance, Unemployment—Germany. 3. Unemployed—Services for—Great Britain. 4. Unemployed—Services for—Germany. 5. Public welfare—Great Britain. 6. Public welfare—Germany. I. Title.

HD7096.G7M33 2004
362.85'82'0941—dc22

                                                                    2003064853

ISBN 1 84376 220 X

Typeset by Manton Typesetters, Louth, Lincolnshire, UK.
Printed and bound in Great Britain by MPG Books Ltd, Bodmin, Cornwall.

# Contents

# Figures

# Tables

# Preface and acknowledgements

This book, a comparison of welfare for the unemployed and its effects on individuals, is based on my doctoral thesis, submitted to Oxford University in early 2001. The analyses in it run until the mid-1990s, and to a large extent I have neither updated the empirical analyses nor added developments in the literature since then, as doing one would have required the other, and doing both would have resulted in a different book.

In the course of writing it I have benefited from the support of a great many people, and it gives me great pleasure to have the opportunity to thank them. In Oxford I would first and foremost like to thank Duncan Gallie, my supervisor, whose encouragement, support and comments have been invaluable. Thanks too to Sheila Jacobs for her good-humoured assistance at many stages, and to Richard Layte, Brendan Halpin and Martin Range for their help with programming. Other people have made a contribution by reading drafts and sharing ideas, including Tony Atkinson, Susanne Choi, Martin Evans, David Firth, Markus Gangl, Gordon Marshall, Helen Russell and Jo Webb. Hans-Peter Blossfeld and Michael Noble gave valuable and careful feedback on the final version of the thesis.

I would like to thank the Economic and Social Research Council (ESRC) for funding my doctoral thesis for three years, and the Data Archive in Essex and the German Institute for Economic Research for permission to use their data.[1] Indeed, the support staff of the German Socio-economic Panel (GSOEP) at the Deutsches Institut für Wirtschaftsforschung in Berlin and of the British Household Panel Survey (BHPS) in Essex responded to my many enquiries with speed and succinctness. I suspect their combined contribution to longitudinal research in both these countries is undervalued.

Having written the doctorate in Britain, the final stages of this book were carried out while I was a post-doctoral fellow at the Max Planck Institute for Human Development, Berlin. I am grateful to Karl-Ulrich Mayer and my colleagues for their intellectual stimulation and for their welcome to me here in Berlin. I would especially like to thank Sven Schubert for his research assistance. I also acknowledge the assistance of my editorial team at Edward Elgar.

On a more personal note, I would like to thank the McGinnity family in Fermanagh, Belfast, Dublin and Mexico for their patient enquiries and long-distance support. My mother Annie and sisters Maria, Colette and Edel deserve a special mention, their phone calls supported me, their example inspires me. Finally I would like to thank Toby Wolfe who, since beginning work on this book, I have met and married. Toby has been of great help in editing the final manuscript, but his help extended much further than this. I would like to thank him for his intellectual, emotional and practical support, his wisdom, his calm, his laughter and his love. It is with the greatest of pleasure that I dedicate this book to him.

Berlin, Summer 2003

## NOTE

1. The data made available through the UK Data Archive was originally collected by the ESRC Research Centre on Micro-social Change at the University of Essex, now incorporated within the Institute for Social and Economic Research. Neither the original collectors of the data nor the Archive bear any responsibility for the analyses or interpretations presented here.

# 1.   Introduction

> Unemployment is probably the most widely feared phenomenon of our time.
> (OECD 1994)

Mass unemployment, the Achilles heel of late capitalism, has become a persistent problem for West European governments in recent decades, as demonstrated by the OECD *Jobs Study* quote. Indeed, unemployment in European Union (EU) countries has risen dramatically since the first oil crisis, from 2.7 per cent in 1973 to 9.2 per cent in 1999 (OECD 1997c, 2000).[1] Concomitant with this rise in unemployment has been increasing concern with social exclusion. The term social exclusion originated in France (Paugam 1996) and has grown in importance to be a key concern in the EU. It embodies the notion of a 'concentration of disadvantage' – of unemployment and poverty, but also of accompanying deficiencies in, for instance, housing and education. In the latter half of the 1990s, it became an important theme of social policy in Britain, Germany and other EU countries (e.g. Room 1995; Kronauer 1998; Littlewood et al. 1999; Büchel et al. 2000). A key component of it is the possibility that a group like the long-term unemployed may become progressively detached from society.[2]

West European welfare states, seen as a spectacular achievement by many, seemed somehow more suited to confronting the problems of the 1950s and 1960s. Labour markets and family structures have changed substantially since then, and some now question the efficacy and appropriateness of welfare states that were built for societies as they were 30 years ago. 'History matters' is the contemporary wisdom, and today's welfare states are limited by the political decisions and institutions of the past. Different countries responded in different ways to the rise of unemployment, resulting in very different policy configurations. This book addresses some of the core policy debates on welfare for the unemployed by comparing two contrasting welfare states and examining how their different approaches to welfare affect the experience of unemployment for individuals and its contribution to social exclusion.

The unemployed have been contentious from the start. From the very beginning of state welfare provision there has been controversy as to whether unemployment is a 'social risk' that should be covered. There has long been agreement that sickness, old age and industrial accidents are legitimate risks for the state to address. The controversy has surrounded unemployment. Those on the right of the political spectrum have tended to support low payments for a very short period in order to overcome the disincentive effects of unemployment benefit. Those on the left have supported higher, longer-lasting payments, out of concern for material deprivation and the importance of maintaining an income whilst unemployed.

Britain and Germany adopted fundamentally different approaches to welfare for the unemployed. Broadly speaking the German welfare state views unemployment as a risk that individuals insure themselves against, with the state administering the insurance and treating the unemployed according to their previous employment record. In Britain, by contrast, the principle of poverty alleviation provides the basis for compensating the unemployed. Benefits for the unemployed are primarily means-tested in Britain, and these are not based on contributions. What are the consequences of this major difference in welfare provision for the lives of unemployed people? This thesis addresses these issues by combining an in-depth analysis of unemployment policies, with a detailed statistical analysis of individual outcomes.

To answer this question, this book examines the experiences of unemployed individuals, using longitudinal data from large, representative panel surveys. The introduction of a time dimension to the comparative analysis of unemployment and welfare states makes it possible to overcome some of the problems of cross-sectional analysis. As Ralf Dahrendorf puts it in his foreword to *Time and Poverty in Western Welfare States*: 'Arguably the most exciting dimension of social analysis is time. Yet it has long been neglected by mainstream sociology' (Leisering and Leibfried 1999). For example, by considering inflows and outflows from unemployment, the longitudinal approach allows us to consider unemployment as a process rather than a state: by comparing income before and after becoming unemployed, we can overcome some of the difficulties of establishing the direction of causality.

The aim of this chapter is to outline our approach to comparing unemployment and to set it in the context of previous approaches. Section 1.1 discusses the comparative perspective and how we apply it to our substantive concerns. It also assesses the advantages of a longitudinal approach for social research. Section 1.2 reviews different theoretical approaches to comparing welfare for the unemployed, stressing the advantages of a focus on consequences for the unemployed themselves. Section 1.3 discusses in more depth the choice of countries, Britain and Germany.[3] Section 1.4 presents our perspective on the family and on the relationship between individuals, the family and unemployment. Section 1.5 discusses the outcome measures we use to compare unemployment in Britain and Germany. Finally, Section 1.6 describes the outline of the book.

## 1.1 THE COMPARATIVE AND LONGITUDINAL PERSPECTIVE

In this section we discuss alternative approaches to comparative research, and we discuss the advantages of the comparative, longitudinal strategy adopted.

Comparative research can force us to be more rigorous in our argumentation, as our concepts and conclusions are required to cross national boundaries; we may thus avoid the temptation to claim that findings for one country are universal truths. There are, however, different traditions in social science as to how cross-national research should be carried out. As Erikson and Goldthorpe (1993) put it, following Ragin (1987), on the one hand there are 'qualitative' comparativists, who treat societies holistically, often working from historical or anthropological sources, emphasising the specificity of the national situation. On the other hand there are 'quantitative' researchers, who may take the nation not as the context of analysis, but rather as the unit of analysis. In the latter approach the ultimate aim is often to 'replace the names of countries with the names of variables' (Przeworski and Teune 1970); differences between countries are analysed using the same multivariate techniques as those used to investigate differences between individuals.[4]

Erikson and Goldthorpe themselves, in their study of class mobility in industrial societies, adopt a mixed strategy. They reject the idea that concepts cannot be compared across countries, and compare mobility rates, patterns and trends across nations. In this respect they follow a more quantitative approach. However, they refrain from ignoring the national context altogether, and often in their explanation of quantitative results rely on analyses of a more 'internal' and historical kind.

The approach adopted in this book follows a similarly 'mixed' strategy – a combination of a small-N case study approach with detailed multivariate analysis of individuals within countries. There is extensive comparison of the level, composition and duration of unemployment in Britain and Germany, all the time striving to maintain the highest level of comparability and assuming that unemployment is fundamentally comparable across countries. However, the details of the national context, such as differences in welfare policy, labour market policy and education systems, are brought into explanations. As a reflection of this strategy, we never put the two countries in the same multivariate model. We most often include the same variables to account for differences between individuals within countries, and try to interpret their effects in their national context. This approach does not imply that trends may not be similar in the two countries, but it does mean that the similarity is something we discover rather than assume. In this way, the names of the countries do not disappear from the narrative – the 'cases' and their uniqueness are preserved.

The overall approach of this book is to begin with similarities and differences in principles at the macro-level, develop hypotheses about their effects, test these hypotheses using data on individuals, and then generalise the results to describe patterns and results at the 'macro-' (in this case national) level. We examine the differences in welfare state provision primarily by their effects as experienced by individuals – 'individual outcomes'. By focusing on individual outcomes we can also see how the state interacts with the market and the family at the micro-level. As our aim is to conduct detailed analysis at an individual level, we limit the number of countries in the analysis. The small number of units lets us examine national patterns in detail – analysing a large number of countries risks superficiality and tends to constrain the elements of variation to a small number of variables.

We argue that longitudinal data is superior to cross-sectional data for the analysis of social processes. As Coleman (1990) claims, if individuals relate causes and effects through their actions, then research into social processes is best carried out using longitudinal individual data. Only with this kind of data can one trace the course of action of each individual over time. Longitudinal data puts us in a stronger position to make inferences about causality, and the identification of causal mechanisms has been one of the classic concerns of sociology. As Davies (1994) argues, there are frequently doubts about the direction of causality in social research, and in these cases cross-sectional data is unable to resolve the ambiguity in correlations. For example, there is strong cross-sectional evidence that the unemployed have poorer physical health than those in employment, but we do not know if this is because ill health leads to unemployment or because unemployment leads to ill health. Similarly, cross-sectional analysis may reveal an association between poverty and unemployment. But how do we know whether it is that unemployment leads to poverty or that poorer people are more likely to become unemployed? To overcome uncertainty in such cases we need information about the health and wealth of individuals both *before and after* they become unemployed. Indeed Lieberson (1985) makes the general point that the normal control approaches in cross-sectional research will rarely be successful in isolating the influence of some specific causal force.

In addition there is the problem that few social scientists are in a position to perform control experiments. We rely on observational data, and thus the burden of explanation rests on the statistical methods used. Davies warns us that one of the dangers of using repeated cross-sectional analysis to look at change is the tendency to overestimate the effect of explanatory variables, such as policies. If we omit a relevant variable, we may overestimate the effect of other variables. What is more, cross-sectional analysis 'cannot characterize the inertial characteristics of behaviour' (1994, p. 32). Put simply, it cannot account adequately for the effect of previous behaviour on current behaviour. For example, the employment status of a woman in any given month partly depends on her status the previous month, not just on current influences such as the availability of childcare. Thus we need to consider the history of individuals when interpreting their current situation. The strength of longitudinal data analysis is that inferences are based not only on variation *between* cases, as in cross-sectional analysis, but also on variation *within* cases.

Another important benefit of longitudinal analysis lies in the issue of duration dependence (Blossfeld and Rohwer 1995). Longitudinal data can tell us much more than cross-sectional analysis about the 'distribution of disadvantage'. A 10 per cent unemployment rate could mean that each individual in the labour force has a 10 per cent chance of being unemployed at any given time, or it could mean that a specific group that makes up 10 per cent of the labour force is permanently unemployed. While the truth is likely to lie somewhere in the middle, the duration of unemployment has important consequences for the distribution of disadvantage and social exclusion, and hence for social policy.

This is not to say that longitudinal data is a panacea, nor that longitudinal data does not have its own problems. And indeed no amount of sophisticated data will inform us about causation if we do not have theoretical predictions to test. Nor do we wish to argue that cross-sectional data is not informative: for many problems this approach is adequate – indeed we use cross-sectional analysis in one section of our analysis. Nevertheless some of the problems of cross-sectional data can be overcome using longitudinal data.

Comparing Britain and Germany allows us to address some of our key questions from a longitudinal perspective. The two cases chosen are similar enough to be comparable (in terms of the size of their economy and labour force, the level of industrial development, and participation in education) but have policies different enough – particularly in respect of the unemployed – to shed light on how social policies affect individuals. Though there are a growing number of longitudinal datasets in Europe and the US, the choice is limited.[5] Britain and Germany are two countries with panel datasets excellently suited to comparing unemployment from a longitudinal perspective: the British Household Panel Survey (BHPS) and the German Socio-economic Panel (GSOEP). The surveys have a similar focus on socio-economic issues such as labour force status and income. The two datasets also provide detailed information on individuals' work histories, information excellently suited to the analysis of labour market transitions. From a methodological perspective, the surveys are carried out in a very similar way and the data is organised using the same principles. Indeed, the BHPS, which began some time after the GSOEP, adopted much of the German methodology in terms of survey design and data structure. Details of the choice and design of the data sources, sampling methods, data collection and topics covered are provided in the final Appendix, which also discusses the representativeness of the surveys, panel attrition and weighting.

## 1.2   TYPOLOGIES OF WELFARE FOR THE UNEMPLOYED

In this section we review different approaches to comparing welfare for the unemployed from a cross-national perspective. Although some of these approaches take the form of typologies, it is not the purpose of this book to 'test' typologies of welfare in order to establish which one is superior. Rather, we use the typologies and approaches discussed below to sensitise us to differences between Britain and Germany in overall principles of welfare for the unemployed. The strength of typologies for comparative analysis lies in isolating principles, helping us to understand the empirical pattern of welfare provision. Using these theoretical approaches, we can abstract from the complex plethora of policies to generate hypotheses about how differences in state provision affect 'outcomes' for the unemployed. How we address these hypotheses is the subject of Section 1.5.

The weakness of typologies is that the abstraction required to construct them creates 'ideal types', which often do not reflect the complexity of institutional arrangements in different countries. As Daly puts it: 'Typologizing has high costs, forcing one to forfeit especially the richness and complexity of welfare state provision within and across national contexts' (2000, p. 52). It is in the nature of typologies that they concentrate on a limited number of principles, or variables. In so doing some variation is missed. This omission gives rise to another typology, which stresses variation on another dimension, and so the process continues. The very fact that we discuss a number of typologies of welfare states below is evidence of this. None of the approaches may be wrong – they just emphasise different facets of variation. Our approach is to combine insights from a variety of typologies to inform the case study analysis. In this way we can capitalise on the strengths of typologising, while avoiding some of its weaknesses.

The approaches presented in this section focus on welfare provision by the state, though it is a central concern of this book to situate state provision in the context of the market and the family. Approaches to the family are discussed in Section 1.4, while the role of the market, and market differences, are discussed in Chapter 2.

We begin our review of comparative approaches to welfare states by summarising two principles, which, we argue, these approaches share and that form core assumptions of this book. In Section 1.2.1 we continue our review by introducing a major work in the field of comparative welfare states, Esping-Andersen's *The Three Worlds of Welfare Capitalism* (1990), and discuss how Britain and Germany fit into its typology. We then discuss some important criticisms of this work. The feminist critique (Section 1.2.2) is probably the most radical. Another important critique for us is that of Gallie and Paugam (2000) (Section 1.2.3), who reject Esping-Andersen's 'integrated perspective' in favour of a specific focus on welfare for the unemployed. We continue by considering two further approaches, which, while they do not address Esping-Andersen or his critics, also divide state treatment of the unemployed into 'types'. Schmid and Reissert (1996) (Section 1.2.4) make an important contribution for this book in pitting insurance-based against means-tested welfare systems. Finally, we draw on the field of economics in presenting an approach that sees rigidity and flexibility as crucial concepts in comparing unemployment and welfare states (Section 1.2.5). As we present each of the approaches below, we note how in each case Britain and Germany fall into different categories and because of this are two countries excellently suited to the purpose of exploring the various approaches. This point is discussed in more depth in Section 1.3, where we consider the choice of countries.

The first principle that these approaches all share, we argue, is that institutions matter. This principle is an important thread running through the book and stands in contrast to earlier approaches to welfare states, both the industrialisation approach (Kerr et al. 1960; Wilensky and Lebeaux 1965) and the Marxist tradition (O'Connor 1973; Ginsburg 1979). While industrialisation and Marxist models differ radically in their explanations of welfare states, they both assume that welfare states are fundamentally similar across countries (van Kersbergen 1995). The approaches described below in general reject this notion of convergence. In contrast, their perspective is that welfare state institutions – in particular those dealing with the unemployed – differ fundamentally between countries.

A second central principle is that welfare states 'stratify outcomes'; while the institutions of the welfare state are shaped by society, politics and history, they themselves have a direct role to play in determining 'outcomes'.[6] This principle implies that policies concerning the unemployed do affect the situation of individual unemployed people. This is not to argue that state policy is the only distributive mechanism in society but rather that state policies play a role, in conjunction with the family and the market.

Combining these two principles we reach the claim that different welfare states stratify outcomes in different ways. These differences in outcomes are the focus of our analysis. Having discussed principles that the different approaches share, we now consider the approaches in more depth.

### 1.2.1    Three Worlds of Welfare Capitalism

A landmark study in the comparison of welfare states was Esping-Andersen's *The Three Worlds of Welfare Capitalism* (1990). Esping-Andersen asks two related questions: what are the causal forces behind the development of welfare states, and can the welfare state transform capitalism? Welfare states are both the independent and dependent variable – they shape and are shaped by society. His focus is on qualitative variation between states – not only in terms of how welfare programmes are organised, but also in terms of their relationships with other institutions (like the market and the family) and political configurations. He argues that welfare states cluster into three, now familiar, types of regime: liberal, conservative and social democratic. The basis for his classification of 18 countries rests on three key concepts: the degree of decommodification, the principle of stratification and the nature of state–market–family relations.

Decommodification is based on Marx's concept of commodification. With the rise of capitalism, labour becomes a commodity, forced to sell itself in the market place. People's right to survive outside the market is at stake (Marx [1864] 1978). As markets become universal and pervasive, the welfare of individuals comes to depend entirely on the cash nexus. Decommodification, in Esping-Andersen's terms, is when the state intervenes in the workings of the market so that 'a person can maintain a livelihood without reliance on the market' (Esping-Andersen 1990, pp. 21–2). For his operationalisation of decommodification, Esping-Andersen looks at 'summary measures' – indices of old-age pensions, sickness benefits and unemployment insurance – in 18 countries.[7] Thus unemployment benefits form one, but not the only one, of his criteria. Indeed, a crucial part of his argument is to treat welfare for the unemployed as governed by the same overall principles as welfare in other domains, such as sickness benefit and pensions.

On Esping-Andersen's criteria, different welfare regimes exhibit different degrees of decommodification. The liberal regime (loosely defined as the Anglo-Saxon nations) is characterised by heavy reliance on means-tested programmes. This type of state pays modest social transfers to low-income groups and encourages private insurance. State regimes are conditional and discretionary, underpinned by the 'Poor Law' philosophy of deserving and undeserving poor. Britain falls into this category.[8] In the conservative-corporatist regimes of continental Europe (excluding the Netherlands) rights are linked to work performance. Benefits are earnings-related and differentiated by class and status. Thus welfare provision maintains class and status differentials, producing a highly stratified system of welfare. Germany is an excellent example of the conservative-corporatist welfare regime. The third type of regime, the social democratic (Scandinavian), is characterised by universal benefits covering the entire population, a weakening of the influence of the market, and a strong commitment to full employment.

According to Esping-Andersen, welfare systems are not only institutions, they are powerful societal mechanisms which shape the future of employment and stratification, and each type of welfare state shapes society quite differently; different welfare states produce different outcomes. Thus we would expect Britain and Germany, falling into two different categories, to produce different outcomes in all domains of welfare provision. Though this idea is developed in his work, he does not subject it to rigorous empirical testing. This weakness is addressed by some of the analysis in this book.

Esping-Andersen's work has been criticised on a range of fronts. Many commentators have argued that various countries are misclassified, including Britain. Others have campaigned for a fourth category (Castles and Mitchell 1993; Ferrera 1996). Perhaps the most far-reaching critique, discussed below, has come from a group of feminists working on welfare states. Partly in response to the feminist critique, more recent work by Esping-Andersen (1999) gives a greater role to the family. A key argument of the book *Social Foundations of Postindustrial Economies* is that the household economy is the most important foundation of post-industrial economies. The result is a revised notion of welfare regimes in which the state, market and family play more equal roles. The question of whether different welfare regimes have created different types of families is not addressed, nor are gender relations more generally. An important point for us here is that Esping-Andersen leaves intact the typology described above. The three welfare regimes remain the liberal, conservative and social democratic, and the position of Britain and Germany in this schema remains unchanged.

### 1.2.2    Comparing Welfare States: a Gender Perspective

The thrust of the gender critique is that Esping-Andersen (1990) does not take sufficient account of how welfare states embody differentiation between men and women. It is not that women are neglected, but class inequalities are prioritised over gender inequalities.

For an approach that sees gender as the core inequality, all three of Esping-Andersen's dimensions are problematic. The decommodification criterion does not properly capture the complex and varied ways in which welfare states relate to women. For example decommodification does not always imply independence for women (Lewis 1992; Orloff 1993; Sainsbury 1994; Ostner and Lewis 1995; Daly 1996). Women may indeed wish to commodify their labour, and the degree of provision of public services can directly and indirectly enable women to participate in the labour market. The second dimension, stratification, sees class as the crucial cleavage and ignores the question of how welfare states contribute to gender inequality. And thirdly, although Esping-Andersen (1990) proposes to consider the state–market–family nexus, in the tradition of mainstream power resource analysis the key relationship that Esping-Andersen considers is between the state and the market, and the family is rendered relatively unimportant in his initial typology (Orloff 1993).

The feminist critique suggests that typologies of welfare states need to be revised or adapted to take into account the relationship between unpaid work, welfare and citizenship, and to incorporate differences into the welfare/work choice (Lewis 1992; Orloff 1993; Lewis and Ostner 1994; O'Connor 1996; Daly 2000).[9] The male breadwinner typology as developed by Lewis and Ostner (1994) and Lewis (1992) is the best known. Lewis and Ostner compare a number of states on the basis of whether they recognise and cater for women solely as wives and mothers or as workers. They derive a three-fold typology of welfare states: strong, moderate or weak breadwinner models. They find Britain, Germany and the Netherlands strongly committed to the breadwinner form, France less so and Sweden and Denmark only weakly so, tending to the dual breadwinner form. In both Britain and Germany then we would expect the welfare system to prioritise the male breadwinner family model.

Daly's (1996) gender typology also focuses on support for the traditional male breadwinner model. Her range of countries is more comprehensive, though she only focuses on cash benefits. In contrast to Lewis and Ostner (1994), Daly argues that the British benefit system less strongly favours the male breadwinner household than continental European systems like Germany, Belgium or France. In this and later work (2000), she argues that social insurance benefits linked to employment, which have a high potential for gender inequality, play much less of a role in Britain than in Germany (Daly 1996, 2000). She categorises Britain as an intermediate 'more-than-one bread-winner' welfare regime, where 'labour market participation for all is encouraged and indeed rendered necessary by low social payments' (Daly 1996, p. 21). In Daly's typology, Germany is an example of a strong breadwinner model.[10]

Examining welfare states from a gender perspective, one might not choose unemployment as the focus of analysis. Lone parents, caring services or even pensions might be seen as more appropriate. Indeed one might argue that the choice of unemployment as a focus is fundamentally gendered; part of the feminist critique of welfare states is that they prioritise the state–market axis, and the question of how the state compensates the individual for labour market failure (unemployment) relates to this axis. To be 'at risk' of unemployment one needs to participate in the labour market. Men and women tend to differ substantially in their labour market participation, and the rate and conditions of that participation vary substantially between countries. For example, in 1997 the labour force participation of women in EU countries ranged from 59.0 per cent in Denmark to 34.8 per cent in Italy (Eurostat 1998).

While unemployment may be a limited lens through which to view gender inequalities in welfare states, at the very least the preceding analysis implies that we should take care in examining gender differentials in state provision for the unemployed. It is particularly important to compare how different patterns of labour market participation affect entitlements to benefits for men and women in different countries.[11] A second implication is that, when examining outcomes for the unemployed, we need to be sensitive to how these outcomes may differ for men and women. The choice of outcomes is discussed in more detail in Section 1.5.

Finally, an important theme in the gender debate on welfare states, as mentioned above, is the relationship between the state, market and family – and how the family is often omitted from mainstream discussions of welfare states. The importance of the family in mediating the experience of unemployment is an important theme of this book. Whereas the unemployed, particularly in economic debates on unemployment, are often seen as individuals acting 'free of context', we attempt here to examine the state–individual relationship in the context of the family. This issue is discussed further in Section 1.4 below.

### 1.2.3 Unemployment Welfare Regimes

Having considered some general theories of welfare states, in this and the following sub-sections we narrow our focus to theories that address welfare for the unemployed. Gallie and Paugam (2000) draw on Esping-Andersen's work in their discussion of welfare regimes for the unemployed, but their approach is also a critique of his 'integrated perspective' on social welfare. Whereas Esping-Andersen stresses similarities between different domains of welfare such as sickness benefit, unemployment benefit and pensions, Gallie and Paugam argue that in any given regime the principles underlying welfare for the unemployed may differ from those underlying other welfare domains. Gallie and Paugam focus solely on aspects of welfare regimes that deal with labour market risks, particularly financial support for the unemployed, and the regulation of employment and unemployment (Gallie and Paugam 2000, p. 4). Also, whereas Esping-Andersen (1990, 1999) uses the term welfare 'regime' to mean how welfare production is distributed between states, markets and families, Gallie and Paugam (2000, p. 4) confine their criteria for defining regimes to aspects of provision by public authorities.

Gallie and Paugam restrict their classification of 'unemployment welfare regimes' to three criteria of welfare provision for the unemployed: the degree of coverage, including the balance between insurance and means-tested benefits; the level of financial compensation; and the extent of active labour market programmes. Using these criteria they identify four unemployment welfare regimes in Europe: the sub-protective regime, the liberal/minimal regime, the employment-centred regime and the universalistic regime (2000, p. 5).[12] A sub-protective regime offers the unemployed less than the minimum needed for subsistence. Few unemployed people receive benefits, and the amount they receive is very low. The Southern European welfare states of Greece, Italy, Portugal and Spain fall into this category. The liberal/minimal regime offers a somewhat higher level of protection to the unemployed, but not all the unemployed are covered. The emphasis is on poverty alleviation. Britain and Ireland are examples of the liberal/minimal regime. The employment-centred regime provides a much higher level of protection than the liberal/minimal regime and also provides more extensive active labour market measures. However, such a system strongly favours those with a good employment record, and eligibility to benefits is strongly determined by previous employment. Germany, Belgium, France and the Netherlands are examples of employment-centred regimes. Finally, the universalistic regime is characterised by more comprehensive coverage of the unemployed and higher levels of compensation, and benefits are granted with little or no regard for the earnings of other household members. Denmark and Sweden come closest to the universalistic regime.

As regards the position of women, Gallie and Paugam (2000) suggest that women are disadvantaged in both the employment-centred and the liberal/minimal regimes. In employment-centred regimes (such as Germany) they are disadvantaged because interruptions to their career for family reasons affect their contribution record and thus their entitlement to benefits. In liberal/minimal regimes (such as Britain) they are disadvantaged because the system of means-testing takes account of family income. In this respect their typology differs from that of Daly (1996) who argues that women will be more disadvantaged in the German system.

### 1.2.4   Means-tested Versus Insurance Benefits

A rather more specific 'typology', which is also restricted to welfare compensation for the unemployed, sees a crucial distinction between insurance-based and means-tested benefits. This is the approach adopted by Schmid and Reissert in their analysis of unemployment compensation and labour market transitions:

> There are two basic principles governing unemployment compensation: the insurance principle and the welfare principle. In the former, support is deter-

mined by insurance contributions paid prior to unemployment and by previous earnings (unemployment insurance). In the latter, the unemployed are provided with a guaranteed minimum level of income (unemployment assistance). (1996, p. 236)

Schmid and Reissert go on to describe the salient characteristics of these two principles. They differ in financing, in who is covered, in how level of benefit is determined, and in its duration. Typically, insurance benefits are financed by wage-linked insurance contributions from employers and/or employees; unemployment assistance benefits are funded by general taxation. Insurance benefits are available only to those who have paid contributions, regardless of individual need; unemployment assistance is paid regardless of contributions, and only if certain need criteria have been fulfilled. The level of insurance benefits is also linked to previous earnings, while the level of assistance benefit is linked to need. Finally, the duration of insurance benefits is limited and is often linked to previous employment, whereas the duration of assistance benefit is usually unlimited.

Atkinson (1989) notes how a central criticism levelled at social insurance is that in general it privileges those with good employment records, and is not good at protecting the vulnerable from poverty. Webb (1994) echoes this by suggesting that social insurance schemes are not likely to meet the needs of today's poor, as the poor today are increasingly unlikely to have a contribution record that would entitle them to social insurance benefits. In the conclusion to their comparison of the two systems, Schmid and Reissert stress the differences between the two 'models' of compensation, and the implications of these differences for the unemployed:

Welfare-oriented unemployment insurance systems (the United Kingdom being a model) are less effective at providing income protection but more effective at being equitable and, possibly, at restricting moral hazard than insurance-oriented systems are. Insurance-oriented unemployment insurance systems (Germany being a model) are effective at protecting income, but tend to exclude marginal groups when there is persistent mass unemployment. Such systems are also more prone to moral hazard, especially if they provide practically indeterminate income protection. No convergence of these principles was observed. (1996, p. 273)

The question this book addresses is: can the impact of these principles be observed at the level of individuals? Schmid and Reissert's argument suggests we should find more income poverty among the unemployed in Britain than in Germany. Meanwhile if the British system is more 'equitable' we should find less inequality among the unemployed in Britain than in Germany. This argument also suggests that we should find a stronger negative effect of benefits on unemployment durations in Germany than in Britain because of the 'moral hazard' referred to by Schmid and Reissert.

A further difference between insurance-based and means-tested systems is that means-tested benefits are said to be more flexible (Webb 1994) as both the levels of payment and the structure of the benefit system can be changed more readily. Arguably an insurance-based system requires a longer period of adaptation, as it is related to contributions. Whether flexibility is in the interests of the unemployed is open to debate. On the one hand it means that governments can cut the levels of payments dramatically in response to changing policy goals. On the other hand it means that the system can be quickly adapted to serve the sector of the population most in need. We discuss historical changes in the unemployment welfare systems in Britain and Germany in Chapter 3.

### 1.2.5    Rigid and Flexible Labour Markets

A somewhat different approach to the comparative analysis of unemployment comes from the field of economics, where a distinction is drawn between 'rigid' and 'flexible' labour markets. Though in some ways this approach is a clear departure from some of the work described above, as it involves analysis of a range of labour market institutions as well as the welfare state, it also highlights differences in welfare for the unemployed and shares an emphasis on institutional variation. The 'eurosclerosis' debate, which draws on the distinction made here, has contributed much to recent policy debates on unemployment, particularly on unemployment benefits (see, for example, OECD 1994). The following is a brief summary of the main issues relevant to us.[13]

A rigid labour market stands in contrast to a freely clearing labour market, and rigidities are, broadly speaking, impediments to the efficient functioning of the labour market. What are defined as labour market rigidities varies, but they may include: generous unemployment benefits and/or unemployment benefits of long duration; employment protection measures such as difficult and expensive dismissals; high levels of unionisation; high overall taxes impinging on labour; and high minimum wages. The argument is made that institutional rigidities restrict the labour market's ability to respond to external shocks, such as intensified competition in a global economy or technological changes.

This contrast between a rigid and a flexible labour market is often seen as the crucial difference between some European labour markets and the US, and as the cause of higher unemployment in the EU (Siebert 1997; Mortensen and Pissarides 1999). Britain is regarded as having many of the features of the US labour market, particularly following reforms during the 1980s (Siebert 1997). So, as well as having substantially different welfare systems, Britain and Germany are judged by many commentators to differ in terms of labour market rigidity, with the British labour market seen as much less rigid (Grubb and Wells 1993; Siebert 1997; Nickell 1997).

This approach suggests that, although welfare systems may play a role in reducing the financial deprivation caused by unemployment, they may also contribute to unemployment's existence and persistence. So, to understand unemployment from a comparative perspective it is crucial to consider not only the level of unemployment but also its duration, and to compare not only welfare institutions but also labour market institutions. In spite of much research, however, not many conclusive findings have emerged as to how labour market regulation affects unemployment. In particular, no simple relationship has been established between labour market regulation and the overall level of unemployment (OECD 1999). It is not always the case that countries with high levels of labour market regulation have high levels of unemployment, as some proponents of this approach would argue.

However, one vein of research has argued that labour market regulation affects the structure of unemployment (Esping-Andersen 1998; OECD 1999). In other words the regulatory structure produces a higher level of unemployment among some socio-economic groups than among others. In labour markets with stronger regulation, the groups among which we would expect high long-term unemployment with low chances of mobility into jobs are the weakest groups in the labour force. The weakest labour market groups are argued to be women, the low-skilled and the young (Esping-Andersen 1998). This argument suggests that in Germany the duration of unemployment should be particularly long for such groups, and that in Britain we should not expect such a strong effect.

In addition to the general analysis of labour market rigidities, some authors argue that we should focus on specific rigidities. One crucial factor often cited is the duration and level of unemployment benefits. The argument at its crudest runs as follows: high and long-lasting benefits mean the unemployed will raise their reservation wage and prefer to be unemployed than to take low-paid jobs. On the demand side the high contributions needed for generous unemployment benefits also raise the cost of labour for employers. If we lower benefits, it is argued, we will reduce unemployment. However, this argument has not gone uncontested. Atkinson and Micklewright (1991) argue that the empirical support for the argument is not as convincing as its proponents claim. Given the complex criteria for claiming benefits and eligibility rules, Atkinson and Micklewright criticise the assumptions that all the unemployed receive benefits and that they do so under the same conditions. In addition, if an active job search requires financial resources, then generous compensation for the unemployed will increase the resources available for searching for jobs, and may thus increase the probability of returning to work, offsetting the disincentive effect of higher benefits (Atkinson and

Micklewright 1991). So higher unemployment benefits may not necessarily cause longer durations. In fact a direct empirical evaluation of the disincentive effect of unemployment benefit is not possible in this book, given the data available. To properly test the disincentive effect of unemployment benefits the unemployed would need to be randomly assigned benefits and their durations of unemployment compared. Here we can only compare the unemployment durations of those who receive benefit and those who do not.

## 1.3   THE CHOICE OF COUNTRIES

Though the classifications above focus on different elements of variation in the state and unemployment, Britain and Germany appear in contrasting categories in each of them.[14] For Esping-Andersen, Germany is a conservative welfare state and Britain a liberal welfare state. For Daly, Britain is a 'more than one breadwinner' state, while Germany is a 'male breadwinner' state, with more potential for gender inequality. For Gallie and Paugam, in their 'unemployment welfare regimes', Britain is a liberal/minimal regime and Germany an employment-centred regime. Schmid and Reissert single out Britain and Germany as 'models' of the two types of unemployment compensation scheme: Britain as a model welfare-oriented scheme and Germany as a model insurance-oriented scheme. In terms of labour market rigidities, Germany is argued to be considerably more rigid than Britain. Thus if we are setting out to explore different approaches to welfare for the unemployed, Britain and Germany provide a good contrast.

Each typology contributes in a different way to an understanding of how the state interacts with the unemployed. A two-country case study in which the two countries differ in terms of each typology puts us in an excellent position to explore the different dimensions of variation thrown up by these approaches. For example, from Esping-Andersen we may gain insights into how welfare regimes allow the unemployed to retain an income independently from the market, encouraging us to look at the financial dimension of unemployment. By contrast the rigidities argument focuses not on deprivation but on the disincentives of the welfare system and the duration of unemployment. Our approach here is to draw on the full range of typologies, permitting a comprehensive and balanced comparison of welfare for the unemployed.

For a two-country comparison of unemployment, the unification of Germany in 1990 poses a special problem. Should the former East Germany be analysed as part of a unified Germany, should we exclude it and simply focus on West Germany, or should we treat it separately and in effect have a three-'country' comparison?

The transformation of East Germany from a soviet-style planned economy to a market economy took place almost overnight. Economic and currency union took place in summer 1990, complete political reunification took place three months later. The effects of the economic changes in the East were dramatic. Between 1990 and 1991 the GDP of East Germany declined by almost 30 per cent (Rothschild 1993). An estimated 4.14 million jobs were lost in East Germany between 1989 and 1992.

In labour market and social policy, as in all other spheres, the institutional framework of West Germany was accepted – and implemented – almost wholesale in the East. The Federal Labour Office in Nuremberg took over the administration of labour market policy, and administrative structures were rapidly transferred. Though institutions were now almost identical, some special labour market measures were introduced and used extensively to cushion the collapse of the economy and employment (see Chapter 2). Bosch and Knuth (1993) report that of the 4.14 million East Germans not in regular employment in December 1992, 1.75 million were in some form of labour market programme – early retirement, job creation (350,000), short-time work, further training and retraining (479,000). If the large numbers of people on these schemes were included in the unemployment figures, the East German unemployment rate would have been much higher. These programmes also mean that identifying transitions between unemployment and employment is more difficult.

On the one hand this situation provides a remarkable opportunity to capitalise on almost experimental conditions by comparing outcomes when one social policy system is applied to two very different labour markets. On the other hand the trauma of the early years after reunification and the massive scale of labour market intervention make it difficult to include East Germany in the analysis of German unemployment. We choose a compromise strategy. For analysis of the latter half of the 1990s we include East Germany but distinguish it carefully from West Germany. For the analysis of work histories in Chapters 5 and 6, which relies on data from the early 1990s and earlier, we omit East Germany from the analysis.

Before we discuss our measures of outcomes, we turn to consider an issue that is important for our comparison of unemployment, but previously only hinted at in the discussion – the relationship between unemployment and the family.

## 1.4 INDIVIDUALS, THE FAMILY AND UNEMPLOYMENT

Most labour market analysis is at the level of the individual, and in this vein unemployment is often interpreted as an individual phenomenon – i.e. studies consider how benefits replace individual income, how the unemployed individual becomes re-employed. Our analysis is at the individual level, but the surveys we use allow us to consider the role of the family. Throughout our analysis we use the detailed information we have on the household and family situation of individuals to examine how unemployment as a social risk is distributed across families, and the role of the family in mitigating some of its consequences.

A valuable concept for capturing the role of the family in the welfare mix is 'defamilialisation'. As discussed above, the male breadwinner model has been used to highlight the male bias in social policies. Esping-Andersen's concept of decommodification has been criticised for failing to take into account women's experience of welfare states and how women need to be able to commodify their labour before they decommodify it. Orloff (1993) argues that as a prelude to decommodification women need to be freed from dependence on the family – 'defamilialisation' is a precondition for decommodification. Defamilialisation is a term used to indicate the degree to which social policy renders women autonomous from the family. If we broaden to the notion of 'familialism', we can talk more generally about dependence on the family and about cross-national differences in how responsibilities are shared between state, market and family. At one end of the spectrum there are countries and welfare systems in which many family responsibilities are collectivised and looked after by the state. At the other end there are countries where the family still plays a principal role in caring for the social needs of its members. These differences are likely to be particularly salient for women, in determining how they can combine employment and family life. These issues are discussed in more depth in Chapter 2, where we discuss labour market participation rates and the distribution of employment and unemployment.

As regards the relationship between the family and the state in the sphere of unemployment compensation, there are a number of ways in which the two can interact. Families may be treated differently in each benefit system, and this may influence outcomes. It is important when considering the details of state support for the unemployed to look at the details of how unemployment regulations affect families (see Chapter 3). How are dependants defined, and what benefits are paid for them? How much more do the unemployed with children receive than those without?

In general, eligibility to means-tested benefits – the principal type of benefit for the unemployed in Britain – depends on family income, and the benefits are paid to the family. If one or more other individuals in a household are working, an unemployed individual may not receive a means-tested benefit. This is in contrast to insurance-based benefits – the principal type of benefit in Germany – which are paid to the individual (though in some cases, particularly in Britain, insurance benefits are paid with dependants' allowances). As long as all relevant contribution conditions have been met, an unemployed individual may receive an insurance-based benefit regardless of whether others in the household are working.

However, we also need to consider the effect of state benefit conditions on the behaviour of families. It may not be entirely correct to take the family structure as given. For example, where benefits are means-tested, if a woman is working part-time when her husband becomes unemployed, her working may mean that her earnings are deducted from his benefit. She may therefore choose to stop work, and be no worse off financially. This effect of the state on the family is the subject of Chapter 6.

It is not only the family situation per se that is of importance, but also the family's engagement with the market. For this we need to consider the distribution of household employment.[15] In a society in which all families are single-earner households, the effect of unemployment will be very different to its effect in a society with many dual-earner households. An unemployed person living in a household where others are employed – be they a spouse/ partner or other family members, such as parents – is less at risk of financial deprivation than an unemployed person who lives either alone or in a household where no other adult is employed. We test whether this effect varies between two countries with very different benefit systems.

## 1.5 OUTCOMES FOR THE UNEMPLOYED

Although the claim is often made that welfare states stratify outcomes – and as noted above it is an assumption that underlies the typologies we discuss – much of the work comparing the performance of welfare states lacks a focus on outcomes for individuals.[16] As Mitchell notes in her discussion of the literature on transfer programmes of welfare states: 'What the literature lacks, however, is a clear assessment of how, and whether, these variations result in tangible differences in the impact of these programs on, for example, poverty and inequality' (Mitchell 1991, p. 1). Mitchell's own work focuses on outcomes of transfer programmes, though not specifically on the unemployed. Daly (2000) too notes that practically all comparative welfare state typologising has focused on macro characteristics, but has failed to analyse micro-level outcomes systematically. The analysis in this book is on micro-level outcomes, with the individual – situated within the family or household – as the unit of analysis.

The tools we use reflect the variety of approaches we draw on; the aim of this book is to explore different aspects of unemployment from a comparative perspective, not to test any one typology. In the rest of this chapter we begin the discussion of the outcome measures we use. Further details of the individual measures used appear in each individual chapter.

The main types of outcome measured in this book are: firstly, relative income poverty rates and income change; secondly, the duration of unemployment until exit to employment; and thirdly, the effects of unemployment on the labour market transitions of partners of the unemployed.

An important theme running like a watermark through many of the approaches to the study of welfare states and unemployment is that of the financial consequences of unemployment. Esping-Andersen focuses on decommodification and how welfare states replace income from the market, covering the contingency of market failure. The male breadwinner typology is primarily concerned with how welfare states treat men and women differently, but one key issue here, we argue, is (unemployed) women's access to an independent income. Gallie and Paugam (2000) refer specifically to how they expect different types of welfare state to be associated with different levels of poverty among the unemployed. Schmid and Reissert (1996) also explicitly predict that the welfare-oriented system is less effective at protecting the income of the unemployed than the insurance-based system. A powerful indicator of the financial consequences of unemployment is income poverty, and income poverty is a central concern in this book.

Another important theme running through many approaches to welfare and unemployment is the duration of unemployment. Discussions of rigid and flexible labour markets emphasise the importance of looking not just at the level but also at the duration of unemployment. It is particularly important to compare the durations of unemployment for different groups of the unemployed (Esping-Andersen 1998; OECD 1999). Only through a comparative analysis of unemployment durations can we begin to illuminate the complex impact of institutions – both labour market and welfare institutions – on unemployment.

This focus on labour market transitions is also reflected in our analysis of the behaviour of partners of the unemployed. Since a key concern of this book is to incorporate the family into the analysis of unemployment, we compare how different conditions of benefit receipt affect the wider family unit. A crucial difference between insurance-based and means-tested benefits is that in the former the basis of entitlement is the individual, while in the latter it is the family (or more precisely the 'benefit unit'). We seek to look not only at how family situation affects entitlement to benefit, but also at how benefit entitlement affects family situation, i.e. family employment.

In addition through these three outcome measures – poverty among the unemployed, the duration of unemployment, and unemployment and partner's employment – we also approach analysis of an outcome that is less easy to measure, namely social exclusion. At the beginning of this chapter we noted the rising concern with the problem of social exclusion. At the core of the concept of social exclusion is the idea that a disadvantaged group may become increasingly marginalised – detached from society, without the necessary means to participate. That said, it should be noted that the notion of social exclusion is much wider than simply long-term unemployment and poverty. It is precisely the concentration of many forms of disadvantage that the concept is designed to capture. It is not the intention of this book to compare the full extent of social exclusion in Britain and Germany, but we do point to factors that are important in explaining its extent.

One type of outcome measure that is not addressed here is the non-material consequences of unemployment. These include, for example, the psychological distress caused by unemployment or the disruption of marital or family relations.[17] The non-material consequences of unemployment are an important component of the experience of unemployment, and their study has a long history (Jahoda et al. [1933] 1975). We argue here, however, that the financial consequences of unemployment are those most directly affected by cash transfers and that none of the typologies of welfare that we explore explicitly address the non-material consequences of unemployment.[18]

## 1.6   OUTLINE

The empirical analysis that forms the core of the book is presented in Chapters 4, 5 and 6. Chapters 2 and 3 are background chapters, providing the context for the empirical analysis. Chapter 7 draws conclusions.

Chapter 2, the first background chapter, provides a picture of the labour markets and unemployment in Britain and Germany. We consider macroeconomic developments in both countries, and how these have affected the overall level of unemployment. We discuss the definition of unemployment, and we examine the composition of the unemployed by gender, age and duration. Thirdly, we consider differences between the British and German labour markets, focusing particularly on the labour market participation of women and of older workers. Then we discuss the differences between the education systems and the implications for employment and unemployment. Finally, we look at the relation between the family and both employment and unemployment in Britain and Germany.

In Chapter 3 we compare state provision for the unemployed in Britain and Germany. We first look at the development of unemployment-related benefits over the course of the 20th century. We concentrate particularly on changes to these benefits in both countries during the 1980s and 1990s. We then examine the level and coverage of benefits in detail in 1996, investigating what proportion of the unemployed receive means-tested and insurance benefits in

Britain and Germany. We pay particular attention to eligibility and the conditions for receipt of benefits. We compare coverage and replacement rates in detail. Finally, we briefly consider active labour market policies and their role in labour market policy.

Chapter 4 examines income poverty among the unemployed. Drawing on some of the different approaches described above, we develop general hypotheses about differences in overall poverty incidence among the unemployed in the two countries. We then develop more specific hypotheses about poverty *among* the unemployed, distinguishing the recipients of different benefits. We also explore gender differences in poverty among the unemployed. One important concern of the gender typologies is the idea that different welfare states prioritise different types of household structure, and in our analysis we compare poverty rates of individual unemployed people living in different family situations. Finally we use the panel element of our data to look at changes in income following a move to unemployment, to examine the robustness of our findings.

Chapter 5 looks at the process of escape from unemployment. In the debate over rigid and flexible labour markets, discussed above, the role of institutions in explaining the persistence of unemployment is a key issue. Esping-Andersen (1998) argues that in regulated labour markets, weaker labour market groups – such as women, young people and the low-skilled – will be disadvantaged in the competition for jobs and will have longer durations of unemployment. We test this hypothesis with comparative data on work histories from our national datasets, using event history modelling. We also consider the effect of unemployment benefit on escape from unemployment.

Chapter 6 focuses on the unemployed as members of households, as unemployment benefits may affect the labour market participation of other household members. In particular, means-tested benefits, as they are 'household' benefits based on 'need', may act as a disincentive for other household members to work, as benefits are withdrawn if others in the 'benefit unit' are employed. We investigate this hypothesis using event history modelling by looking at the labour market participation of the wives of unemployed men in Britain and Germany. We consider the type of benefit the man receives – means-tested or insurance-based – and the influence of this on the wife's participation.

Chapter 7 brings together the findings of the previous chapters on the differential consequences of unemployment for British and German men and women. We discuss the implications of these differences for the welfare typologies described above. We also relate our findings to issues of social policy. We discuss methodological issues arising from our current work, and suggest some avenues for future research.

In the final Appendix we discuss data issues. We describe the data used in the study, in particular the problem of attrition that arises when using panel data, and the weighting methods used to overcome it. We also address the measurement of unemployment from a cross-sectional and longitudinal perspective, and compare the samples of unemployed used with those from other data sources.

## NOTES

1.  Figures quoted are an average for the 15 countries of the EU.
2.  One of the best-known examples of the study of marginalisation as a consequence of long-term unemployment is the work of Marie Jahoda et al. in Marienthal ([1933] 1975).
3.  In this book 'Britain' is used to mean England, Scotland, Wales and Northern Ireland for any discussion of theory, legislation or official statistics. For the empirical analysis the term Britain refers to England, Wales and Scotland south of the Caledonian Canal, as this is how Britain is defined in the data used, the British Household Panel Survey (BHPS). Germany is taken to mean the Federal Republic of Germany, i.e. West Germany before reunification in 1990 and reunited Germany after reunification, unless otherwise stated. The term East Germany refers to the former German Democratic Republic.
4.  However, even radically different approaches to comparative research need not imply different conclusions, as Kangas (1994) illustrates.
5.  The European Community Household Panel (ECHP) is coordinated by the statistical office of the European Union and covers 12 countries (Eurostat, 1998). However, the first wave was carried out in 1994 and at the time the analysis in this book was carried out only three waves were available for public use.
6.  The main alternative approach to social policy research is to study the influences on the policy-making process (e.g. Baldwin 1990; Pierson 1994). Rake describes this latter approach as 'society makes policy' rather than 'policy makes society' (Rake 1998, p. 6). While it is important to recognise the two-way link between social structure and policy-making, the focus of this book is on the impact of social policy on social stratification.
7.  Details of the indices differ but in general the focus is on: the extent to which the benefit replaces income; qualification conditions; the number of waiting days before the benefit is paid; duration of benefits; and crucially the benefit coverage, i.e. what proportion of the population is covered by the benefit (Esping-Andersen 1990, Chapter 2).
8.  It does so somewhat uneasily, though, and the categorisation of Britain has been the subject of dispute. Some commentators argue that in the area of service provision, for example, Britain more closely resembles a universal welfare regime. In general the liberal category has proven more contentious than the others. However, Britain, unlike Germany, has never been classified as conservative.
9.  Lewis and Ostner (1994) is a later version of a 'tour de force' conference paper presented to the Centre for European Studies, Harvard University in 1991.
10. Daly also discusses benefits for caring, arguing that the principle of caring work is better established in Britain than in Germany.
11. This view is shared by Russell and Barbieri (2000), who compare gender and the experience of unemployment in Britain, Denmark, France and Italy.
12. Though they propose their own typology, Gallie and Paugam (2000) point out that typologies are ideal types and that their classification of countries is tentative.
13. The rigid/flexible distinction is also one of many economic approaches to explaining the causes and persistence of unemployment. It is not the purpose of this book to give a comprehensive review of these.
14. With the exception of Lewis and Ostner (1994).
15. We discuss the distribution of employment and unemployment within families in greater depth in Chapter 2.

16. The exception here is Gallie and Paugam (2000), whose edited volume does compare a variety of outcomes for individuals.
17. For examples of this work see McKee and Bell 1985; Gallie et al. 1994; Lampard 1994; Whelan 1994; Russell 1996; Whelan and McGinnity 2000.
18. Gallie and Paugam's edited volume does include work on the non-material consequences of unemployment, but these non-material consequences play no part in the rationale for their typology of unemployment welfare regimes.

# 2. Comparing labour market trends and the composition of the unemployed

This chapter compares unemployment and labour markets in Britain and Germany at a macro-level. The primary aim of this and the next chapter, which compares welfare provision for the unemployed, is to provide the background to allow us to interpret the empirical findings that form the core of the book. As the empirical analysis presented later in the book is longitudinal, some of the material in this chapter compares changes in the labour markets and unemployment over time. Where changes over time are not so relevant, we compare the labour markets from a cross-sectional perspective, normally in 1996 as this is at the end of the period analysed. Where data from other years is used, the year is specified. For the most part we compare Britain and Germany, but where relevant we distinguish East and West Germany after 1992.

Section 2.1 gives a brief account of recent macroeconomic change in Britain and Germany. Section 2.2 discusses the measurement of unemployment and compares trends in overall unemployment and the composition of the unemployed. Section 2.3 examines trends in employment, particularly labour force activity rates, since the 1980s. Section 2.4 considers the role of the education and training systems in understanding unemployment. Section 2.5 looks at the distribution of employment and unemployment within households. We conclude by reflecting on some of the differences between the British and German labour markets.

## 2.1 PATTERNS OF MACROECONOMIC CHANGE IN BRITAIN AND GERMANY

In Britain, the 1980s were characterised by considerable macroeconomic turbulence (see Figure 2.1). Margaret Thatcher's government, which came into office in 1979, introduced a tight monetary policy, intended to reduce inflation. Interest rates were allowed to rise (to 13.9 per cent in 1981) and recession took hold. The rise in the exchange rate, resulting from the high interest rates, had a strong negative effect on exports. Manufacturing industry was hit particularly hard and unemployment rose rapidly, reaching 14.8 per cent of the labour force

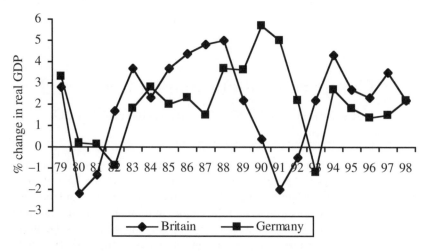

*Note*:   Up to 1991 data refer to West Germany only.

*Source*:   Economic Outlook, OECD (1995, 1997a and 1999).

*Figure 2.1    Economic growth in Britain and Germany: percentage change
in real GDP, 1979–98*

in 1983 (according to the International Labour Organisation [ILO] definition –
see the next section for details of this definition). Although GDP began to rise
in 1982, earlier than in other countries, employment was slow to pick up, an
indication of the depth of the recession. In the second half of the 1980s, GDP
growth accelerated and employment recovered: GDP grew by 5 per cent in
1988, and total employment grew rapidly from 24.2 million in 1985 to 26.8
million in 1990 (Eurostat 1987, 1990, 1992). However, the boom was not
sustainable; in the early 1990s the economy plummeted back into recession and
unemployment rose dramatically.

The crisis on the financial markets in 1992, leading to the forced withdrawal of sterling from the Exchange Rate Mechanism and a major currency
devaluation, eventually brought about a restimulation of the economy. After
adjustment to the lower exchange rate, the economy saw a period of buoyant
export growth, accompanied by low inflation and moderate output growth
(OECD 1996b).

West Germany was also hit by negative GDP growth in the early 1980s,
though somewhat later than Britain (see Figure 2.1). Economists have argued
that the strength of German exports meant that the recession there in the early
1980s was not as traumatic as after the previous oil shock in the 1970s. In
particular, the recession did not have as marked an impact on employment

(OECD 1982, 1983). Indeed, by the mid-1980s the economy was showing signs of recovery, and robust growth continued to the end of the decade, reaching a high of 5.7 per cent in 1990.

In that same year, 1990, the Deutschmark was introduced to East Germany, causing a massive upheaval in the German economy. The currency union meant that the East German economy, which had previously been protected from world markets, was suddenly exposed to international competition without having time to restructure. The East German economy collapsed. The collapse was cushioned somewhat by massive transfers from West Germany, which far surpassed initial estimates of the cost of reunification.[1] Until mid-1992, however, West Germany was not affected by the recessionary tendencies that emerged in Britain in 1990, profiting instead from a boom in exports to East Germany. But this temporary boom was followed by recession, with negative growth in 1993, and the transition in the East was slow. Employment in East Germany fell dramatically, particularly in manufacturing, and unemployment soared. Although there was an upswing in the economy after 1993 – particularly in 1994, with more modest GDP growth after that – there was weak investment and low employment growth, as enterprises focused on rationalisation.

The fact that unemployment in Germany persisted through the economic upturn of 1994–95 was very different from the experience in Britain, where unemployment responded to recovery. Some commentators attribute the persistence of unemployment to low wage dispersion and inflexible working patterns in Germany (OECD 1996b). In any case, by the late 1990s the German and British economies were in very different situations. In Germany, unemployment was still rising and the economy was burdened with the massive restructuring in the East and with the associated financial transfers from the West. In Britain, by contrast, the late 1990s saw a sustained boom, though much higher wage inequality (OECD 1996c).

## 2.2  UNEMPLOYMENT

Narrowing our focus to unemployment, this section compares different measures of unemployment before examining trends in unemployment since the early 1980s. We then consider the composition of the unemployed in terms of gender, age and the duration of unemployment.

### 2.2.1  Measuring Unemployment

Measuring unemployment is fraught with difficulties, and no measure is perfect; any measure excludes groups that we might wish to include, and vice versa. We compare the official registered definition and the ILO definition of unemployment, arguing that the ILO measure is superior for comparative purposes. We also briefly consider self-defined unemployment.

A common measure of unemployment is the live register of the unemployed, which is often used as the 'official' national unemployment rate. The advantages of this definition are that it is cheap to collect and available for very small geographical areas. However, the measure has a number of disadvantages for cross-national research. One is the difference in national definitions at any given time. For example, in 1996 the German Federal Labour Office counted as unemployed those persons under 65, registered at local employment offices, looking for a job and available for work for at least 18 hours a week. They did not need to be actually claiming benefit. In Britain, since 1982, only people who claim insurance or assistance benefits (or national insurance credits) are counted as unemployed, and for this they need to prove that they are actively seeking work.[2] This measure is also known as the 'claimant count' in Britain.[3] While in Germany this definition is still widely used in public discourse, in Britain the claimant count has been somewhat discredited in recent years and is no longer popular as a measure of unemployment (Nickell 1999).

A second problem with official definitions is that they may not be consistent over time. Coverage changes when adjustments to the rules and procedures regarding benefits are made. Regulations governing benefit entitlement have changed many times in the last two decades, particularly in 1980s' Britain, as we discuss in Chapter 3.

A further problem is the exclusion of certain groups of the unemployed. In Britain, the claimant count excludes those who do not claim benefit, which includes those who previously had part-time jobs, those with discontinuous employment histories and those with a partner in employment. Thus many women, particularly married women, are excluded from the claimant count. In Germany, the national definition excludes those seeking employment on their own initiative, not through the public employment service. Those not receiving benefits and seeking employment on their own initiative are known as the 'silent reserve' (*Stille Reserve*). Holst (2000, p. 205) distinguishes between a 'highly labour market oriented silent reserve' – those who wish to take up employment immediately or in the coming year – and those intending to take up employment in the next two to five years. She estimates that in 1996 the highly labour market-oriented group formed 2.4 per cent of the German population aged between 16 and 59.[4] Those in active labour market programmes are also not included in the official unemployment count in Germany – another example of the so-called 'hidden unemployed' (Düll and Vogler-Ludwig 1998). In addition, since 1985, older workers who receive benefit but are not immediately available for work have not been included in the official German count.

One of the major alternatives to official national definitions of unemployment is the ILO definition, introduced in 1982. The ILO defines the unemployed as those who:

- have no paid work in the current week, and;
- are available to start work within the next two weeks, and;
- have actively sought employment in the previous four weeks, or have been waiting to start a job already obtained.

The ILO definition too has problems. It defines *employment* much more broadly than the German national definition; it counts as employed anyone who has done a few hours casual work in the past week. The ILO's availability criterion is strict: somebody who needs a few weeks to sort out child-minding is not counted as unemployed. Discouraged workers, who have not been seeking work actively in the past four weeks are excluded. Indeed, the ILO measure may underestimate unemployment in times of high unemployment. Robinson (1997) argues that the differences between the British claimant count and the ILO unemployment rate are consistent with an added worker/discouraged worker effect. During the upswing of the late 1980s, the claimant count fell faster than the ILO measure because the improved employment prospects brought more people back into the labour force, swelling the ILO measure. In the recession of the early 1990s, by contrast, the deteriorating employment situation resulted in discouraged jobseekers giving up active job search, so the ILO measure rose less quickly than the claimant count. An additional disadvantage of the ILO definition for the longitudinal analysis in this book, which requires measuring unemployment using retrospective data, is that it is not feasible to expect people to answer questions about their search activity and availability for each month in the past year, or for past years. This issue is discussed in more detail in the final Appendix, Section A.2.1, where we discuss how unemployment is measured for the empirical analysis in this book.

In spite of these limitations, the ILO definition is a superior measure of unemployment for comparative purposes. Since 1983, Eurostat's European Labour Force Survey has provided standardised unemployment rates based on survey data using the ILO definition, and this is the source of most of the unemployment data in the rest of this chapter. One problem with the Eurostat data is that it does not distinguish East and West Germany after 1992. Where East/West differences are relevant, we use special tabulations from the German Microcensus provided by the Statistisches Bundesamt. The Microcensus also uses the ILO definition but its estimates for Germany differ from Eurostat because its sample is bigger and slightly different, though the differences are negligible for the most part.[5]

Table 2.1 compares unemployment rates – the percentage of the labour force that is unemployed – using different measures of unemployment in Britain and Germany from 1985 to 1998. The national rate in Britain is similar to the Eurostat data, with only small deviations in both directions. However, the similarity does not mean that the two measures define the same people as unemployed. In Britain, unemployed women, particularly married women, often do not claim benefits and are thus not counted as unemployed under the national definition. Compared to the European Labour Force Sur-

*Table 2.1    Unemployment rates using national and Eurostat data*

| | Britain | | Germany** | |
|---|---|---|---|---|
| | National rate* (%) | Eurostat (LFS) (%) | National rate (%) | Eurostat (LFS) (%) |
| 1985 | 11.8 | 11.5 | 8.2 | 6.9 |
| 1986 | 11.8 | 11.5 | 7.9 | 6.0 |
| 1987 | 10.6 | 11.0 | 7.9 | 6.8 |
| 1988 | 8.4 | 9.0 | 7.7 | 6.3 |
| 1989 | 6.3 | 7.4 | 7.1 | 5.7 |
| 1990 | 5.8 | 7.0 | 6.4 | 4.9 |
| 1991 | 8.0 | 8.6 | 5.7 | 4.1 |
| 1992 | 9.8 | 9.7 | 7.7 | 6.3 |
| 1993 | 10.3 | 10.3 | 8.9 | 7.7 |
| 1994 | 9.4 | 9.7 | 9.6 | 8.7 |
| 1995 | 8.1 | 8.7 | 9.4 | 8.2 |
| 1996 | 7.4 | 8.2 | 10.4 | 8.8 |
| 1997 | 5.6 | 7.1 | 11.4 | 9.9 |
| 1998 | 4.7 | 6.3 | 11.0 | 9.9 |

*Notes*:
*   Claimant count. Since May 1998 official statistics in Britain (produced in *Labour Force Trends*) have also reported the ILO measure of unemployment.
**  Until 1992, figures are for West Germany only. Since then, Eurostat has not provided separate estimates for East and West Germany. For Germany the national figures reported are with respect to civilian employment, as are all the German national figures reported in this book. Note that official rates within Germany are often quoted with respect to *dependent* civilian employment, excluding self-employed and family workers. This measure results in a higher unemployment rate.

*Sources*:   *Employment Gazette*, various issues for Britain (Office for National Statistics 1985–98); *Amtliche Nachrichten der Bundesanstalt für Arbeit*, various issues for Germany (Bundesanstalt für Arbeit 1985–98); European Labour Force Surveys, Eurostat 1987–99.

vey, the claimant count seriously underestimates female unemployment in Britain (see also Russell 1996).

The German national rate has been consistently higher than the Eurostat estimate. Klös and Lichtbau (1998) argue that the official German rate tends to overestimate the number unemployed, at least compared to international estimates. Firstly, jobseekers working very short hours may be considered unemployed on the national definition. Secondly, registered unemployment also includes persons who are de facto not available for work, or only available to a limited extent. On the other hand, the national statistics take no account of those unemployed individuals who do not register with the public employment service, though the latter effect is not large enough to counter the previous effects (Düll and Vogler-Ludwig 1998).

A third commonly used definition of unemployment is self-defined unemployment. Retrospective surveys often use this categorisation; respondents are asked to fill in a monthly 'calendar' of their principal economic status in the past year or longer.[6] Although self-defined unemployment often includes discouraged workers, unlike the ILO category, it often excludes many women. Indeed, Russell (1996) argues that this measure most clearly illustrates the ambiguities surrounding the definition of female employment. She discusses three reasons why women often do not define themselves as unemployed in Britain. Firstly, women are more likely to be ineligible for unemployment benefit, and for this reason some may not count themselves as unemployed. Secondly, the fact that female jobseekers do not label themselves unemployed may be linked to their domestic responsibilities. The label of being unemployed implies 'without work', and many women do not feel themselves to be without work even though they may be actively seeking it.[7] Thirdly, many women do not feel themselves to be unemployed because they are looking for part-time work.

Some of the unemployed may not be captured by any of the three types of measure. In particular, the older unemployed who view their job chances as slight may withdraw from the labour market completely. Those with health problems may claim sickness benefit, while others may take early retirement. These individuals will not be counted as unemployed using the registered definition, and it is highly unlikely that they will be counted as unemployed using either the ILO definition or the self-definition. The propensity of the unemployed to use these 'exit routes' may be influenced by the regulations surrounding unemployment benefit, sickness benefit and early retirement. These regulations may differ between countries and over time (see Section 2.3.3).

### 2.2.2 Trends in Unemployment

What are the consequences for unemployment of the patterns in economic change in Britain and Germany discussed in Section 2.1? During the 1960s and early 1970s Britain and Germany enjoyed more or less full employment, since when they have both seen an upward trend in unemployment. In 1975 the ILO unemployment rate was 3.2 per cent in Britain and 3.5 per cent in Germany (European Commission 1997). Twenty years later, in 1995, the unemployment rate was 8.2 per cent in Britain and 9.0 per cent in Germany. The trend has been common to their European counterparts. Unemployment in the European Union (EU) as a whole rose from 3.7 per cent in 1975 to 9.9 per cent in 1998 (European Commission 1999).

Figure 2.2a presents a more detailed picture of the evolution of unemployment in the two countries since 1983 (using the ILO definition). While in the late 1990s the unemployment rate was higher in reunified Germany than in Britain, the average rate for the whole period 1983–98 was higher in Britain (9.3 per cent) than in Germany (7.1 per cent).

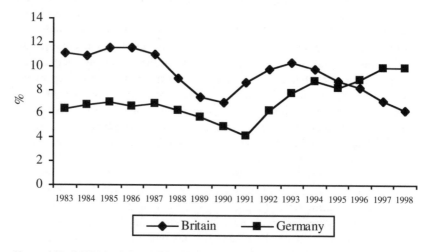

*Note*:   * Until 1991 the figure refers to West Germany only.

*Source*:   European Labour Force Surveys (Eurostat 1985–99).

*Figure 2.2a   Harmonised ILO unemployment rates, Britain and Germany\*, 1983–98*

In Britain, fluctuations in unemployment have been sharper than in most other industrialised countries, reflecting the British experience of two very sharp recessions punctuated by a very rapid recovery in the second half of the 1980s. From a high of nearly 11.5 per cent in the mid-1980s, unemployment fell to 7 per cent in 1990, as total employment grew rapidly. In the recession of the early 1990s the unemployment rate rose again, reaching a peak of 10.3 per cent in 1993. The rate then started falling again, and in 1998 stood at 6.3 per cent of the labour force, well below the EU average. The periods of rising unemployment were different in character. While the recession of the 1980s hit the manufacturing areas in the North particularly hard, exacerbating the traditional North/South divide, the recession in the early 1990s hit the South-East, London in particular. As regional unemployment rates converged in the 1990s, Jackman and Savouri argue that the traditional North/South divide 'all but disappeared' (1999, p. 29).[8]

In Germany, the pattern of unemployment was somewhat different. In the early 1980s unemployment in Germany, at an average of around 6.5 per cent, was considerably lower than in Britain. The rate decreased further in the late 1980s to a low point of around 4 per cent in West Germany in 1991. However, reunification had a huge impact on German unemployment, in large part because of the collapse of the East German economy. From 1990 to 1996, overall German unemployment more than doubled, to 8.8 per cent in 1996, and in 1998 stood at 9.9 per cent.

Figure 2.2b compares unemployment rates in East and West Germany from 1992, and also includes the overall German unemployment rate, using data from the German Microcensus (which uses the ILO definition). Here we see

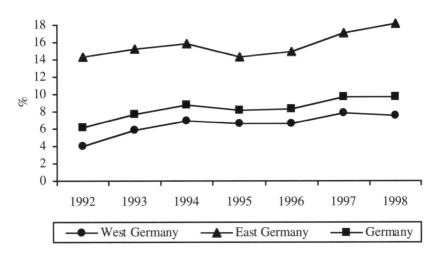

*Source:* German Microcensus.

*Figure 2.2b   ILO unemployment rates, East and West Germany, 1992–98*

how much of the overall rise in German unemployment is accounted for by the very high unemployment in East Germany. Since 1992 the unemployment rate in East Germany has not fallen below 14 per cent of the labour force, and for many years was three times the rate in West Germany. In 1998, the ILO unemployment rate was estimated to be around 7.4 per cent in West Germany and 18 per cent in East Germany.

In the former West Germany, unemployment has to be seen against a backdrop of rapid economic growth and high economic output in the post-war period, combined with long-term structural change and increasingly 'jobless growth' since the mid-1970s.[9] In the former East Germany, by contrast, unemployment in the 1990s is the result of the sudden, nearly complete collapse of the former economic system and labour market. An estimated 40 per cent of jobs in East Germany were lost between 1989 and 1992, and a wide range of labour market groups were affected. The unemployed in East Germany show much greater differentiation in terms of qualifications, work history and age than they do in West Germany (Hahn and Schön 1996). We return to this point in Chapter 4.

So far we have only looked at the overall unemployment rate, but this masks important differences in the composition of the unemployed. The following sections compare unemployment by gender, age and duration in Britain and Germany.

### 2.2.3   Gender and Unemployment

Identifying women's unemployment presents a number of problems, some of which were discussed above. Women's frequent transitions in and out of the labour market mean that it can be difficult to distinguish between spells of unemployment and spells of economic inactivity. In some countries, eligibility criteria often mean that women do not qualify for benefits, and unemployment registration figures seriously underestimate the number of women unemployed. National estimates of female unemployment are much lower than estimates using the ILO definition. Russell (1996) argues that because unemployment in Britain is seen as primarily a male problem and is so strongly linked to male patterns of participation in the labour market, many women do not define themselves as unemployed even though they are seeking work. Holst (2000) draws our attention to the importance of the *Stille Reserve* in Germany, described above. Figure 2.3 compares the unemployment rate by gender in Britain and Germany in 1996.

In Germany, the unemployment rate is higher for women than men; in Britain the converse is true – indeed the unemployment rate for British men in 1996 (9.7 per cent) was much higher than that for women (6.3 per cent). Of the two countries only Germany follows the general European pattern of

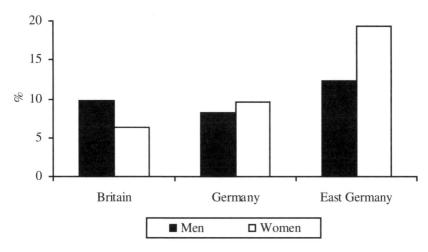

*Note*: Microcensus estimates differ very slightly from the European Labour Force Survey because of sample differences, see endnote 5.

*Sources*: European Labour Force Survey 1996 for Britain (Eurostat 1997); Microcensus 1996 for Germany.

*Figure 2.3*     *Unemployment rate by gender, 1996, Britain and Germany, distinguishing East Germany*

higher unemployment for women (Rubery et al. 1998) – though note that in West Germany in 1996 the ILO unemployment rate was rather similar for men and women (at around 7 per cent). It is the very high unemployment rate among East German women – just under 20 per cent of the female labour force in 1996 – that underlies the higher unemployment rate among women in Germany. Many writers, East and West, argue that East German women are bearing the brunt of reunification, suffering particularly high rates of unemployment. Indeed, Ina Merkel, a leading figure in the Independent Women's Association – the first feminist women's organisation in East Germany, founded in 1989 – described unification as 'three steps back' for East German women (Chamberlayne 1994). In the face of high and rising male unemployment, a large number of men have begun entering jobs that were traditionally done by women. The female employment rate in East Germany has been extremely high, amounting to more than 85 per cent of those aged between 25 and 60 in 1989, in comparison with a rate of only 60 per cent in West Germany (Ostner 1993). Only a small number of East German women have withdrawn from the labour force, and many register as unemployed (Holst and Schupp 1995).

### 2.2.4   Age and Unemployment

Figure 2.4 compares the unemployment rates for different age groups in
1996. In Britain, the youth unemployment rate, at just under 15 per cent, was
much higher than that for older age groups. In Germany, the unemployment
rate was higher for under 25s than for 25–44-year-olds, but we see from
Figure 2.4 that it is the oldest age group – over 55s – who were particularly at
risk of unemployment, especially in East Germany. Germany is unusual in
the EU in having higher unemployment among older than younger workers
(Pischner and Wagner 1995). Older workers have been particularly badly hit
by economic restructuring, particularly in the East. Falling labour demand,
discrimination against older workers by employers, and a reluctance to re-
train have all contributed to the high unemployment rate. In addition, some
authors have related the high unemployment among older people to a number
of features of the German unemployment compensation system, in particular
the longer benefit durations and special benefit conditions for older workers
(see Chapter 3) (Hunt 1995; Steiner 1997). It is also important to note how
selective withdrawal from the labour market may influence the comparison of
unemployment for the older age. This is discussed further in Section 2.3.3.

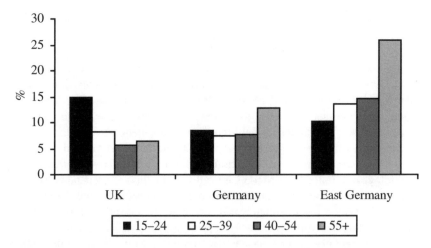

*Note*:  Microcensus estimates differ very slightly from the European Labour Force Survey
because of sample differences, see endnote 5.

*Sources*:  European Labour Force Survey 1996 for Britain (Eurostat 1997); Microcensus for
Germany.

*Figure 2.4    Unemployment rate by age in Britain, Germany and East
             Germany, 1996*

Youth unemployment rates for Britain and particularly for Germany were lower than the EU average for the period (see Figure 2.5).[10] The average rate of youth unemployment in the EU during the period 1983–98 was just under 20 per cent, compared to an average of 8.0 per cent in Germany and 15.4 per cent in Britain.

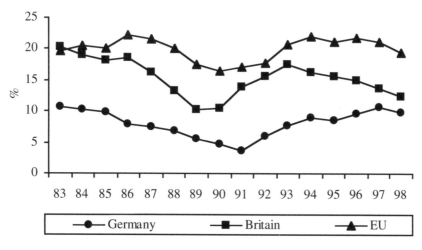

*Notes*:
* Figures from 1992 include the new German *Länder*.
** EU is an average of 10 countries in the period 1983–85, 12 countries in 1986–94 and 15 in 1995–98.

*Source*: European Labour Force Surveys (Eurostat 1985–99).

*Figure 2.5 Youth unemployment rates, Germany\*, Britain and EU\*\*, 1983–98*

One key explanation of the low rate of youth unemployment in Germany is the apprenticeship system (see Section 2.4). Whereas a very small proportion of British 16-year-old school leavers go on to an apprenticeship, in Germany very few school leavers receive no further training, most going into highly structured, three- or four-year apprenticeships. These apprenticeships confer certified marketable skills, and there is a high level of retention, i.e. apprentices being kept on in the firm where they did their apprenticeship. The relationship between school, training and employment is clear and 16-year-olds in Germany do not emerge anonymously into the labour market, as they often do in Britain. The first transition into the labour market is thereby facilitated, and young people are less likely to become unemployed (OECD 1998; Müller and Shavit 1998).

### 2.2.5   Duration of Unemployment

Any consideration of unemployment cannot be disconnected from its length.[11] High short-term unemployment may just indicate high labour turnover and may not require specific policy attention. Long-term unemployment, defined as those who are unemployed for a year or more, is a much more serious problem. As the percentage of long-term unemployed in the EU rose to 48 per cent of the total, the OECD (1994) and the European Commission (1994) identified long-term unemployment as a major aspect of the problem of unemployment in Europe. OECD evidence suggests a duration effect of unemployment – the probability of re-employment decreasing as duration increases, pushing the long-term unemployed to the bottom of the jobs queue and leading to severe problems of marginalisation and social exclusion. Many of the long-term unemployed in both Britain and Germany are older, have low qualifications and a much higher incidence of health problems (OECD 1996a; Robinson 1997). This concentration of disadvantage means they constitute a particularly intractable problem for policy-makers.

Figure 2.6 shows the percentage of the unemployed who were long-term unemployed in the period 1983–98. Despite yearly fluctuations, the percentage is rather similar in both countries.[12]

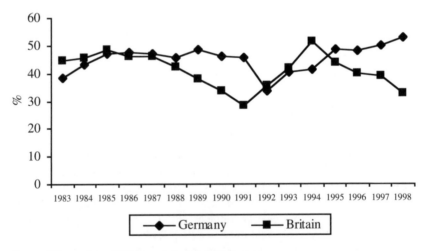

*Note*:   * Figures from 1992 onwards include East Germany.

*Source*:   European Labour Force Surveys (Eurostat 1985–99).

*Figure 2.6    Percentage of unemployed who were long-term unemployed, Britain and Germany\*, 1983–98*

In Britain, for most of the period, the percentage of long-term unemployed among the unemployed was well above 30 per cent. In 1991, as overall unemployment began to rise again, the new influx of unemployed people meant that the percentage of long-term unemployed fell to under 30 per cent, but, as the recession deepened, long-term unemployment rose. In West Germany, the percentage fluctuated slightly around a mean of 46.5 per cent for most of the 1980s, falling at the end of the decade as unemployment fell. After reunification, the percentage started rising, and in 1998 stood at 52.6 per cent of all the unemployed. Estimates from the Microcensus point to a somewhat higher proportion of long-term unemployed in East Germany than in West, though the difference is small.[13]

The most striking difference between Britain and Germany in long-term unemployment is the gender difference. Unlike in Germany, long-term unemployment in Britain is primarily a male phenomenon. In 1996 over three-quarters of the long-term unemployed in Britain were men; in Germany over half were women. Indeed, in East Germany around 60 per cent of the long-term unemployed were women.[14] This is an issue we return to in Chapter 5, where we compare gender differences in the duration of unemployment.

## 2.3 COMPARING LABOUR MARKETS AND LABOUR MARKET TRENDS

We now turn to a brief comparison of the British and German labour markets more generally. Of particular interest is how differences in the structure of employment and labour market activity might affect unemployment and escape from unemployment. After looking at trends in employment and the sectoral composition of employment, we examine the labour market activity rates of different age groups and of women, and compare part-time work in the two countries.

### 2.3.1 Employment Trends

Overall trends in employment reflect the demand for labour and affect how difficult it is for those who are unemployed to find a job. Notwithstanding differences between individuals, a period of job scarcity in the labour market makes it more difficult for the unemployed to find employment.

In Figure 2.7 we compare percentage changes in total employment in Britain and West Germany. (The focus here on West Germany provides useful background for Chapter 5, when we specifically compare exit from unemployment in Britain and West Germany.)[15] Figures are taken from the *Statistisches Jahrbuch* for Germany as there is no separate series available

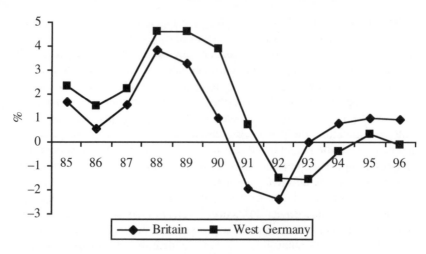

*Sources*:   OECD Labour Force Statistics 1976–96 for Britain (OECD 1997c); *Statistisches Jahrbuch*, various years for West Germany.

*Figure 2.7    Percentage change in total employment, Britain and West Germany, 1985–96*

from international statistics for West Germany: both sources use the ILO definition of employment.[16] Looking at Figure 2.7 we see similar trends in the two countries, with employment growth in times of macroeconomic growth and employment falling at the beginning of the 1990s during recession (compare Figure 2.1). In Germany, the recession came slightly later than in Britain, and total employment in West Germany did not show positive growth until later in the 1990s, some time after reunification, nor indeed was the growth in employment in the 1990s as strong as in Britain.

### 2.3.2    Sectoral Changes in Employment

Both countries have undergone significant changes in the nature of employment in the last 25 years. Table 2.2 presents the share of total employment by broad sector of the economy since the mid-1970s, drawing on estimates from *Employment in Europe* (European Commission 1997). The table shows a trend away from industry and agriculture towards services in both Britain and Germany.

Growth in employment is now concentrated in the service sector. Service sector employment has been more sustained in Britain, and in 1996 it accounted for just over 70 per cent of employment. In Germany this figure was 61.8 per cent. It has been argued that the lower service sector growth in

*Table 2.2    Share of total employment in agriculture, industry and services in Britain and Germany\*, selected years, 1975–96*

|      | Britain | | | Germany | | |
|------|---------------|-----------------|------------------|---------------|-----------------|------------------|
|      | Agric. (%) | Industry (%) | Services (%) | Agric. (%) | Industry (%) | Services (%) |
| 1975 | 2.8 | 40.4 | 56.8 | 6.8 | 45.4 | 47.8 |
| 1985 | 2.4 | 34.7 | 63.0 | 5.2 | 41.0 | 53.8 |
| 1991 | 2.1 | 29.4 | 68.5 | 4.2 | 40.3 | 55.5 |
| 1996 | 2.0 | 27.5 | 70.6 | 2.9 | 35.3 | 61.8 |

*Note*:    * Figures from 1992 onwards include East Germany.

*Source*:    *Employment in Europe* (European Commission 1997).

Germany is related to the relatively high cost of labour and to wage compression (e.g. Appelbaum and Schettkat 1990). In Germany the industrial sector has not undergone as rapid a decline as in most West European countries, and 35 per cent of total employment was in industry in 1996, compared to 27 per cent in Britain (European Commission 1997). Manufacturing, at 24 per cent of employment, was still significant in the West German labour market.

In general, older, quite often male, workers have lost out from restructuring in manufacturing in both Britain and Germany. The decline of manufacturing and expansion of services has significant consequences for women's employment, part-time work and unemployment, the implications of which are discussed throughout this book.

### 2.3.3    Labour Force Activity Rates by Age Group

Another salient issue when considering the nature of employment, unemployment and escape from unemployment is labour force activity rates (or participation rates), i.e. the labour force expressed as a percentage of the population of working age. As Table 2.3 shows, there are significant differences in participation rates for different age groups in both countries, participation rates being highest for the 25–49 age group. The differences between the countries for this 'prime-age' group are not large.

For the younger age group (15–24), British activity rates are higher than German for both men and women. It is assumed that most of this difference is accounted for by differences in the education and training systems. Firstly, the average age of leaving school is higher in Germany. Secondly, a much

*Table 2.3    Labour force activity rates, percentage of working age*
*population (15–64 years) by age group, 1984 and 1996*

|  | Britain | | Germany | | West Germany | East Germany |
|---|---|---|---|---|---|---|
|  | 1984 | 1996 | 1984 | 1996 * | 1996 | 1996 |
| 15–24 (All) ** | 60.4 | 64.5 | 52.6 | 52.5 | 51.6 | 56.1 |
| Men | 65.6 | 68.4 | 55.1 | 56.7 | 55.5 | 61.0 |
| Women | 55.1 | 60.3 | 50.1 | 48.1 | 47.5 | 50.4 |
| 25–49 (All) | 80.5 | 84.0 | 77.3 | 85.0 | 82.9 | 94.4 |
| Men | 95.5 | 92.8 | 94.7 | 93.9 | 93.5 | 95.7 |
| Women | 65.6 | 75.1 | 59.5 | 75.7 | 71.9 | 92.9 |
| 50–64 (All) | 60.3 | 61.5 | 50.6 | 56.3 | 56.2 | 56.7 |
| Men | 76.6 | 71.9 | 72.0 | 67.7 | 69.3 | 61.1 |
| Women | 45.0 | 51.5 | 32.7 | 45.0 | 43.0 | 52.6 |

*Notes*:
\*   Microcensus estimates differ very slightly from the European Labour Force Survey because of sample differences, see endnote 5.
\*\*   In 1984 this age group was 14–24.

*Sources*:   European Labour Force Surveys for Britain and for Germany 1984 (Eurostat 1986, 1997); Microcensus for Germany 1996.

greater proportion of German young people are in apprenticeship training, and therefore counted as out of the labour force by Eurostat (see Section 2.4).

As Table 2.3 also shows, participation rates for the 50–64 age group are much lower than for the 25–49 age category in both countries. Participation rates for women of this age group are very low in both countries, which is discussed in more detail below (Section 2.3.4). For men the activity rate fell in both countries between 1984 and 1996. While the fall in participation rates, particularly of men, has recently received much attention in Britain (e.g. Gregg et al. 1999; Disney 1999), the participation rates for both men and women of this age group are actually lower in Germany. Possible explanations for the lower participation rate among men in the older age group are early retirement, special benefit regulations and incapacity/invalidity.

Early retirement is more common in Germany. Kruppe et al. (1999), using data from the European Labour Force Survey for 1995 (Eurostat), find that while in Germany 50 per cent of exits to retirement from dependent employment are by people under 60, only 27 per cent in Britain are under 60. There are a number of early retirement schemes in Germany. Those with a long contribution history (35 years) can retire at 63 (Bloendal and Scarpetta 1997), and from 1984 to 1988 Germany had a special early retirement scheme in which workers were granted an early retirement pension from the age of 58 if they were replaced by an unemployed or young person. Particularly relevant for this book is that those who were long-term unemployed could receive a pension at 60.[17] Kruppe et al. (1999) find a particularly high rate of transition in Germany from unemployment to early retirement in both 1985 and 1995 – in fact the highest rate of transition among all the EU countries they examine. As noted in Chapter 1, following the collapse of the East German labour market in the early 1990s, many special labour market programmes that included early retirement were put in place in East Germany, especially for the 50–64 age group, whose participation rate was particularly low (see Table 2.3).[18] In Britain there was an early retirement scheme in the 1980s, but it was abolished in 1988, though early retirement continued to be seen, especially among those with occupational pensions (Disney 1999). And Casey (1996) would argue that there is 'de facto' early retirement for unemployed men over 60 in Britain: the fact that unemployed men over 60 were not required to register as jobseekers to receive means-tested benefit 'meant that older unemployed men are treated effectively as being old-age pensioners' (Casey 1996, p. 386). At the introduction of this measure in the early 1980s, registered unemployment among 60–64-year-olds fell by two-thirds (Casey 1996).

In addition, the claiming of benefit for incapacity/invalidity, which particularly in Britain has received increasing attention as a means of labour market exit, is often linked to local labour market conditions. The incentive for an individual to take up incapacity/invalidity benefit may be linked to the replacement rate, which is often higher than for unemployment benefit. In Britain in 1996, long-term incapacity benefit was 27 per cent higher than unemployment benefit. The high take-up of incapacity/invalidity benefit may also be linked to the less stringent eligibility conditions than for unemployment benefit, particularly the lack of a requirement to search actively for a job. The conditions for receipt of incapacity/invalidity benefit in Germany explicitly take local labour market conditions into account (Casey 1996; Bloendal and Pearson 1995). This is not the case in Britain, but Disney and Webb (1991) provide strong evidence that the receipt of incapacity benefit in Britain is nevertheless linked to the local unemployment rate. They suggest that the tightening of conditions for unemployment benefit in Britain in the late 1980s may explain why the rate of incapacity benefit receipt did not fall during this period.[19] Though it is difficult to estimate the extent to which incapacity/invalidity benefit influences the unemployment rate, it does seem that its impact is greater in Britain. Estimates from the European Labour Force Survey in 1996 show that whereas 6.7 per cent of all inactive men in Germany were not seeking work because of illness or disability, this was true of 21.7 per cent of inactive men in Britain.[20]

The fact that there is more early retirement in Germany and greater movement to incapacity benefit in Britain may affect our subsequent analysis, though it is difficult to assess the magnitude of this effect: we can merely speculate on the direction of the effect. If a substantial number of those at high risk of unemployment move into early retirement or incapacity, this will tend to lower the unemployment rate. If this were happening in one country to a greater extent than in the other, the comparison of unemployment rates might be biased. We might expect that those moving to incapacity benefit in Britain are at higher risk of unemployment than others remaining in the labour market, so this may lower the unemployment rate for the older age group there. Those retiring on the general early retirement schemes in Germany do not clearly have a higher risk of unemployment, so it is not clear that they will affect the analysis of unemployment. The impact is different though for those on the early retirement scheme for long-term unemployed in Germany, or the de facto early retired in Britain (i.e. older unemployed men who receive means-tested benefits but do not register as unemployed) – in both cases the effect might be to lower the overall unemployment rate. However, one might note that over-57-year-olds entering unemployment in Germany have an incentive to remain unemployed to qualify for an early pension. This, combined with long benefits durations for this age group, may increase the duration of unemployment in Germany for those over 57. We return to this point in Chapter 5.

### 2.3.4   Labour Force Activity Rates of Women

In both Britain and Germany the labour force activity rates of women are lower than those of men, though the gender gap is small for the youngest age group (Table 2.3). The trend during the period covered by this book is very similar in the two countries: men's activity rates fell over the period while women's rose significantly, for all age groups in Britain and for all but the youngest in Germany. The persistent rise in female participation, largely undeterred by downturns in the economic cycle, is remarkable.

Between 1984 and 1996 the female activity rate in Britain rose by nearly 10 percentage points for the 25–49 age group. In 1996 the overall female participation rate was one of the highest in the EU. Part of the explanation for this is the changing nature of employment in Britain; employment growth has been in non-manual professional and personal services and in part-time employment (discussed in the next section), jobs which are more attractive to women. Crompton (1997) notes how most of the recent rise in women's employment in Britain has been part-time work.

Germany has seen a similar rise in female labour force participation, although here the picture is somewhat more complicated as participation rates are very different in East and West Germany (Table 2.3). Although female participation in East Germany has fallen since reunification in the face of high and rising unemployment, it has remained much higher than in the West, and in 1996 the rate for the prime age group (25–49) was almost 93 per cent in the East compared to around 72 per cent in the West.[21] Even for the older age group (50–64) female participation is considerably higher in the East than in West Germany.[22] Indeed, part of the reason for the rise in the figure for German women as a whole between 1984 and 1996, as shown in Table 2.3, is that East German women are included in the 1996 figure.

If we exclude East Germany, we can see that in 1996 the participation rate of West German women was significantly lower than that of British women, in all age groups. What might explain this? Some authors have focused on the extent to which state policies facilitate women's employment. For example the burden of childcare almost always falls on women, and there is likely to be a smaller difference between men's and women's labour market participation in countries with good public provision of childcare. Empirical evidence does indeed suggest that increased provision of public childcare is associated with an increase in paid employment of women (Connelly 1992).

Table 2.4 shows the proportion of young children in publicly funded childcare and at school. Both Britain and Germany have limited childcare provision, restricting the employment opportunities for women with young children. Both countries have a very low level of provision for the nought to two age group. German provision for three-year-olds is better, with an extensive network of kindergartens. For five-year-olds this pattern is reversed, with the early school age in Britain meaning that all five-year-olds spend the day in school, whereas in Germany, school does not start until children are six or seven.

*Table 2.4   Proportion of young children in publicly funded childcare and at school*

|  | Aged 0–2 (%) | Aged 3–school age (%) | Children (age 5) in pre-primary or school (%) |
| --- | --- | --- | --- |
| Britain | 2 | 38 | 100 |
| Germany | 2 | 78 | 85 |

*Source*:   Gornick et al. 1997.

In addition, Gornick et al. (1997) note how low weekly school hours are particularly incompatible with employment schedules, especially when the school hours are discontinuous. Though pre-school childcare provision is low in both countries, school schedules in Britain are more compatible with women's employment than they are in Germany, where school hours are low.

While childcare is seen as particularly significant for the participation of mothers, other institutional factors are also salient. Extended unpaid maternity leave in Germany allows a mother who can afford it to stay at home with her child for up to three years after the child is born (Gauthier 1996; O'Reilly and Bothfeld 2002). In Britain, shorter maternity leave and informal childcare arrangements mean women tend to return to employment sooner. Daly (2000) highlights the role of tax-splitting in Germany (*Ehegattensplitting*), whereby spouses' incomes are added together, halved and then taxed as two separate incomes, in privileging the single male breadwinner family model. In Britain the absence of tax-splitting reduces the advantage in tax terms of being married. Daly concludes that although there are some premiums to marriage in Britain, the role of a dependent, non-earning wife is more supported in Germany (Daly 2000).

Other authors stress cultural arguments for differences in the labour force participation of women (Höllinger 1991; Pfau-Effinger 1998). Pfau-Effinger argues that the primary explanation is differences in gender culture, particularly in cultural ideals about the work of mothers and the appropriate sphere for bringing up children. Höllinger observes that the participation of women in Britain, while falling with the birth of children, rises again after children go to school, whereas this does not happen in Germany. Höllinger links this difference to evidence of strong attitudes in Germany against working mothers with pre-school and school-age children.

One conclusion might be that it is a combination of factors – welfare and employment institutions, cultural differences and also labour market demand – that explains differences in women's labour market participation between Britain and Germany. In any case, as Meyer (1997) notes, in the context of the overall rapid rise in women's labour market participation it is important to reiterate the terms of this participation. Women's capacity for independence is limited by both low incomes (especially in Britain) and the lack of work for women (especially in Germany). When women participate in the labour market, they often do not do so on the same terms as men.

### 2.3.5    Part-time Work

In the analysis of employment, an important distinction, which is particularly salient for women, is between full-time and part-time work. Table 2.5 shows the growth between 1983 and 1996 in both Britain and Germany in the

*Table 2.5    Percentage of people in employment working part-time, 1983 and 1996, by sex*

|  | Men | | Women | |
|---|---|---|---|---|
|  | 1983 | 1996 | 1983 | 1996 |
| Britain | 3.3 | 8.1 | 42.1 | 44.8 |
| Germany* | 1.7 | 3.8 | 30.0 | 33.6 |

*Note*:    * 1996 figures include East Germany.

*Source*:    European Labour Force Surveys (Eurostat 1985 and 1997).

proportion of people in employment who were working part-time. The table also reveals that part-time work is more prevalent in Britain than in Germany, among both men and women. Indeed, Rubery et al. (1998) show that 68 per cent of new jobs in Britain in the period 1983–92 were part-time, compared to only 40 per cent of new jobs in West Germany during the same period.[23] This difference should be borne in mind when we observe the higher female participation rate in Britain, shown in Table 2.3.[24]

But it is the gender difference in the extent of part-time work that is most striking. In 1996, just under 45 per cent of British women and 34 per cent of German women were working part-time as opposed to 8 per cent and 4 per cent of British and German men respectively.[25] Blossfeld and Hakim (1997), using longitudinal data, stress the importance of part-time work for the mothers of young children in a range of countries, Britain and Germany included.

While part-time work may be associated with low pay and less favourable conditions in both countries, in an analysis of unemployment such as this it may be most useful to consider it as a route out of unemployment, especially for women trying to combine work and family life, rather than as a route into unemployment. In a comparison of transitions from part-time work in Britain and Germany, O'Reilly and Bothfeld (2002) show that part-time work is actually quite stable, particularly for women, and is not disproportionately associated with transitions to unemployment, either in Britain or Germany.

## 2.4    EDUCATION, TRAINING AND UNEMPLOYMENT

The education system is an important mediator between supply and demand in the labour market (Halsey et al. 1997). According to human capital theory, employers ranking potential candidates have imperfect information about applicants, and education is used as a screening device. Those with lower qualifications do worse in the competition for jobs, receive lower wages and are more vulnerable to unemployment (Becker 1993). Though the human capital approach suggests that these processes will be rather similar in different labour markets (in this sense it is to be interpreted as a 'universal' theory), the relationship between education and unemployment may vary according to the education system, or the interaction between the education system and the labour market. There has been much cross-national research to show how education systems shape unemployment in different ways (e.g. Müller and Shavit 1998; Brauns et al. 1999).

Müller and Shavit (1998) contrast the highly stratified German education system with the unstratified British one.[26] The German education system is also classified as highly standardised (i.e. quality of education the same nationwide), though here Britain is an ambiguous case, having a fairly standardised general education system, but low standardisation of vocational and post-secondary qualifications (Müller and Shavit 1998). The largest difference between the education systems, though, is in the extent of vocational training. Vocational training may be viewed as a way of improving matching between individuals and employers by providing individuals with specific skills that they can use on the job. Britain lacks a standardised and widespread system of vocational training; there is much stronger vocational orientation in Germany, and segmentation along occupational lines (Müller and Shavit 1998). This difference is most manifest in labour market outcomes among young people – youth unemployment has been consistently lower in Germany than in Britain, and much of this difference is attributed to the apprenticeship system in facilitating the transition from school to work in Germany (OECD 1998; Brauns et al. 1999). In Britain, as Bernardi et al. (2000) note, attending a vocational course instead of a more regular school course is often thought to be a sign of educational failure.

While there are clear effects of the vocational training system on early labour market outcomes, less work has been done on the effects of vocational training on unemployment for older people. There is certainly a strong expectation in Germany that once trained in a certain occupation in the vocational training system, the individual will stay in this occupation. It is conceivable that such a vocational training system could lead to longer durations of unemployment for older individuals due to the difficulty of making transitions between different occupations where qualifications are highly formalised. This idea is consistent with previous empirical work that highlights low occupational mobility in Germany across the life course (e.g. Blossfeld et al. 1993).[27]

Retraining is possible in the German system, though, as Schömann (2002) notes, the incidence of this is rather low in comparative perspective. Particularly for those over 55, retraining is often seen as futile by both employers and employees. Indeed Schömann (2002) concludes that though the initial transition from school to work functions well in Germany, later transitions do not. For Britain, the opposite is true: Green (2000) has argued that, in general, Britain does not have a problem with the system of continuing training, but with its initial skill formation system.[28]

In conclusion, we would argue that attachment to occupation is not as marked in Britain, and qualifications are not as formalised. We would therefore expect it to be easier to move between occupations in Britain, particularly for older workers who lose their job. But this lower level of attachment to occupation should be seen in the context of the more general lower level of skills in the British labour market and a more difficult school to work transition than in Germany.

## 2.5 EMPLOYMENT, UNEMPLOYMENT AND THE FAMILY

As we argued in Chapter 1, while employment and unemployment are largely viewed as affecting individuals, it is important to consider the role of the family in understanding them. The family is an important mediating structure between individuals and the labour market (Saraceno 1997); family structure and patterns of relationships between husbands, wives, young and adult children can affect labour market activity greatly.

What are the principal differences between Britain and Germany in family structure? In terms of the main demographic indicators, we saw in Chapter 1 that Britain and Germany have undergone changes similar to many Western countries in recent decades. While the marriage rate has remained stable and similar in the two countries,[29] the divorce rate has increased significantly. The proportion of marriages ending in divorce for those married in 1980 was 42 per cent in Britain and 33 per cent in Germany (Gallie and Paugam 2000, p. 14). In terms of relations between the generations, young adults in Britain and Germany tend to live separately and are for the most part autonomous from their parents. Gallie and Paugam (2000) characterise the family model in both countries as one of 'advanced intergenerational autonomy'.

Regarding policies towards the family, Gauthier (1996) characterises the German approach as a 'pro-traditional model', for which the preservation of the family is the main concern (Gauthier 1996, p. 203). The state provides moderate support for the family, while encouraging the traditional male breadwinner family. Public childcare provision is generally low, and the state gives preference to extended leave for childcare, as discussed in Section 2.3.4. For Gauthier, the British model is 'pro-family but non-interventionist' – belief in the self-sufficiency of families and the merits of the market results in a system with very low levels of state support for the family (Gauthier 1996, p. 204). The British state is not opposed to women's participation, but childcare is not seen as the state's responsibility. That said, recent moves by governments in both countries suggest that public provision of childcare may improve.[30]

Table 2.6 illustrates how employment, unemployment and inactivity are distributed among families in the two countries. The table compares the labour market position of couples; in a later discussion we consider lone mothers.[31] The proportion of couples with both spouses employed ('dual breadwinner' couples) is similar in Britain and Germany. Disaggregating East and West Germany, however, we find a much higher proportion of dual

*Table 2.6    Percentage of couples in Britain and Germany in different labour market situations, both spouses 25–54-years-old*

|  | Britain 1994 | Germany 1994 | West Germany 1996 | East Germany 1996 |
|---|---|---|---|---|
| Both spouses employed | 63.9 | 63.2 | 61.1 | 70.1 |
| One employed, one unemployed | 5.1 | 4.9 | 3.3 | 11.6 |
| One employed, one inactive | 23.3 | 30.1 | 31.9 | 13.4 |
| Both unemployed or inactive, | 7.7 | 1.8 | 3.8 | 4.0 |
| of which: | | | | |
| *Husband*          *Wife* | | | | |
| Unemployed      Unemployed | 0.9 | 0.3 | 0.7 | 2.3 |
| Unemployed      Inactive | 3.9 | 0.8 | 1.0 | 0.4 |
| Inactive            Unemployed | 0.2 | 0.1 | 0.0 | 0.7 |
| Inactive            Inactive | 2.7 | 0.6 | 2.6 | 0.7 |
| No. of couples with complete information | 1,710 | 1,720 | 1,763 | 706 |
| Data source | ECHP 1994 | ECHP 1994 | GSOEP 1996 | GSOEP 1996 |

*Sources*:   De Graaf and Ultee (2000) using data from the European Community Household Panel (ECHP), Table 13.1 for 1994; and own calculations from the German Socio-economic Panel (GSOEP), weighted, for 1996.

breadwinner couples in East Germany than in West. Germany has a higher proportion of couples than Britain in which one spouse is employed and one inactive.

Compared to Germany, Britain has a relatively high proportion of couples with both spouses unemployed or inactive ('workless couples'). For Germany there is some difference in the proportion of workless couples in the two years (and data sources) cited in the table, though under both estimates the proportion of workless couples is considerably lower than in Britain. Looking more closely at these workless couples in Britain, we find that in most cases the husband is either unemployed or inactive, and the wife is inactive. 'Workless households', a term that includes single people and lone parents as well as workless couples, have received considerable attention in Britain (e.g. Gregg et al. 1999). In contrast to Britain, in workless couples in East Germany both spouses tend to be unemployed. In West Germany there is a higher proportion of workless couples where both partners are inactive. The table shows that a greater proportion of the unemployed in Britain are not supported by another earner, which is a theme to which we return in both Chapter 4, when examining poverty rates among the unemployed, and Chapter 6, when we look at the labour force transitions of the wives of unemployed men.

And what of other family forms? Lone motherhood has increased in both countries, though is much more common in Britain than in Germany. Pedersen et al. (2000) estimate that 10 per cent of mothers in Germany are lone mothers, compared to 16 per cent in Britain.[32] Indeed, Britain has the highest rate of lone motherhood in Europe. Pedersen et al. (2000) also note the particularly low employment rate of lone mothers in Britain. They estimate that in 1994 only 37.6 per cent of lone mothers in Britain were in employment, compared to 74.8 per cent in Germany. Lewis (1997) notes that the low labour market participation of lone mothers in Britain is relatively unusual in a country where the participation of other women with children is relatively high. She attributes this to two factors: firstly the lack of comprehensive childcare provision, and secondly the nature of the social security system – a flat-rate, non-stigmatising, means-tested benefit. In Britain there are national guidelines for benefits for lone mothers and there is much less scope for discrimination in the administration of benefit than there is in other social assistance schemes, such as Germany's. Lewis with Hobson (1997) note how German lone mothers are much more likely to work outside the home. In Germany, social assistance payments are low and wages better than in Britain.

Summarising the distribution of family employment, we find a somewhat lower participation of women in the West German labour market and a correspondingly lower proportion of dual-earner couples. East Germany has a relatively high proportion of dual-earner couples and a structure of employment less oriented towards the male breadwinner model, but also more unemployment than Britain or West Germany. In comparison with West Germany, Britain has a somewhat higher proportion of both dual-earner and workless couples, implying a polarisation of couples' employment (Gregg et al. 1999).

## 2.6   CONCLUSION

The main purpose of this chapter is to give the context for the analysis of outcomes for unemployed individuals in later chapters. To this end the chapter compares a range of aspects of unemployment and the labour markets in Britain and Germany, sometimes making cross-sectional comparisons, but mostly with a focus on change over time.

We discuss some of the difficulties of measuring unemployment, especially from a comparative perspective. All measures of unemployment have strengths and weaknesses, though we argue that the ILO measure is superior for comparative purposes, where it is possible to use it. However, for all measures of unemployment we need to consider who is excluded from the chosen measure. We consider how the rise in long-term sickness benefit receipt in Britain and the high rate of early retirement in Germany, particularly retirement from unemployment, might affect unemployment rates. Using the data we have, it is difficult to judge the extent to which unemployment is affected by these trends.

Looking at change over time we see that there was considerable volatility during the period under scrutiny (1983–98) in both macroeconomic performance and harmonised unemployment rates. An important feature of this volatility for our analysis is that the periods of high and low unemployment did not coincide in the two countries, nor did changes in overall employment. This has a number of implications. One is that our modelling needs to take into account macroeconomic variation, as changes in the demand for labour affect exit from unemployment. Secondly, when carrying out cross-sectional analysis, as we do in Chapter 4, rather than choosing the same calendar year we choose years of high unemployment in both countries.

Our focus on change over time has the benefit of preventing us from being misled by short-term fluctuations. However, the longitudinal perspective can make cross-national comparisons more complex, particularly where there is greater variation over time than there is between the countries, as is the case with the proportion of long-term unemployed in Britain and Germany (Figure 2.6). Given the variation over time, in the following summary of similarities and differences in unemployment between Britain and Germany we use averages for the period 1983–98.

Using our preferred measure of labour force status – the ILO definition – the average unemployment rate was 9.3 per cent in Britain and 7.1 per cent in Germany.[33] The proportion of the unemployed who were long-term unemployed was relatively high in both countries, relative to other EU countries. It was, on average, somewhat higher in Germany, with 41.0 per cent long-term unemployed in Britain and 45.2 per cent in Germany, though this difference is not large and at times the proportion was higher in Britain.

A smaller proportion of women were unemployed in Britain than in Germany, and a higher proportion worked part-time. We argue that the more rapid growth of the service sector in Britain provided more jobs for women. Unemployment was particularly high among East German women, many of whom were long-term unemployed. Regarding different age groups, youth unemployment was a more pressing problem in Britain. The average rate of youth unemployment during this period was 15.4 per cent in Britain, compared to only 8.0 per cent in Germany. We argue that the apprenticeship system in Germany seems to guarantee more jobs and a more fluid transition for young people, and that it is important to consider how different education systems may influence unemployment. The very high rate of unemployment among older Germans by contrast has been particularly marked in recent years, particularly in East Germany, and reunified Germany currently faces a large problem of how to reintegrate the older, long-term unemployed.

A theme that runs through this chapter is the differences between unemployment in East and West Germany. Following reunification, the massive restructuring of the East German economy led to very high unemployment there, with particularly high unemployment among women and the older age group, as these groups bore the brunt of economic restructuring. The high unemployment among East German women has to be seen in the context of the much higher female labour market participation in East Germany, which suggests a 'dual breadwinner' model rather than the 'male breadwinner' model seen in West Germany. The combination of high female labour market participation and high unemployment in the East leaves a somewhat different constellation of household situations from that seen in West Germany, which is particularly important for our investigation of poverty in Chapter 4.

## NOTES

1. In 1992 about 173 billion DM flowed from West to East Germany, equivalent to about half of East German and 7 per cent of West German GNP (Bosch and Knuth 1993).
2. There are exceptions to the 'actively seeking work' condition for unemployed over 60 in Britain, see Section 2.3.3.
3. Before 1982 the definition of unemployment in Britain was similar to that in Germany (Clasen, 1994a). The claimant count includes a small number of unemployed who claim

benefit but do not receive insurance or assistance benefit because they do not fulfil the entitlement criteria (see Figure 3.2). The advantage in claiming is that their national insurance payments are covered. However, many of the unemployed who know they are not eligible for benefit do not make a claim at all.

4. The concept of the *Stille Reserve* particularly applies to West Germany; in East Germany individuals are much more likely to register as unemployed (Holst 2000).

5. The Microcensus sample is more than twice as big as the European Labour Force Survey sample and it also includes residents of institutions. Those on military and national service are counted as employed. For 1997, this resulted in a 0.1 per cent difference in the overall unemployment rate (9.8 in the Microcensus, 9.9 in the European Labour Force Survey). The proportion of unemployed who are long-term unemployed in Germany is somewhat overestimated by the Microcensus (55 per cent in 1997) relative to the European Labour Force Survey (at 50 per cent) (Statistisches Bundesamt, 2001).

6. The British Household Panel Survey (BHPS), one of the datasets used in Chapters 5 and 6, is an example. The final Appendix discusses some of the advantages and disadvantages of this measure.

7. In addition, women returning to the labour force after a period of absence lack any formal procedure to mark the transition from housewife to being unemployed if they do not receive benefit.

8. By the turn of the century the North/South divide was becoming more salient again.

9. In this respect the West German experience was quite similar to Britain's.

10. The only exception to this was Britain in 1983, when the youth unemployment rate was 20.2 per cent, compared to an EU average of 19.7 per cent.

11. The duration of unemployment is here defined as either (1) the duration of a search for a job, or (2) the length of time since the last job (if this period is shorter than the duration of the job search).

12. On average during this period (1983–98) the long-term unemployed made up a slightly larger share of the unemployed in Germany (45.2 per cent) than in Britain (41.0 per cent).

13. According to the Microcensus, 45 per cent of the West German unemployed were long-term unemployed in 1996, compared to 51 per cent in the East. As noted in note 5 above the Microcensus may slightly overestimate the proportion of long-term unemployed relative to the European Labour Force Survey.

14. From estimates using the German Microcensus.

15. In addition, employment in East Germany underwent such a massive fluctuation during this period that it is not easily compared in the same graph.

16. The *Statistisches Jahrbuch* uses data from the Microcensus.

17. The conditions of this pension were that the unemployed person be 60-years-old, have been unemployed for 52 weeks in the past 18 months and have paid sufficient pension contributions (in most cases for a minimum of 15 years). This measure was amended in 1996.

18. As well as early retirement, other programmes included ABM (Job Creation Schemes), short-time work, further training and retraining programmes.

19. Eligibility conditions for unemployment benefit are discussed in more detail in Chapter 3.

20. The figures for women were 3.5 per cent in Germany and 10.3 per cent in Britain (Eurostat, 1997).

21. A range of measures were in place to promote the labour market participation of women in East Germany, and women's labour market participation was high (Trappe, 1995).

22. Some of the difficulties of estimating female unemployment discussed in Section 2.2.1 also apply to labour force participation. In particular, frequent moves between unemployment and economic activity may distort the picture.

23. Table 2.5, p. 35, from special tabulations provided by Eurostat.

24. Indeed, at 45 per cent in 1996, the proportion of women working part-time in Britain was one of the highest in the EU, second only to the Netherlands (68 per cent) (Eurostat, 1997).

25. Among German women the percentage working part-time is higher in West Germany than

in East Germany; in 1996 around 38 per cent of West German women and 20 per cent of East German women were working part-time.

26. In this they follow Allmendinger (1989), who defines 'stratification' as the proportion of the cohort that attains the maximum number of school years provided by the education system, coupled with the degree of tracking within given educational levels.

27. Additional support for this argument comes from evidence that reaction to structural change takes place by means of 'cohort exchange' (Blossfeld 1989; DiPrete et al. 1997). Using life course data for a series of German cohorts, Blossfeld (1989) shows that, while for the older cohorts the distribution of occupations remains relatively stable, big changes are seen in the younger cohorts in the transition to their first job. In this way structural adjustment is achieved without older workers changing occupation.

28. However, in both countries low-skilled older workers tend to be excluded from further training, and this is the group who is most at risk of unemployment (Schömann 2002).

29. In 1995 the marriage rate was 5.5 per 1,000 in Britain and 5.3 per 1,000 in Germany (Gallie and Paugam 2000, p. 14).

30. The National Childcare Strategy was launched in Britain in May 1998, while in January 2001 the German Minister for Family Affairs, Senior Citizens, Women and Youth announced an increase in spending on kindergarten places ('Bund will neue Kitaplätze massiv fördern', *Berliner Zeitung*, 21 January 2001).

31. In Chapter 4 we focus specifically on the household situation of the unemployed.

32. Lone mothers include dependent single mothers, i.e. those living with partners or their own parents.

33. From 1992 onwards the average for Germany includes East Germany. The average ILO unemployment rate for this period in West Germany was 6.2 per cent.

# 3. Welfare for the unemployed in Britain and Germany

The overall aim of the book is to compare welfare provision and outcomes for the unemployed in Britain and Germany. The purpose of this chapter is to uncover the institutional frameworks with which to interpret the empirical comparison of outcomes conducted in later chapters. This chapter also aims to flesh out the bare bones provided by the typologies of welfare we reviewed in Chapter 1, drawing on these typologies in explaining both historical developments and current provision of welfare.

This chapter traces the development of welfare for the unemployed from the beginning of the 20th century until the present day, in the form of cash transfers and measures to assist the unemployed back into the labour market. The material has been chosen with later chapters in mind, and the emphasis is on the main period covered by analysis in this book: 1991–96 for Britain, and 1984–96 for Germany. We do, however, also include a brief historical account, arguing that past policy choices had a considerable impact on subsequent and current structures of provision.

After comparing the origin and evolution of benefits for the unemployed in Britain and Germany, we present an overview of the principles of unemployment compensation. We then focus on the 1980s, a period characterised by changes in the welfare systems – particularly in Britain – that have had a big impact on current provision. The next section presents an overview of benefit provision in 1996, comparing in detail the balance of means-tested and insurance benefits, as well as the conditions for the receipt of benefit, partly following Atkinson (1999). We then compare coverage and replacement rates for different groups of the unemployed, before very briefly looking at the provision of active labour market programmes. Finally, we conclude by reflecting on the differences in welfare for the unemployed for our subsequent analysis.

## 3.1   ORIGINS AND EVOLUTION OF SOCIAL SECURITY FOR THE UNEMPLOYED

Current welfare provision differs considerably between Britain and Germany. These differences have historical roots. Although structures and principles have changed over time, certain characteristics have remained since unemployment schemes were first implemented. The analysis in this section is very much in keeping with Esping-Andersen's view (1990) and that of the new institutionalism, which stresses the path dependency of social and political structures. The function of this section is to trace the development of welfare for the unemployed, and sketch the principles of welfare provision in both countries. In the first part we look at the evolution of policy in Germany and Britain separately, concluding with an overview of principles of welfare for the unemployed. In a separate section we then look more closely at developments in the 1980s in the two countries.

### 3.1.1 Germany

Germany led the way in Europe in introducing social insurance as a way of dealing with the costs and consequences of industrialisation. The rise of the labour movement was seen as the greatest threat to the newly established German Reich of 1871, and Bismarck set up the world's first social insurance scheme in the 1880s with the intention of reducing the growing influence of social democrats over the workers. Although unemployment insurance was not introduced until later, the first legislation was important in setting a precedent in Germany and throughout Europe. A succession of laws were passed, introducing compulsory insurance against sickness (1883), industrial accidents (1884) and invalidity and old age (1889). Contributions by employers and employees were the main sources of funding. Although benefits were initially at a low level, they established the principle of a legal claim to protection and gave workers a financial stake in the system (Rosenhaft 1994). By the turn of the century more than half of all wage earners were members of social insurance schemes. Subsequent measures included special provision for civil servants (*Beamte*), who still enjoy a privileged position in the German welfare system.

It is important to note that Bismarck's legislation did not cover the risk of unemployment. In the 1880s unemployment was still seen as what would now be termed 'voluntary', and insuring against unemployment was not approved. It was only in later decades, under pressure from the trade unions (who began to compensate members for unemployment as early as 1896) and in the face of growing unemployment, that unemployment became seen as a social rather than an individual problem, one for which the state needed to assume responsibility. It was not until 1927 that a fully-fledged national unemployment insurance system was established. Nevertheless, unemployment insurance had much in common with earlier policy choices. It was financed partly by contributions shared equally between employers and employees, and partly by central government. Corresponding to the three sources of funding it was governed on a tripartite basis, thereby giving trade unions an influence over unemployment insurance, which they retain today. By the end of the 1920s the structure of today's social welfare system was in place, though it was interrupted by the National Socialists' seizure of power.

In the 'take-off' phase after the war, with high economic growth rates, social security spending increased considerably (Clasen 1994b). During the reform period between the mid-1950s and the early 1960s, the existing 'three-tier' benefit structure was reshaped; in the post-war period three types of cash payment for the unemployed have been in operation: *Arbeitslosengeld*, which is linked to contribution records; *Arbeitslosenhilfe*, which is linked to contributions but is also means-tested; and *Sozialhilfe*, a means-tested scheme.

The take-off phase came to an end after the first oil price shock in the mid-1970s. Rising unemployment meant simultaneously less income from contributions and increased social security spending, to which the government's response was cutbacks. This trend continued into the 1980s, which is the subject of more detailed discussion below.

### 3.1.2   Britain

The development of the British welfare state was dominated by other priorities. The first measures were introduced to stem the rising tide of poverty, rather than the fear of workers' revolt, as in Bismarckian Germany. Until the turn of the 20th century, provision had been in the form of the Poor Law,[1] and while Germany introduced radical social reform to deal with its social problems, the British solution to similar problems retained elements and ideology of the Poor Law. Poor Law provision was dominated by the principle of 'less eligibility' – that relief should be inferior in volume and in form to the wages earned by the lowest paid labourer – and provision was restricted to unemployed, able-bodied males (Daly 1994). In the early part of the century, then, the principal concern of welfare was the alleviation of poverty, and with this concern came an emphasis on needs-based provision.

The Liberal Party's National Insurance Act of 1911 created a national insurance system for the first time in Britain. The act introduced accident, unemployment, and sickness and disability insurance. The new benefits were flat-rate, with no means test, were of very limited duration, and were regulated and subsidised by central government (Brown 1990). Though the act's provisions were modelled on the German system (Hennock 1987), the British were first in introducing national insurance specifically for the *unemployed*.

British social insurance was expanded in the next 20 years. Coverage was widened in 1920 from four million to 11.4 million workers at a time of low unemployment. As unemployment began to rise in subsequent years, a 'genuinely seeking work' test was introduced in 1921, shifting the burden of proof of unemployment from the labour exchange to the claimant (Morris 1991, p. 12). The 1934 Unemployment Act established a national Unemployment Assistance Board, to deal with those who had no insurance rights or who had exhausted those rights – effectively taking over many of the public assistance claimants. By 1937 those who were registered as unemployed could receive one of three benefits: unemployment insurance, (means-tested) unemployment assistance or locally administered public assistance.

The Beveridge Report of 1942 was a milestone in the development of welfare for the unemployed in Britain. Beveridge proposed that unemployment insurance be integrated with other benefits, in a compulsory system covering the whole population. Flat-rate contributions were to be financed by employers, employees and a subsidy from the state. Formulated against the backdrop of World War II, the Beveridge Report proved highly popular at the time as a programme for eliminating poverty, and the newly elected Labour government accepted the main structures of Beveridge's proposals in the National Insurance Act of 1946.

However, not all of Beveridge's ideas were implemented. In Beveridge's vision, social insurance was to be the basic compensation for the unemployed and of unlimited duration, with means-tested assistance to be used only in exceptional circumstances (Brown 1990). When the nationally coordinated system came into force, however, benefit duration was limited to 30 weeks. The government argued that indefinite benefits would be open to abuse (Brown 1990). In addition, there was disagreement between the Beveridge Report and the government on the rates to be paid (Brown 1990; Morris 1991). In the end, payments were fixed at a low rate; the subsequent National Assistance Act of 1948 set up a centrally regulated system of means-tested benefits, funded from tax revenues, and most of the unemployed required this support to supplement their inadequate insurance benefit (Morris 1991).

As the economy grew in the 1950s and 1960s, welfare spending grew rapidly. In a historical break with social insurance principles, an earnings-related supplement to unemployment benefit was introduced in the National Insurance Act of 1966 (Morris 1991). It was seen as instrumental in promoting higher mobility of labour and thus economic growth. The existing flat-rate benefit was also increased, and its duration extended to one year. Though the political climate was affected by the oil crisis, the Labour governments of the 1970s in Britain did not undertake any significant reform of benefits for the unemployed.

### 3.1.3 Principles Underlying Welfare Benefits for the Unemployed

In both countries, benefits for the unemployed were introduced 'from above', as states struggled to deal with social problems. The responses differed, however, as did the political actors and social climates. In Germany, the workers' movement was more significant in the development of welfare for the unemployed, and trade unions in Germany have retained influence over unemployment benefits, much more so than in Britain. In Britain the alleviation of poverty, along with social protection, was and has remained a major motivating force behind social policy provision. Distribution based on need continues to underpin the provision of a minimum standard in Britain.

The German system of payments to the unemployed is hierarchical, structured by labour market status. There is a strong sense of earned entitlements, rewarding labour market participation on a scale closely linked to contributions – 'you get what you've paid in'. In Britain there is not the same sense of 'earned' benefit as insurance plays a much smaller role. Uniformity in benefits has meant similar rates of payment, regardless of benefit type. For example, the levels of social insurance and means-tested social assistance are similar in Britain. Also in Britain the idea of 'less eligibility' – the principle that the resources of welfare recipients should be less than the lowest income of the working poor – has influenced the definition of a minimum standard.[2] As a result, benefit rates are by no means generous.

Another key difference between the countries lies in the funding and regulation of benefits. In Germany, funding and regulation depend on the type of benefit. *Arbeitslosengeld* – unemployment insurance – is administered by an autonomous body outside the state apparatus, the Federal Labour Office (Bundesanstalt für Arbeit). Funding is from ear-marked contributions and both unions and employers are strongly involved in the funding and administration. *Arbeitslosenhilfe* – unemployment assistance – is administered by the same body, though it is means-tested and funded by tax revenues. *Sozialhilfe* – means-tested social assistance – is funded and administered separately, at local level by municipalities. This separation of administration and funding does not exist in Britain: insurance and means-tested benefits are part of a centralised system, and the central state has remained fully in control of benefits for the unemployed. These funding differences have important implications for a government's ability to make changes to unemployment benefits, as seen below in the context of the 1980s.

In summary, the German system emerges as an insurance system, as characterised by Schmid and Reissert (1996), though it is an *insurance system with welfare elements*. In contrast, the British system is a *welfare system with insurance elements*. We see below how, under pressure of high unemployment in the 1980s, the systems diverged even further – Germany clinging even more to the insurance principle, Britain moving further down the road of means-testing.

### 3.1.4 The 1980s

The 1980s was a particularly important period in the development of welfare provision for the unemployed. In Britain in particular it was a period of radical change and retrenchment. The changes introduced in Britain were more far-reaching and affected a much greater proportion of the unemployed than did changes in Germany. In Germany those affected were mostly those on the margins of the labour market – those without lengthy and stable records of unemployment insurance. Whereas in Germany those who were long-standing contributors to social insurance funds continued to enjoy barely diminished benefits, in Britain means-tested benefits replaced insurance as the major plank of social welfare.

Three particular factors paved the way for benefit changes in the 1980s in both countries. The second oil crisis triggered recessions and sharp rises in unemployment in the early 1980s. Left-wing governments were replaced by conservative or conservative-dominated governments. And there was an attack on welfare institutions, predominantly from neo-liberals, though Britain saw a much more radical shift to monetarism and anti-welfare ideology than Germany.

In Britain, a large number of major and minor changes were introduced to social security in the 1980s, which affected the unemployed either directly or indirectly. Atkinson and Micklewright (1989) identify 38 such changes between 1979 and 1988. These changes were implemented in a political climate in which social security was seen as a large burden on expenditure, restricting growth.

A number of changes weakened the insurance element of British provision for the unemployed. In 1982 the government abolished the earnings-related supplement to unemployment benefit, which made for an even sharper contrast with the German system, with its strong emphasis on a link to earnings.[3] In 1986 the government abolished lower rate benefits in Britain, which had been paid to those who had not met the full contribution requirements, significantly reducing the total number of benefit recipients. The 1988 Social Security Act tightened the contribution test for unemployment benefit, making it more difficult for claimants to qualify (Atkinson and Micklewright 1989).[4] Throughout the period the level of benefits relative to earnings fell dramatically.[5]

In the political climate of the time, it was widely thought that significant numbers of benefit claimants were not genuinely available for work. As a consequence, various measures were introduced between 1986 and 1989 to check availability for work, through, for example, closer scrutiny of the initial claim and compulsory restart interviews. In 1990 a new test of 'actively seeking work' was introduced for the unemployed. The penalty for refusal of a job offer (or indeed for being sacked for misconduct or voluntarily quitting a job) was increased from six weeks of suspended benefit to 13 weeks, and then subsequently to a six-month maximum (Murray 1995).[6]

The overall thrust of the changes in Britain in the 1980s was to restrict benefits for the unemployed.[7] Not all the changes had an unambiguously negative effect on incomes. For example, Morris (1991) argues that the family premium for income support, introduced in 1988, improved the position of unemployed families with children relative to other unemployed people. Nevertheless, Evans et al. (1994), looking at the 30 per cent income poverty line, find that many more of the unemployed were income poor after the reforms. Atkinson and Micklewright (1989) note how increasing numbers of the unemployed either experienced hardship or were not entitled to unemployment benefits at all. Some of the latter had recourse to other benefits, in particular, disability benefits, as discussed in Chapter 2.

In Germany, the 1980s began with a financial crisis in the Federal Labour Office, and concern with high expenditure led to some cuts in unemployment benefits. The two main changes of the early 1980s were an extension of the minimum contribution period for unemployment insurance from six to 12 months, and a change in the basis for calculating unemployment benefits, to exclude all bonuses and overtime. This latter change meant a real but hidden cut in the rates of both *Arbeitslosengeld* and *Arbeitslosenhilfe*, since the rates of benefit remained the same. The contribution change meant that access to insurance payments was restricted to those with longer contribution periods, excluding more 'peripheral' employees with discontinuous work histories. By the mid-1980s the proportion of those registered unemployed who were receiving unemployment insurance, *Arbeitslosengeld*, was around 35 per cent, the lowest rate in German history (*Statistisches Jahrbuch*, various years; Clasen 1994a).

In the second half of the 1980s the main change in Germany was an extension of the benefit period for older workers receiving *Arbeitslosengeld*, to a maximum period of 32 months for those 54 and over who had contributed for six years, a measure aimed at rewarding the 'loyal and long-term contributors to the unemployment insurance system' (see this chapter's Appendix, Table 3.1.A for further details). This lengthening of the duration of benefits was partly due to increasing concern about hardship among the older unemployed, but also had the effect of shifting the burden of financing unemployment back on the Federal Labour Office – away from the municipalities (Clasen, 1994a). The government had also introduced an early retirement scheme whereby older long-term unemployed could receive a pension at 60, though in practice because the duration of benefits had been lengthened for this group, by the late 1980s those who became unemployed at 57 were eligible for this benefit (see Chapter 2, Section 2.3.3 for further details). The changes in this period were rather selective, rewarding older unemployed with long contribution records.

Though there was initially a decline in the numbers receiving unemployment insurance in both countries in the 1980s (which stopped towards the end of the 1980s in Germany), the changes were of a rather different nature. In their summary of the changes to the unemployment benefit system in Britain, Atkinson and Micklewright conclude that there was 'a major change in emphasis, amounting to the covert abandonment of the insurance principle as far as the unemployed are concerned' (1989, p. 146). In Germany, the insurance principle remained dominant, and indeed the contribution principle was strengthened; those who had good contribution records were virtually unaffected by the changes in Germany in the 1980s.

Part of the explanation for this difference, in addition to the differences in the character of the governments, lies in institutional differences in the regulation of benefits. Firstly, the separation of the insurance fund in Germany reduced the scope for the government changes to benefits. Secondly, the fact that *Sozialhilfe* – social assistance – is administered and funded at a local level in Germany meant that the municipalities and the *Länder* governments played an important role in halting the rise in numbers of social assistance recipients during the 1980s. They argued that unemployment was a national problem and should be dealt with at a national level. Finally, the strong role of the trade unions in Germany in decisions about the level and conditions of unemployment benefit for their members was completely absent in 1980s Britain, where unions had almost no role in decisions about social security for the unemployed. Some authors have also argued that social insurance in Germany enjoys a level of support from the middle classes that unemployment benefits have never received in Britain (e.g. Esping-Andersen 1990).

## 3.2 OVERVIEW OF CURRENT BENEFIT PROVISION

Table 3.1 provides an overview of unemployment benefits in Britain and Germany in 1996. The year is chosen as the final year of empirical analysis in this book. Some relevant changes since then are mentioned briefly below, and some taken up in the concluding chapter.

### 3.2.1 Britain in 1996

Until October 1996 unemployed people in Britain could claim unemployment benefit and/or income support (prior to 1988 called supplementary benefit). The jobseeker's allowance was introduced in October 1996 and

Table 3.1  Benefits paid to the unemployed in Britain and Germany

| Benefit Type / *Benefit Name* | Benefit Unit | Eligibility Requirement for the Unemployed | Final Entitlement based on: | Earnings Disregards for Spouse? (per week) | Duration of Benefit | % of Registered Unemployed in Receipt of Benefit (1996) |
|---|---|---|---|---|---|---|
| **GERMANY** Unemployment insurance *Arbeitslosengeld (ALG)* | Individual | Sufficient contributions | Earnings-linked | N/A | One year* | 50.2 |
| Unemployment assistance *Arbeitslosenhilfe (ALH)*** | Family | Having (previously) received *ALG*, and family means test | Earnings-linked | Yes, approx 150DM *** | Indefinite (in most cases) | 27.9 |
| Social assistance *Sozialhilfe* | Family | Family means test | Flat-rate | Yes, between 30 and 60DM **** | Indefinite | 7.7 (approx – see notes) |

**BRITAIN**

| | | | | | | |
|---|---|---|---|---|---|---|
| Unemployment insurance *Unemployment benefit* | Individual | Sufficient contributions | Flat-rate | N/A | One year (6 mths) ***** | 16.3 |
| Social assistance *Income support* | Family | Family means test | Flat-rate | Yes, £5 | Indefinite | 74.8 |

*Notes:*

\*      The duration is longer for those over 45. See this chapter's Appendix, Table 3.1.A for details.

\*\*      Most German unemployed receive this benefit after having received *Arbeitslosengeld* for one year. In this case the benefit is paid indefinitely. A small proportion of the unemployed receive this benefit if they have some (six months) contributions from having worked, but not enough to qualify for *Arbeitslosengeld*. In this case they receive it for one year.

\*\*\*      The disregard is DM70 higher for those with children. The earnings disregard calculation changed for *Arbeitslosenhilfe* in January 1994. See Section 3.3.2 for further details.

\*\*\*\*      The earnings disregard for *Sozialhilfe* is variable, depending on the earnings of the spouse. See Section 3.3.2 for further details.

\*\*\*\*\*      In October 1996 the maximum duration of unemployment benefit was reduced to six months.

*Sources:*      For Germany, *Statistisches Jahrbuch*, 1996, and own estimates from the GSOEP, 1996, for *Sozialhilfe*; for Britain, *Social Security Statistics*, 1996.

replaced both unemployment benefit and income support, integrating insurance-based and means-tested benefits.

Unemployment benefit was an insurance-based benefit, with eligibility dependent on national insurance contributions (discussed in more detail in Section 3.3.1), granted for a maximum duration of one year. From its introduction, funding had been on a tripartite basis (by employees, employers and the state), but in 1989 the subsidy from general taxation was abolished. Unemployment benefit always covered a smaller proportion of the unemployed than did income support, and the proportion declined in the 15 years prior to 1996. After 1982, with the abolition of the earnings supplement, unemployment benefit became a flat-rate benefit, not linked to earnings. In April 1996 the rate was £48.25 per week for a single adult, and £78 for an unemployed person with an adult dependant (Department of Social Security 1996).[8] The dependant's supplement has since been abolished, with the introduction of the jobseeker's allowance: recipients of insurance-based benefit now need to claim supplementary means-tested benefits if they have a dependent spouse.

The remainder of unemployed claimants in 1996 received income support. This was a means-tested benefit, with the level of the award depending on family circumstances such as the number of dependants and the income and savings of the household. Recipients of income support qualified for a range of additional benefits (see Section 3.2.4 below). In 1996 the rate of income support was £47.90 for single adults and £75.20 for a couple (Department of Social Security 1996).[9] Note how similar these were to the rates quoted above for unemployment benefit – between 96 and 98 per cent of the latter.

Jobseeker's allowance (JSA), introduced in October 1996, has two components: contribution-based JSA replaced unemployment benefit; and means-tested, income-based JSA replaced income support for the unemployed. Unemployed claimants now need to visit just one office, the Employment Service Jobcentre, for both their claims and job search. A new 'Jobseeker's Agreement' was introduced, which all claimants must undertake, and rules relating to disqualification were tightened further.

### 3.2.2   Germany in 1996

In 1996 the majority of German registered unemployed received one of the two main types of benefit administered by the Federal Labour Office in Nuremberg: *Arbeitslosengeld* and *Arbeitslosenhilfe*. If the unemployed person had paid contributions for at least 360 calendar days in the past three years, in employment over 18 hours a week, and if they had shown themselves able and willing to work, they were entitled to *Arbeitslosengeld* – unemployment insurance (see Table 3.1). The duration of benefit depended on the duration of employment, with older workers with long contribution records eligible for longer periods of benefit. For the oldest age group the maximum duration was 32 months (see this chapter's Appendix, Table 3.1.A). *Arbeitslosengeld* was paid at 67 per cent (60 per cent for those without children) of standardised former net earnings, for a standard duration of 12 months.[10] The replacement rate in practice was often lower than 60 per cent as benefits were calculated without bonuses or overtime. Being an insurance payment, *Arbeitslosengeld* was not means-tested against any other income or wealth. Recipients of *Arbeitslosengeld* (and also of *Arbeitslosenhilfe*) could work up to 18 hours per week while in receipt of benefits, provided earnings were not above a given ceiling.[11]

As a rule, *Arbeitslosenhilfe* – unemployment assistance – was granted to the unemployed after their entitlement to *Arbeitslosengeld* was exhausted, and was then paid indefinitely, but at a lower replacement rate.[12] Like *Arbeitslosengeld*, the level of benefit of *Arbeitslosenhilfe* was linked to previous earnings, but, unlike *Arbeitslosengeld*, *Arbeitslosenhilfe* was means-tested against household income. The maximum replacement rate was 57 per cent for those with children and 53 per cent for those without.

Those unemployed who were not entitled to either *Arbeitslosengeld* or *Arbeitslosenhilfe* – usually because they had little or no employment record – and who could prove themselves to be in need, could claim *Sozialhilfe* – social assistance. *Sozialhilfe* is very much the poor relation of other benefits paid to the unemployed in Germany, and is not received by many. All claims for *Arbeitslosengeld*, family maintenance and other forms of income must be exhausted before *Sozialhilfe* is considered.[13] *Sozialhilfe* is a discretionary benefit, and rates of payment vary considerably according to family type and *Bundesland*, though benefit levels are required to be lower than for other unemployment benefits, the stated aim being to keep recipients from destitution. In 1996 the average rate for single claimants or household heads was around DM530 in West Germany, DM510 in East Germany (Brühl, 1996). Although it is a last resort benefit, intended to cover exceptional circumstances rather than standard risks, 687,000 households in receipt of *Sozialhilfe* in 1993 stated unemployment as the main reason for claiming the benefit (Statistisches Bundesamt 1996).[14] The 1980s had seen a rapid rise in the proportion of the unemployed relying on *Sozialhilfe* in West Germany.

Research suggests that *Sozialhilfe* in Germany is heavily stigmatised among unemployed recipients. It is important to appreciate that there is a distinct hierarchy of benefits for the unemployed in Germany: *Arbeitslosengeld* is seen as superior to *Arbeitslosenhilfe*, which in turn is seen as superior to *Sozialhilfe*. Clasen (1994b) draws our attention to the institutional, administrative and ideological divisions that exist in Germany between insurance-based benefits and social assistance. Whereas the former have the legitimacy of the 'joint insurance of the insured', *Sozialhilfe* is stigmatised, has generally much lower levels of both payment and take-up and is not based on any criterion of achievement.[15] Germans are proud of *Arbeitslosengeld*, while *Sozialhilfe* slips between the lines of most accounts of welfare for the unemployed.

As discussed in Chapter 1, West German laws, regulations and institutions were introduced in East Germany immediately after reunification in 1990 (Bäcker, 1991). This was true of all the benefit regulations described above. East German contributions were recognised for insurance purposes, but as many East Germans are not on full earnings, income from taxes and social security contributions is low there. Bosch and Knuth (1993) note how in 1992 the Federal Labour Office received only 3.3 billion DM in unemployment insurance contributions from East Germany, but paid out 42.7 billion DM, while 1.5 billion DM was paid out in unemployment assistance (*Arbeitslosenhilfe*). Labour market policy accounted for the largest single element of West–East transfers.

### 3.2.3  Means-tested Versus Insurance Benefits

From the description above we can see that, for the most part, the characterisation of German welfare provision for the unemployed as insurance-based and British as welfare-based is correct. However, these characterisations need qualification: insurance benefits, battered though they have been, still exist for a substantial minority of the British unemployed. And a small number of the German unemployed receive social assistance (*Sozialhilfe*), which embodies all the principles of means-testing and welfare and has an explicit aim of protecting recipients from destitution. In our historical account we described the German system as an 'insurance system with welfare elements' and the British as a 'welfare system with insurance elements' and it is important to keep in mind these qualifications. In this section, using national statistics and a registered definition of unemployment, we examine the proportion of registered unemployed who receive each type of benefit. It is important to bear in mind that the conditions of registration determine who counts among the registered unemployed, as discussed in Chapter 2.

Figure 3.1a shows the proportion of the unemployed receiving each type of benefit in Germany. While for most of the 1970s well over 50 per cent of the registered unemployed in West Germany received unemployment insurance (*Arbeitslosengeld*), for most of the 1980s the proportion was around 40 per cent. By contrast, unemployment assistance (*Arbeitslosenhilfe*) was relatively more important in the 1980s than in the 1970s, reflecting the rise of long-term unemployment, with recipients moving from unemployment insurance to unemployment assistance after one year. Through the 1980s in West Germany we also see a growth in the numbers having recourse to social assistance

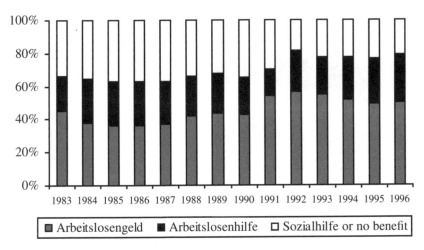

Note: After 1991, figures include the new *Bundesländer*. The *Statistisches Jahrbuch* does not distinguish recipients of *Sozialhilfe* from those receiving no benefits.

Source: *Statistisches Jahrbuch*, various years, quoting figures from the Bundesanstalt für Arbeit. Those classed as receiving *Arbeitslosengeld* or *Arbeitslosenhilfe* can also be in receipt of some *Sozialhilfe*.

*Figure 3.1a    Share of registered unemployment by type of benefit, Germany, 1983–96*

(*Sozialhilfe*) or to no benefit at all.[16] These trends changed somewhat in the 1990s, with the addition of the East German unemployed into the calculations and the changes in benefit regulations in the 1980s. For this reason Figure 3.1b shows the proportion of the unemployed receiving each type of benefit, distinguishing East and West Germany.

After reunification, the different labour market conditions in East Germany strongly influenced the proportion receiving each benefit. Because of their long contribution records, a much larger proportion of East Germans received unemployment insurance – 75 per cent in 1991 (see Figure 3.1b). However, with the growth of long-term unemployment in the East during the 1990s, *Arbeitslosenhilfe* grew in significance there. In 1996, only 50 per cent of registered unemployed were receiving *Arbeitslosengeld*. Combining the figures for *Arbeitslosengeld* and *Arbeitslosenhilfe*, 79 per cent were receiving benefits whose level was linked to their previous earnings.

Turning to Britain, Figure 3.2 shows the importance and growth of means-tested benefit – income support – for the unemployed. Whereas 33 per cent of registered unemployed in 1970 received unemployment benefit only, by 1983 the proportion had fallen to 24 per cent. Through the period 1983–96 this

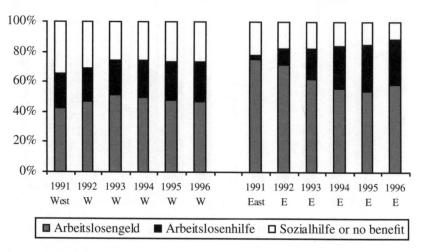

*Figure 3.1b Share of registered unemployment by type of benefit, West and East Germany, 1991–96*

proportion fell further, as shown in Figure 3.2, so that by 1996 only 16 per cent of registered unemployed received unemployment benefit alone (Department of Social Security, various years). The proportion of the unemployed receiving means-tested benefit alone rose from 55 per cent in 1983 to 73 per cent in 1996, in sharp contrast to Germany.

### 3.2.4 Other Benefits Paid to the Unemployed

Fawcett and Papadopoulos (1997) argue that it is crucial to take into account the whole benefit package that the unemployed receive when comparing welfare regimes. In this section we briefly discuss some of the main forms of additional support for the unemployed in Britain and Germany in 1996, of which housing benefit was the most important, particularly in Britain.

In Germany there were two main forms of assistance for housing costs for low-income groups. Firstly, people claiming *Sozialhilfe* normally receive extra amounts to cover the cost of housing (including heating), a benefit known as *pauschaliertes Wohngeld*, paid at the discretion of local authorities within general guidelines. Secondly, there was a housing benefit scheme

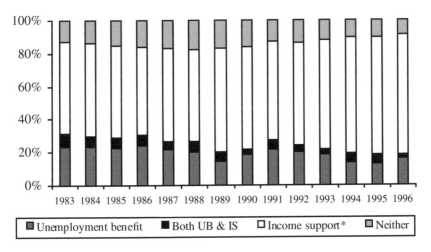

Note: November figures are quoted in each case.
* Income support replaced supplementary benefit in 1988.

Source: Department of Social Security (1983–98).

*Figure 3.2 Share of registered unemployment by type of benefit, Britain,*
*1983–96*

(*Wohngeld*) to assist low-income households with paying rent.[17] Housing benefit, administered by local authorities and financed equally by the federal government and the *Länder*, was available to people living in both private and public rented housing and also to owner-occupiers.[18] In 1996, 7.3 per cent of all private households (i.e. excluding people living in institutions) were in receipt of some housing assistance and about 45 per cent of these were receiving either *Sozialhilfe* or state assistance for victims of World War II (Statistisches Bundesamt 1999).

In Britain there were also two main forms of housing assistance. Firstly housing benefit, administered by local authorities, provided help with rent for those on low incomes or income support living in private or public housing. Those on income support or with a level of net income at the level of income support usually had 100 per cent of their rent paid, while housing benefit was reduced for every pound of additional income above this level.[19] Secondly, mortgage interest payments were covered for people on income support, though this assistance was scaled back in the late 1990s (McKay and Rowlingson 1999). In 1993 approximately 19 per cent of households were receiving housing allowances, about two-thirds of whom were receiving income support. This is a considerably larger proportion than in Germany.

In Germany there were two forms of benefit payable for children. *Kindergeld* comprised universal and income-dependent components, with payments depending on income and the number of children (Schluter 1995). *Erziehungsgeld* was a separate means-tested transfer payment. Those receiving *Arbeitslosengeld* were not eligible, nor were those in full-time work. It was paid at a generally higher rate than *Kindergeld*: an eligible parent could receive up to 600DM per month per child for the first 24 months (Brühl 1996). In Britain, child benefit was a cash payment for all children, paid to the mother without regard to means.

In both countries there was a range of other benefits available to the unemployed. In Germany these benefits – paid at the discretion of staff in local offices – included free medical prescriptions, free school milk and reduced cost public transport, and in some cases national insurance contributions could be paid. A second type of payment, in the form of either grants or loans, was help with one-off or special payments, such as essential furniture, clothing and household needs, and emergency or crisis payments. Some were grants, some were loans: they were all discretionary.[20] In Britain there were a number of benefits known as 'passport' benefits, which were available for all those in receipt of income support.[21] These included free school meals, free medical prescriptions, free dental treatment and eyesight tests, and free travel to hospital. Local taxation, known as Council Tax, was also paid. For one-off payments in Britain claimants could apply to the Social Fund.

As can be seen, the extra benefits available to the unemployed covered similar contingencies in the two countries. There were, however, differences between the countries, particularly in the greater degree of discretion in Germany. While we see some discretion creeping into the British system, for instance within the Social Fund, there are more benefits paid as of right. Another difference is that, given the often lower rate of compensation for unemployment in Britain, for most of the unemployed these other benefits played a greater role in the incomes and lives of the unemployed in Britain than in Germany. This was particularly true of housing benefit. The role of housing benefit in Britain will be discussed further when we look at the effect of replacement rates and housing benefits in Section 3.4.2.

## 3.3   COMPARING ELIGIBILITY AND CONDITIONS FOR RECEIPT OF BENEFIT

While in previous sections we have outlined the basic principles of compensation for the unemployed, in this section we focus on conditions for the receipt of benefit.

### 3.3.1 Contribution Conditions for Insurance Benefit

In Germany, if contributions had been paid for at least 12 months in the past three years, the unemployed were entitled to *Arbeitslosengeld*. The duration of benefit depended on the duration of employment, and older unemployed people were eligible to longer periods of benefit.[22] Contributions of six months in the preceding year and proven need made the unemployed eligible to the 'hybrid' benefit, *Arbeitslosenhilfe*. Up until 1997 the maximum length of eligibility for *Arbeitslosengeld* for the oldest age group was 32 months. Employment must have been over 18 hours per week, and there was a ceiling on monthly (gross) earnings liable for insurance contributions – in 1996 this threshold was DM8,000 in West Germany, and DM6,800 in East Germany (Bundesministerium für Arbeit und Sozialordnung 2000).[23]

In Britain, two contribution conditions must be met. Firstly, claimants must have paid contributions on earnings at least 25 times the weekly lower earnings limit in at least one of the previous two years. Secondly, they must also have paid contributions (from either employment or from registering as unemployed) on earnings equal to 50 times the lower earnings level in the past two relevant tax years (Department of Social Security 1996). The lower earnings limit in 1995–96 was £58, the upper limit £440.

Evans (1996) points out that it was much easier to requalify for benefit through short periods of work in Germany than in Britain. There were many more people in Germany entitled to insurance benefit there (see Figure 3.1a) and there was also, as we have seen, more of an advantage in Germany in qualifying for insurance benefit than there was in Britain.

In both Britain and Germany, entitlement to unemployment benefit was contingent on meeting weekly working-time conditions while in previous employment. The 'over 18 hours a week' condition in Germany excluded marginal part-time workers (*geringfügige Beschäftige*) from benefits.[24] In Britain there was a minimum earnings threshold, rather than an hours limit. Below this threshold employees neither made contributions nor received benefit payments. In 1996, as noted above, this 'lower earnings level' was £58 per week (Child Poverty Action Group 1997).

In both Britain and Germany there was the additional requirement of being able and willing to seek full-time work, although some exceptions applied for workers caring for children or others (Grimshaw and Rubery 1997). The clear implications of this are that women, who are much more likely to work part-time in both countries, are more likely to be excluded from benefits. They may also be discouraged from taking up part-time work, as it does not carry benefit rights with it.

### 3.3.2    Conditions for Receipt of Means-tested Benefit

The conditions for means-testing in both countries are complex and include many exceptions. What follows is a summary of the main conditions.

For means-tested benefits for the unemployed in Britain, the 'benefit unit' is normally made up of an adult living alone or independently within a large household, a couple living together as 'husband and wife', or either of these with dependent children.[25] Children are normally defined as dependent until the age of 16 or up to the age of 19 if in full-time education. In Germany the unit of entitlement for both *Arbeitslosenhilfe* and *Sozialhilfe* is the claimant, plus partner if there is one, and dependent children. However, the principle of subsidiarity means that the resource unit (those people expected to support the family) can be wider than the family unit, though how the resource unit is defined is at the discretion of the social assistance officer. In practice, claims on parents or working children are rarely made for *Arbeitslosenhilfe*, but are more commonly applied for *Sozialhilfe*.

In both countries there is both an assets and an income test. In both countries the assets test refers to cash, savings and the net market value of land or property, excluding the house of residence, and capital held by couples is added together. In Britain the first £3,000 of capital was ignored, while capital between £3,000 and £8,000 was taken into account by making a small deduction from benefit. Capital over £8,000 excluded the claimant from benefit entitlement. In Germany, for *Arbeitslosenhilfe*, assets could not exceed DM8,000 (similar to the £3,000 test in Britain). For *Sozialhilfe* the assets test was much lower, at DM2,500.

Regarding income, in both countries most forms of income were taken into account. In Britain most unearned income, like social security benefits such as child benefit, was taken into account. Income from earnings is counted net of income tax and national insurance contributions.[26] There are important earnings disregards in the income test, noted in Table 3.1. The earnings disregard for income support was low, £5 per week in most cases.[27] In Germany the earnings disregard for *Arbeitslosenhilfe* in 1993 was higher than in Britain, at DM150 or around £50, with a DM70 addition for children.[28] For *Sozialhilfe* the earnings disregard was variable, at around DM130–260 per month, or DM30–60 per week.[29]

In some ways the German system applied more stringent criteria to means-testing than the British. In principle at least, the unemployed in Germany could be required to seek help from those outside the household. For *Sozialhilfe* the amount of assets allowed was much lower than for income support. However, one area where the British system seems to be more stringent is in allowing earnings disregards. Earnings disregards are much lower in Britain than in Germany. Given that a large proportion of the unemployed in Britain

receive means-tested benefits, this may have consequences for the employment of partners of the unemployed, which is the subject of further discussion
in Chapter 6.

### 3.3.3 'Actively Seeking Work' and Disqualification

In addition to contribution conditions, there were also conditions relating to
availability for work and job search in both countries. As well as promoting
job search, these sanctions may have acted as a deterrent to registering as
unemployed for those who did not wish to fulfil the criteria. For most of the
period in question (1990–96), conditions were stricter, sanctions more common, and claimants under more pressure to find a job in Britain than in
Germany. The difference in climate can be seen from differences in the
proportion of unemployed who are refused benefit or otherwise sanctioned
(Table 3.2). A much higher proportion of the unemployed in Britain were
sanctioned than in Germany.[30]

In Germany, claimants had to show ability and willingness to work in
order to qualify for unemployment compensation. For those receiving
*Arbeitslosengeld* and *Arbeitslosenhilfe*, this willingness to work was most
often certified by regular registration at the local Federal Labour Office
(*Arbeitsamt*), which functions as both benefit office and labour exchange.[31]
The claimant had to register in person every three months, and in addition
present themselves whenever requested to do so. The claimant was obliged
to accept 'suitable work' or take part in training courses offered by the
Labour Office. Up until 1994, only jobs requiring the same level of occupational qualification and experience as the previous job were deemed suitable
in the first four months of unemployment.[32] Since then, in 1994 and then
again in 1998, criteria for claiming benefits have become somewhat more
stringent.[33] However, once again the distinction between the benefits of the
Federal Labour Office and *Sozialhilfe* become apparent. While recipients of
*Arbeitslosengeld* and *Arbeitslosenhilfe* could wait until a 'suitable' job was
offered, recipients of *Sozialhilfe* had to accept any job, or otherwise face
penalties from the social welfare office.[34]

In Britain, until October 1996, unemployed claimants had to appear in
person in the benefit office every two weeks, an action known as 'signing on'.
Claimants had to be willing and able to accept any suitable job offer at once.
For those with a usual occupation, they could look for work in this occupation for 13 weeks, after which they had to be prepared to accept any job
(Child Poverty Action Group 1997). Claimants were required to take 'active
steps' to find work each week and random checks could be conducted by
benefit officers to ensure the claimant was actively seeking work.[35] Following
the changes to regulations about job search in the 1980s, discussed in Section

3.1.4, these job search requirements were quite stringent. The new regime introduced in October 1996 was even tougher on claimants. Claimants now have to sign and keep to a 'Jobseeker's Agreement'.

Penalties for not fulfilling these criteria existed in both countries.[36] In Germany, *Arbeitslosengeld* was suspended for up to 12 weeks if the insured had left the previous employment without due cause (as defined by law), or if the claimant rejected a suitable job offer.[37] In Britain, unemployment benefit could be suspended from one to 26 weeks in cases of 'voluntary' unemployment,[38] which included losing a job because of misconduct or leaving without good cause, refusing to take up a suitable job or a place on a training scheme, or losing a place on a training scheme because of misconduct (Child Poverty Action Group 1997).

Table 3.2 compares the incidence of unemployment benefit refusals and sanctions in Britain and Germany. While there is not a large difference in the countries in the rate of sanctions for behaviour before the benefit period starts, in Britain there is a much higher rate of sanctions for behaviour during the benefit period. While the data in the table relates to a slightly later period than that under discussion, the findings are consistent with the regulations described above.

*Table 3.2   The incidence of unemployment benefit refusals and sanctions*

|  | Germany | Britain |
|---|---|---|
|  | % of flow of claimants | |
| **Sanctions for behaviour before benefits start:** | | |
| Voluntary unemployment | 3.62 | 4.32 |
|  | Annual rate as a % of average stock of benefit claims | |
| **Sanctions for behaviour during benefit period (total):** | 1.14 | 10.30 |
| Refusal of work | 0.64 | 1.23 |
| Active labour market programme or related action plan | 0.50 | 2.21 |
| Evidence of active job search | 0.00 | 2.08 |
| Administrative infractions | 0.00 | 4.78 |

*Source*:   Grubb 2000, p. 158, Table 2, from national sources.

Notable exceptions to these conditions were over-58-year-olds in Germany in receipt of *Arbeitslosengeld* or *Arbeitslosenhilfe*, and over-60-year-olds in Britain receiving income support.[39] Both these groups can receive benefit without the associated job search and availability criteria.

## 3.4 BENEFIT COVERAGE AND REPLACEMENT RATES

A key criterion for comparing and evaluating unemployment compensation systems is the extent to which individuals receive a wage replacement when they become unemployed. One indicator of this is the beneficiary rate – the proportion of the unemployed in receipt of benefits. Another is the replacement rate, which relates to the size of compensation. Gallie and Paugam (2000) use these two indicators, along with spending on active labour market programmes, as criteria for defining their 'unemployment welfare regimes'. Schmid and Reissert (1996) in their work on unemployment compensation and labour market transitions, focus on these aspects as important indicators in evaluating unemployment compensation systems.

### 3.4.1 Comparing Benefit Coverage

As Atkinson points out, in the typical economic treatment of unemployment benefit, 'all of those out of work are assumed to be in receipt of unemployment compensation' (1999, p. 84). Given the conditions for eligibility, it is not surprising that this is far from the truth. Table 3.3 compares the beneficiary rates in Britain and Germany using the ILO definition of unemployment. The ILO definition (which is discussed in more detail in Section 2.2.1 in

*Table 3.3*   *Percentage of ILO unemployed receiving insurance-based and means-tested unemployment compensation, by gender*

|  | 1996 | | | 1985 |
| --- | --- | --- | --- | --- |
|  | (1)<br>All | (2)<br>Men | (3)<br>Women | (4)<br>All |
| Britain | 58.6 | 69.9 | 36.4 | 71.8 |
| Germany* | 74.1 | 78.6 | 69.1 | 58.4 |

*Note*:   * 1985 figures for Germany are for West Germany only.

*Source*:   European Labour Force Surveys 1996 and 1985 (Eurostat 1987, 1997).

Chapter 2) allows us to compare the coverage of the unemployment compensation systems with a definition of unemployment that is independent of those compensation systems. In column (1) we see that in 1996 the beneficiary rate was considerably higher in Germany (74.1 per cent) than in Britain (58.6 per cent).

Comparing these figures to the mid-1980s, in column (4), when the beneficiary rate was 58.4 per cent for Germany and 71.8 per cent for Britain, we see a marked change in 11 years. During this period, discussed in Section 3.1.4 above, changes to the benefit system in Britain restricted the number of recipients, while changes towards the end of the 1980s in Germany had the opposite effect. The shift may also be related to reunification with East Germany, a region of high unemployment where many more of the unemployed receive benefits, particularly women. Though we have tended to contrast Britain and Germany as two different types of welfare regimes, these contrasting figures for the 1980s and 1990s should serve as a caution against seeing welfare regimes as fixed. As Daly (1997) points out, a risk of the welfare state regimes perspective is to take a relatively static view of welfare states, oversimplifying questions of development and change.

Comparing the beneficiary rates for women in column (3), we see that in 1996 unemployed women clearly fared better in Germany than in Britain. The rate for women in Britain was only 36.4 per cent, compared to 69.1 per cent in united Germany. The low figures for Britain would seem to be at least partly explained by the extension of household means-testing there, as argued by Gallie and Paugam (2000). These figures do not seem to support Daly's (1996) observations about the disadvantage suffered by women in continental European systems such as Germany relative to liberal systems such as Britain.[40] However, an important caveat is that unemployed women in East Germany now make up a large proportion of unemployed German women and they typically enter unemployment with very good employment records, making them eligible for *Arbeitslosengeld*, which is not the case for West German women.[41]

Table 3.4 compares the beneficiary rates among young people in 1996. The relationship between unemployment and age in insurance systems is influenced by two opposing forces (Schmid and Reissert 1996). On the one hand younger people are less likely to satisfy eligibility criteria. On the other hand, the probability of being long-term unemployed and therefore having exhausted benefit entitlement is lower for younger people. As we saw in Section 3.1.4, unemployment compensation in Germany was strengthened for older people in the late 1980s in response to persistent high unemployment in this group. 'Welfare-oriented' systems like Britain, Schmid and Reissert argue, are largely designed to provide a minimum income, regardless of age, limiting the differences in provision for different age groups. We do indeed see

*Table 3.4*   *Percentage of ILO unemployed receiving insurance-based and means-tested unemployment compensation, by age*

|  | All | | | 15–24-Year-Olds | | |
|---|---|---|---|---|---|---|
|  | (1)<br>All | (2)<br>Men | (3)<br>Women | (4)<br>All<br>young | (5)<br>Young<br>men | (6)<br>Young<br>women |
| Britain | 58.6 | 69.9 | 36.4 | 51.8 | 59.5 | 37.3 |
| Germany | 74.1 | 78.6 | 69.1 | 58.1 | 60.7 | 54.4 |

*Source*:   European Labour Force Survey 1996 (Eurostat 1997).

less of a difference in beneficiary rates for 18–24-year-olds between Britain (52 per cent) and Germany (58 per cent) than we see for all the unemployed (59 and 74 per cent respectively). Indeed, in Britain the rate is actually slightly higher for young unemployed women than it is for all unemployed women. These figures seem to support the claim that younger people fare better relative to their older unemployed counterparts in more means-tested systems like Britain, at least in terms of coverage of benefit. The story is different when we look at replacement rates (see below).

In conclusion, the insurance or employment-centred regime, Germany, is somewhat biased towards protecting core workers (mostly male and older) rather than marginal workers (young, female, casual). In the British welfare-oriented liberal regime, we do not find such strong privileging of core workers. The important exception to this is unemployed women, who, as we saw in Table 3.3, do not fare very well in the British system. In our subsequent examinations of income poverty among the unemployed (Chapter 4) and the duration of unemployment (Chapter 5) it will be important to consider the impact of these differences in beneficiary rates. However, in our discussion thus far we have not considered the level of benefit paid, and we now turn to this important aspect of unemployment compensation.

### 3.4.2   Comparing Replacement Rates

Replacement rates, which measure the extent to which benefits replace wages, have been the subject of much discussion, not least by economists in the debate discussed in Chapter 1 on 'rigid versus flexible labour markets'. High benefits paid to the unemployed are often believed to damage work incentives and ultimately to contribute to high unemployment rather than ameliorate it (for example, OECD 1994 and Siebert 1997). Gallie and Paugam (2000) consider replacement rates a key component in comparing welfare for the unemployed. They stress the 'insider/outsider' divisions in employment-centred regimes like Germany, where benefits vary greatly according to previous employment status: long-standing contributors (insiders) are given priority, marginal workers (outsiders) are disadvantaged. Liberal regimes like Britain show no such division amongst the unemployed according to Gallie and Paugam: here all the unemployed fare badly.

As a comparative illustration of replacement rates, Table 3.5 gives replacement rates for a single person and a married couple with two dependent children, for two durations of unemployment.[42] For a single person who has been unemployed for six months, German unemployment insurance is considerably more generous than British. The replacement rate for a single person, at 61 per cent of average earnings, is considerably higher than in Britain (41 per cent). For long-term unemployed single people, German benefits are still considerably more generous, though falling to 55 per cent of average earnings. In Britain the benefit remains the same for long-term unemployed single people, at 41 per cent of average earnings. While single unemployed people receiving benefits are clearly better off in Germany, the long-term unemployed fare better in Britain *relative to the short-term unemployed* than they do in Germany. This is consistent with the work described above, which predicted that the long-term unemployed will be better served by means-tested or liberal systems, relative to the short-term unemployed (Webb 1994; Schmid and Reissert 1996; Gallie and Paugam 2000).

*Table 3.5*    *Income replacement rates\* by family type in Britain and Germany, after six months and two years of unemployment (1993)*

|  | Single Person | | Married (two children) | |
| --- | --- | --- | --- | --- |
|  | 6 months (%) | 2 years (%) | 6 months (%) | 2 years (%) |
| Germany | 61 | 55 | 72 | 69 |
| Britain | 41 | 41 | 70 | 70 |

*Note*:  \* Income replacement rates as a percentage of the average industrial wage. Worker is assumed to be 35, and have worked continuously for 10 years. Replacement rates for those unemployed for six months refer to unemployment benefits. For those unemployed for two years, it is assumed they have satisfied the household means test, and are in receipt of either income support (Britain) or *Arbeitslosenhilfe* (Germany).

*Source*:  European Commission 1995.

For a married person with a dependent spouse and two dependent children, the comparison looks somewhat different. In Germany they receive 72 per cent of average earnings after six months of unemployment; in Britain the replacement rate, at 70 per cent of average earnings, is only slightly lower. The long-term unemployed with a dependent spouse and two children are actually slightly better off relative to average wages in Britain, where they still receive 70 per cent of average earnings, than they are in Germany, where the replacement rate falls slightly to 69 per cent for the long-term unemployed. Here once again we see the long-term unemployed faring better relative to the short-term unemployed in the means-tested/liberal system.

In addition, when we compare the replacement rates of single and married unemployed, we see that dependants have a much greater influence on replacement rates in Britain than in Germany, so that whereas for single people the German system is much more generous, this is not the case for married unemployed with dependent children. This seems indicative of the fundamental differences between the systems we identified earlier in this chapter, that benefits in Germany respond to an 'earned right' rather than a perceived need. Benefits replace the income of individuals; there is less emphasis on maintaining the income of families. In Britain there is more emphasis on need and thus on protecting families from hardship.

Though estimates for those with little or no employment record were not available from this database, we could infer that the rates for Britain would be close to those for the long-term unemployed, as they too would be entitled to income support if they satisfied the means test. German unemployed with some contributions would have benefit rates similar to those for *Arbeitslosenhilfe*, while those with no contribution record at all and no other means of support would have to rely on *Sozialhilfe*, the rates of which vary by region and are considerably lower than those implied by Table 3.5.

Replacement rate calculations are useful but they have their limitations. Firstly, the unemployed with certain characteristics are selected in order to illustrate the operation of benefits, yet there are so many factors to be considered it is inevitable that many contingencies and circumstances are not illustrated, many household types left out. This is particularly true when comparing countries, as what is a representative household in one country may be far from representative in another.

Secondly, the calculations make certain assumptions about other benefits payable, such as housing benefit. Assumptions are made about how much rent an individual or family pays, and this may greatly influence the replacement rate. The rates quoted in Table 3.5 assume that the individual pays average rent, though estimates of what constitutes an average are approximate because of lack of reliable data. Rents vary considerably by region and by the size of town or city of residence. As we saw in Section 3.2.4, housing benefit assumes a greater role in Britain than in Germany. Estimates in European Commission (1995) indicate that housing benefit has quite a marked effect on replacement rates in both countries when compared to the lower earnings level (50 per cent of average income).

Thirdly, the calculations above are based on hypothetical situations, and assume that people claim the benefits to which they are entitled, which is often not the case (see for example van Oorschot 1991). It is the task of Chapter 4 to compare data on the income of unemployed individuals and their families to see if these differences are confirmed in reality. How do these replacement rates translate into rates of poverty and deprivation? Is it the case that the single unemployed are considerably less likely to be poor in Germany? What about the welfare of families – are families headed by an unemployed person better or worse off relative to the single unemployed in each country? In the empirical analysis of survey data in Chapter 4 we aim to come closer to the lived reality of welfare.


## 3.5   ACTIVE LABOUR MARKET PROGRAMMES

In terms of labour market policy, it has become conventional to distinguish between passive measures, which provide protection for unemployed workers, and active measures, which are designed to improve the skills and competencies of the unemployed and support the search process in the labour market. The treatment of active measures here is very brief as they are not investigated elsewhere in the book. Active labour market programmes include: job placement services to improve matching between vacancies and jobseekers; labour market training to enhance the skills of jobseekers; and employment programmes, which may be either direct job creation schemes in the public sector or the subsidising of jobs in the private sector.

Gallie and Paugam (2000) argue that employment-centred regimes such as Germany are characterised by a higher level of effort and spending on active labour market programmes than liberal regimes such as Britain, and their argument is supported by Figure 3.3, which compares the proportion of GDP spent on active labour market programmes. Active and passive benefits are also more integrated in the German system, though their common funding has been a focus of criticism.[43] British efforts at active labour market programmes dwindled in the 1990s, to be revived in the new Labour government's package of New Deal programmes, which falls outside the scope of this study.

In Figure 3.3 we see that although spending on active labour market programmes was similar in Britain and Germany in the mid-1980s, spending diverged sharply in the period covered by this book. From an average of

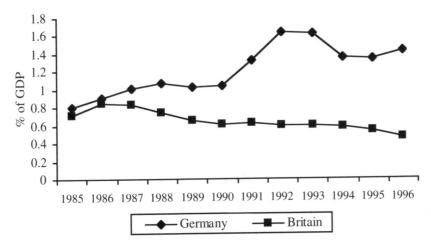

*Note*: Figures from 1991 onwards include East Germany.

*Source*: OECD Employment Outlook (1991 and 1997b).

*Figure 3.3*   *Public expenditure on active labour market programmes as a percentage of GDP*

around 1 per cent of GDP in West Germany in the late 1980s, spending in Germany rose rapidly after reunification, as labour market programmes were extensively used in East Germany to ease the transition. Spending peaked in 1992 at 1.6 per cent of GDP, and in 1996 it was 1.4 per cent of GDP. Britain spent much less relative to Germany and OECD counterparts. The OECD average in 1992 was 0.9 per cent of GDP, while in Britain it was only 0.6 per cent of GDP in 1992–93. Indeed, spending was under 0.6 per cent of GDP for most of the decade, and by 1995–96 had fallen to below 0.5 per cent of GDP. As a proportion of GDP, in 1996, Germany spent three times as much on active labour market programmes as Britain.

## 3.6 CONCLUSION

In this chapter we have seen how the British and German governments responded in different ways to the problem of unemployment throughout the 20th century. Different principles structure the provision of welfare for the unemployed in the two countries, and this provision has been shaped by history. The main principle of unemployment benefits in Germany, now and throughout the 20th century, is that unemployment insurance is an earned right, its function to replace income from the market. In Britain, benefits are based on need, to protect the unemployed from hardship, with need assessed through means-testing. This 'welfare' principle became even stronger in Britain through changes in the 1980s.

In line with these principles, and in keeping with the predictions of some typologies discussed in Chapter 1 (Esping-Andersen 1990; Schmid and Reissert 1996; Gallie and Paugam 2000), we find a stronger link between unemployment compensation and previous employment in Germany than in Britain. In Germany so-called 'core workers' – those with long and full-time employment histories – fare well if they lose their jobs relative to others who are unemployed, in terms of both coverage and replacement rates. In Britain there is not such a contrast. The important exception to this observation is the coverage of women in the two countries, which is discussed below.

In our review of benefit coverage and the conditions of benefit payment, we saw that in both Britain and Germany not all the unemployed are entitled to benefits, and benefits are often of limited duration. There is an array of eligibility conditions in both countries. Looking at replacement rates, which are a key concern in several of the typologies discussed in Chapter 1, we observed that benefit rates in Germany are relatively high for single people entitled to insurance benefits. However, the British emphasis on needs-based provision shows up in benefits to families: the replacement rate for families is much higher than for single people and here there is little difference between British and German benefits.[44]

Comparing the impact on men and women, we see evidence of a 'male breadwinner' effect in unemployment compensation in both Britain and Germany. Insurance benefits in both countries tend to place women at a disadvantage relative to men, because women more often work part-time or discontinuously. This effect is more pronounced in Germany as insurance benefits are more salient there, consistent with Daly (1996). Means-tested benefits also place women at a disadvantage however, as they tend to provide for married women as dependants. As predicted by Gallie and Paugam, the greater reliance on means-tested family benefits in Britain means coverage of women is very low there. Women are most often the second earners in families, and do not qualify for means-tested benefits in their own right if they are unemployed and their spouse is earning. So although Daly predicted that the German system would be worse for women, in terms of coverage at least, the British system is worse. In the German benefit system women are disadvantaged because of their work histories, in the British because of their economic dependence on men.

In countries where families at the bottom end of the income distribution are increasingly finding that both couples have to work, household means-testing may create an in-built disincentive for the wife to participate in the labour market, leading to a situation of contrasting work-rich and work-poor households. The issue of means-testing and the employment of partners is the subject of more detailed empirical investigation in Chapter 6, where we compare the effect of the labour force status of husbands on their wives/ partners' labour force transitions, and what role the benefit system plays.

Also in keeping with Gallie and Paugam's predictions, Germany, the employment-centred regime, has tended to devote more resources to active labour market programmes than Britain. Here too we find that the 'insiders', those who have paid their insurance contributions, have privileged access to these programmes.

While it was the purpose of this chapter to sketch out the differences in welfare provision, it is the purpose of our subsequent empirical chapters to disentangle the implications of these differences in welfare provision for individual and household outcomes in the 1990s. The task of Chapter 4 will be to investigate how differences in provision translate into different rates of income poverty for the unemployed. Do we find for example that there are strong differences in poverty rates between different groups of the German unemployed, while there is more 'equity in deprivation' among the British unemployed?

## NOTES

1. The Poor Law Amendment Act of 1834 (see Daly, 1994).
2. The 'wage stop', which lasted from the 1950s to the early 1970s, is a particularly good example of this. Aimed particularly at unemployed people with larger families, it ensured that those on benefits could not receive more than they would when in work.
3. Indeed, this change made Britain the only member of the European Community with no element of unemployment benefit linked to past earnings (Atkinson and Micklewright, 1989).
4. The new social security regulations meant that benefit entitlement depended on paid (rather than paid or credited) contributions in the two preceding tax years (Atkinson and Micklewright 1989).
5. How the benefit level is set in Britain is particularly salient given that benefits are all flat-rate and are not linked to an individual unemployed person's previous earnings.
6. This applied to both unemployment benefit and income support.
7. Other changes included the taxation of both insurance and means-tested benefits (in 1982), and the exclusion in 1988 of 16–17-year-olds from income support (the means-tested benefit that replaced supplementary benefit). The rate of means-tested benefits for 18–25-year-olds was also reduced.
8. No additional payment was available for children.
9. The rates were somewhat lower for 16–17 and 18–24-year-olds (Department of Social Security, 1996).
10. The addition for children, introduced in 1984, constituted a slight deviation from the insurance principle in accounting for assumed need.
11. The limit was changed to 15 hours per week in 1998.
12. A small proportion of the unemployed receive this benefit if they have some (six months) contributions from having worked, but not enough to qualify for *Arbeitslosengeld*.

13. In cases where low contributions mean a very small amount of other benefits, *Sozialhilfe* is used to top up payments to the *Sozialhilfe* level.
14. This is the most detailed information provided by the Bundesanstalt für Arbeit about *Sozialhilfe*, and is only available up to 1993. There are no estimates of the proportion of the unemployed receiving only *Sozialhilfe*, so it is not clear how many unemployed recipients of it also receive other unemployment benefits.
15. Voges and Rohwer (1992) show how those most liable to become claimants for social assistance are single mothers, non-citizens and dependent relatives.
16. With this data we cannot distinguish between those who receive social assistance and those who receive no benefits.
17. Although this benefit is means-tested on income, assets are not counted.
18. Normally, a very small proportion of owner-occupiers claim. In 1993 only 7 per cent of all claimants were owner-occupiers (Eardley et al. 1996).
19. The capital limit was £16,000, twice the limit for income support (see Section 3.4.5).
20. The 'Help in Special Circumstances' (*Hilfe in besonderen Lebenslagen*) is a second type of social assistance, paid for extraordinary life situations, such as dependence on care for the elderly, disability or homelessness.
21. Other people on low income could apply for help towards these costs.
22. The following durations applied from July 1987 to March 1997 for the unemployed aged under 40. See this chapter's Appendix Table 3.1.A for further details.
23. And a corresponding ceiling on earnings-related unemployment benefits.
24. In 1997 this threshold was lowered to 15 hours by the Employment Promotion Act (*Arbeitsförderungsreformgesetz*).
25. The couples can be married or living together as if they were married.
26. In Germany essential work costs such as travel and clothing are taken into account. In Britain it has not been possible to offset work expenses since 1988.
27. The disregard was £15 in cases of unemployment over two years. Note that income support was aimed more widely at those on low incomes, not only the unemployed.
28. In January 1994 the calculation of the earnings disregard for *Arbeitslosenhilfe* was changed. While the minimum disregard remained of similar magnitude to the pre-1994 level, above this minimum the disregard was variable and dependent on the earnings of the spouse. It was normally calculated as the hypothetical *Arbeitslosenhilfe* entitlement of the spouse, with additional disregard for those with responsibility for children. The focus here is on the pre-1994 regulations, as the analysis for Germany in Chapter 6 is based on the period up until December 1993.
29. Specifically, the earnings disregard was 25 per cent of the basic rate of *Sozialhilfe*, plus 15 per cent of earnings thereafter. The total earnings disregard could not exceed 50 per cent of the standard rate of *Sozialhilfe* paid. Additional costs such as travel to work could also be disregarded.
30. However, as noted below, these figures refer to a slightly later period than the rest of the discussion.
31. For those receiving *Sozialhilfe*, the *Sozialamt* is the benefit office. However, the job search requirements for *Sozialhilfe* recipients are more stringent, and the *Sozialamt* may encourage them to register at the *Arbeitsamt* in case they are eligible for even a small amount of *Arbeitslosengeld/Arbeitslosenhilfe*, as this will take the pressure off the *Sozialamt*'s (local) funding.
32. After this initial period the level of qualification was gradually reduced, as the period of unemployment lengthened. This process was codified by special regulations and known as the *Zumutbarkeits-Anordnung*.
33. The 1998 act abolished the qualification regulation altogether. Now the unemployed can be obliged to accept any job offers, provided they do not fall below a certain percentage less than the salary of the previous job.
34. The *Sozialhilfe* recipient was also obliged to take up publicly funded work offered by the social welfare office (*Sozialamt*).
35. Note that in Britain the public employment service plays a much smaller role than in Germany.

36. Notable exceptions to these conditions were over-58-year-olds in Germany in receipt of *Arbeitslosengeld* or *Arbeitslosenhilfe*, and over-60-year-olds in Britain receiving income support.
37. If this happened twice, payment could be suspended altogether.
38. Quite often the suspension period was 26 weeks (Child Poverty Action Group 1997).
39. Over-60-year-olds in Britain receiving unemployment benefit were required to 'sign on', but not those receiving income support (Child Poverty Action Group 1997).
40. See Chapter 1 for a discussion of the literature on gender and welfare regimes.
41. Over time the coverage rates may come to look different as a result of more patchy employment histories for East German women.
42. Data is based on results taken from a simulation model developed for Directorate General for Employment and Social Affairs (DGV), and reported in European Commission (1995). The model is designed to estimate the amount payable to unemployed people with different characteristics in terms of age, family situation, employment record and previous earnings, and to compare this to their disposable income when in work. The calculations include the effects of housing benefits by assuming that the individual pays average rent. Alternative estimates of replacement rates are provided by the OECD database – see for example Martin (1996).
43. Schmid et al. (1992) criticise the fact that unemployment insurance contributions fund active labour market programmes. They argue that this engenders programmes that are oriented towards the insured, more privileged unemployed, leaving many social assistance recipients excluded from active labour market programmes in Germany.
44. This finding takes into account other benefits, such as housing benefits.

# APPENDIX

*Table 3.1.A*   *Changes to benefit entitlement periods for German insurance benefit* (Arbeitslosengeld) *since the mid-1980s*

| Months Worked in Base Period | January 1983– Dec. 1984 | January 1985– Dec. 1985 | January 1986– June 1987 | July 1987– March 1997 |
|---|---|---|---|---|
| 12 | 4  | 4        | 4        | 6        |
| 16 | 4  | 4        | 4        | 8        |
| 18 | 6  | 6        | 6        | 8        |
| 20 | 5  | 6        | 6        | 10       |
| 24 | 8  | 6        | 6        | 12       |
| 28 | 8  | 8        | 8        | 14 (>41) |
| 30 | 10 | 8        | 8        | 14 (>41) |
| 32 | 10 | 10       | 10       | 16 (>41) |
| 36 | 12 | 10       | 10       | 18 (>41) |
| 40 | 12 | 12       | 12       | 20 (>43) |
| 42 | 12 | 14 (>48) | 14 (>43) | 20 (>43) |
| 44 | 12 | 14 (>48) | 14 (>43) | 22 (>43) |
| 48 | 12 | 14 (>48) | 16 (>43) | 24 (>48) |
| 52 | 12 | 16 (>48) | 16 (>43) | 26 (>48) |
| 54 | 12 | 16 (>48) | 18 (>48) | 26 (>48) |
| 56 | 12 | 18 (>48) | 18 (>48) | 28 (>53) |
| 60 | 12 | 18 (>48) | 20 (>48) | 30 (>53) |
| 64 | 12 | 18 (>48) | 20 (>48) | 32 (>53) |
| 66 | 12 | 18 (>48) | 22 (>53) | 32 (>53) |
| 72 | 12 | 18 (>48) | 24 (>53) | 32 (>53) |

*Note*:   Age groups to whom the various entitlements apply are in brackets. The changes introduced by the most recent reform of the Employment Promotion Act in 1997 are not included.

*Source*:   Hunt 1995, Table 1.

# 4. Income poverty among the unemployed

As discussed in Chapter 1, an important issue for many comparative approaches to welfare states is the financial consequences of unemployment. Esping-Andersen (1990) focuses on decommodification and how welfare states replace income from the market, covering the contingency of market failure. Gallie and Paugam (2000) refer specifically to how they expect different types of welfare state to be associated with different levels of poverty among the unemployed. Schmid and Reissert (1996) predict that the welfare-oriented systems and insurance-based systems differ in the extent to which they protect the income of the unemployed. The gender typologies discussed are primarily concerned with how welfare states treat men and women differently. One key concern, we argue, is (unemployed) women's access to an independent income. There is also an emphasis in these typologies on which family or household types are favoured, financially or otherwise, by different types of welfare system (Lewis and Ostner 1994; Daly 1996, 2000). In this chapter we address these issues by comparing financial deprivation among individual unemployed people in Britain and Germany.

While there are many consequences of unemployment, the financial consequences are those most directly addressed by cash transfers. This is not to say that other effects of unemployment are not important – unemployment can affect individuals in ways that are non-financial, and a full treatment would look at its impact on psychological distress and on social networks, families and close relationships. Cross-sectional comparative research on life satisfaction suggests that in both Britain and Germany, life satisfaction levels are considerably lower among the unemployed than employees (Whelan and McGinnity 2000). What is more, welfare systems may affect the unemployed in ways that are not financial.[1]

Analysis of the financial consequences of unemployment is important, however, since not only are the unemployed excluded from the market, but their lack of income may also exclude them from participating fully in society (Gallie and Paugam 2000). This is why we compare income poverty rates of the unemployed with income poverty among those who are working in each country. In addition, concern with social exclusion prompts us to compare income poverty among different groups of the unemployed: which groups of the unemployed suffer most financial deprivation in each country?

We start the chapter by presenting a number of hypotheses. We then discuss our approach to the analysis of financial deprivation among the unemployed. The approach used in this chapter has been used to investigate income inequality and poverty more broadly in society (Atkinson 1987, 1995, 1998; Leibfried and Voges 1992; Andress 1995; Hanesch 1996; Jarvis and Jenkins 1996; Hauser 1997). There follows a brief discussion of the choice of year for analysis, which is important given that this is a cross-sectional analysis or 'snapshot' of individual welfare. We then present findings from the British and German data, comparing poverty risk by benefit type, gender and household situation, and draw conclusions about the financial experience of unemployment in Britain and Germany. Finally, we test the robustness of our findings by looking at income change following a move to unemployment, which allows us to overcome some of the problems inherent in cross-sectional analysis. We conclude by reflecting on the implications of our findings for the typologies presented in Chapter 1.

## 4.1   HYPOTHESES ABOUT POVERTY IN A COMPARATIVE CONTEXT

Summarising the differences between the systems of unemployment compensation, in Chapter 3 we characterised the German system as an 'insurance system with means-tested elements' and the British as a 'means-tested system with insurance elements'. What are the implications of this difference for the financial well-being of the unemployed?

Our first group of hypotheses concerns overall rates of income poverty among the unemployed. Gallie and Paugam (2000) argue that employment-centred regimes like Germany are associated with less poverty among the unemployed than liberal-minimal welfare regimes like Britain. Indeed, they predict a strong risk of income poverty among the unemployed in Britain. Schmid and Reissert (1996) also predict that welfare-oriented systems like Britain are less effective at protecting income than insurance-based systems like Germany. In Britain, as we saw in Chapter 3, although benefits are targeted at low income groups through extensive means-testing, benefit levels tend to be low. In keeping with Gallie and Paugam (2000) and Schmid and Reissert (1996), we expect quite a high proportion of the unemployed in Britain to be income poor, with overall rates of income poverty among the unemployed higher in Britain than in Germany.

Our second group of hypotheses concerns differences between the unemployed receiving different kinds of benefit. For both Esping-Andersen (1990) and Gallie and Paugam (2000) the German welfare system is one in which rights are linked to work performance, with benefits linked to earnings, and in which welfare provision maintains class and status differentials, producing a highly stratified system of welfare. The employment-centred welfare regime is expected particularly to disadvantage those without a continuous or lengthy record of employment (Gallie and Paugam 2000, p. 6). By contrast in the liberal systems, of which Britain is an example, modest social transfers are paid to low income groups. Schmid and Reissert (1996) argue that the British welfare-oriented system, which provides a lower level of protection, is more equitable than the German one. The German insurance model provides better income protection overall, but tends to exclude marginal groups who have not paid sufficient contributions.

From each of these typologies we would expect that those with good previous employment records in Germany, who receive insurance benefits, are less at risk of poverty. Specifically we would expect those receiving *Sozialhilfe* (means-tested social assistance) to be most at risk of income poverty, followed by those on *Arbeitslosenhilfe* (means-tested but earnings-linked unemployment assistance), with those receiving *Arbeitslosengeld* (earnings-linked unemployment insurance) least at risk.

In Britain, though we have noted above that we expect a higher risk of poverty overall, we expect less distinction between those with a good employment record, who receive insurance benefit, and those who receive social assistance. This is because, as we argued in Chapter 3, there is not so much difference in the basic amount of insurance and assistance benefit in the British system, and there is less emphasis on previous employment records in determining the amount paid. However, as income support (social assistance) is means-tested, we would expect people receiving it to be at a somewhat greater risk of poverty than those receiving unemployment benefit (unemployment insurance).[2]

Our third group of hypotheses concerns the differential impact of the welfare systems for men and women, and how this is affected by household structure. It is widely argued that women do not have the same financial responsibilities as men, such as providing for dependants, and are therefore protected from the direct financial impact of unemployment (for a discussion see Russell 1996).[3] Women's status as secondary earners is also argued to mean that the wider repercussions of female unemployment are limited. These arguments would lead us to predict much lower rates of poverty among unemployed women than among unemployed men in both countries.[4] However, these arguments have previously been applied in a universalistic way, with little or no consideration of the cultural and institutional differences between countries (Russell and Barbieri 2000).

While the gender-sensitive typologies discussed in Chapter 1 do not explicitly address unemployment, one might infer from them that gender differences in the consequences of unemployment would vary cross-nationally depending on the 'gender welfare regime'. For Lewis and Ostner (1994) Britain and Germany are both examples of a 'male breadwinner' welfare regime, in which women are treated primarily as dependent wives and mothers. This would lead us to expect similar gender differences in the impact of unemployment, with lower female than male poverty in both countries. By contrast in 'dual breadwinner' welfare regimes, where all adults are encouraged to work, the financial impact of unemployment should be rather similar for men and women. Daly (1996, 2000) sees Germany as a clearer example of the male breadwinner model than Britain, as Germany places greater emphasis on 'family solidarity' as a means of female support and pays higher transfers to the wage-earner. Daly's argument would lead us to expect that German women are protected from the financial impact of unemployment to a greater extent than in Britain, which she characterises as a 'more than one breadwinner' state (see Section 1.2.2 in Chapter 1).

Another important area of focus of the gender-sensitive typologies is the idea that different welfare states prioritise different family types (e.g. Lewis and Ostner 1994; Daly 1996, 2000). In our analysis we compare poverty rates of unemployed individuals living in different family situations. For Lewis and Ostner (1994), Britain and Germany are both male breadwinner states, and the traditional single male breadwinner household form is prioritised relative to other household types. So we might expect that male breadwinner families to be less at risk of poverty when the breadwinner becomes unemployed than other household types in both countries. As noted above, Daly (1996, 2000) highlights the differences in the two systems. Daly might argue that single male breadwinner families would be better off relative to other family types in Germany than in Britain (1996).

In addition to the male breadwinner household, another household type of particular concern for gender typologies of welfare states is the household headed by a lone mother. The overall prediction here is that in male breadwinner welfare systems, lone mothers are particularly disadvantaged relative to other family types, and we expect to find very high rates of poverty among lone mothers (Lewis and Ostner 1994; Lewis 1997). Daly's typology, with its emphasis on the differences between the British and German welfare systems, leads us to expect even higher rates of poverty among German lone mothers than among British lone mothers. Our analysis of lone mothers is somewhat limited, however, as the numbers in our sample are low and our definition somewhat narrow,[5] but where possible we speculate as to the implications of our findings for the income poverty of unemployed lone mothers.

## 4.2 MEASURING DEPRIVATION

How we define and measure income poverty can have a significant effect on our findings, possibly influencing the ranking of countries, and is therefore a serious issue. Despite the limitations, we argue that these methods are a useful and comprehensive tool for analysing the financial consequences of unemployment for individuals. In this section we discuss our approach to measuring deprivation. We also discuss the unit of analysis and different ways to adjust for the number of household members. Where possible we try to use international categories and scales in order to maximise comparability.[6] At the end of the section we discuss the samples of the unemployed we use for our analysis, and our choice of specific years on which to base the comparison of Britain and Germany.

### 4.2.1 Choice of Poverty Indicator

How should we measure poverty? For the purposes of this chapter, income is taken as a broad indicator of the standard of living, though it is somewhat restrictive. There may, for example, be differences between countries in terms of service provision that are not captured by a measure of income. If in Britain, medical care is free, and if in Germany, it needs to be paid for by health insurance contributions, then we may underestimate the welfare of British families vis-à-vis German families. Even within Germany the provision of services differs between regions. This is particularly the case for East Germany, where provision of childcare facilities is much better than in West Germany. What is more, even if we accept financial resources as a proxy indicator of the standard of living, income may under- or overstate financial resources. A household may save or borrow, with the result that current income may overstate or understate the standard of living.

Nevertheless, money may be less culturally embedded than other potential indicators, making it more comparable across countries. The fact that one of the primary concerns of this chapter is the effect of cash transfers on the unemployed, further strengthens the argument for using income as an indicator. So although we must recognise the drawbacks of using disposable household income as an indicator of welfare, it is at least a relevant and feasible measure of material resources.

### 4.2.2 Absolute and Relative Poverty

Two different approaches are common in the measurement of poverty. One tries to specify a basket of goods deemed necessary for survival. This is the method followed in the United States to derive an official poverty line, and if we wanted to find out how many unemployed people were below a certain 'absolute' standard of living we would use this approach. Problems with this approach include how we define the basket of goods and who defines it. There are also problems from a comparative perspective: the same proportion of the unemployed may be below an absolute poverty line in two countries, but in one of the countries the same proportion of the population as a whole may be below the absolute poverty line, while in the other, nobody else may be below it. In such a situation the identical extent of 'absolute poverty' among the unemployed in the two countries would not reveal the important difference between the countries in the link between unemployment and poverty.

The alternative approach specifies a 'relative' poverty line, related to contemporary standards of living. If we want to find out how the unemployed fare relative to the rest of the population, we need to use the relative approach. We would also adopt this approach if we want to gauge the means that the unemployed possess to participate in society. The following analysis is therefore based on the idea of relative poverty.

Relative to whom? For most purposes, individuals' standards of living are judged relative to their position in their own country. What is more, most policy-making takes place at the national level. In this analysis, therefore, poverty is assessed relative to the rest of a country. The reunification of Germany poses a special problem in this regard. Should we treat Germany as two different entities and construct two relative income poverty lines, or should we treat it as a single entity and compare incomes with a single poverty line? Certainly, in analysing the first years after reunification, there is an argument for treating East and West Germany separately, which is the strategy followed by Hauser (1995). At that time there were still a large number of subsidies in East Germany, prices were not equivalent in East and West Germany, and the income distribution and overall income levels were very different. In an alternative approach, Krause (1998) rejects both a single poverty line and a separate line, and uses a subjective poverty line for East Germany. This strategy is problematic for comparative purposes – what if people in one country have higher income expectations than in another country? In any case for 1996, the year on which the German analysis in this chapter focuses, the arguments for treating the two separately are less convincing.

The next choice is whether to use mean or median income as a measure of normal living standards from which the relative poverty line is calculated. The mean is perhaps more intuitive and more readily understood by a nonspecialist audience. Its disadvantage is that it is more sensitive than the median to very low and very high incomes, which may vary from year to year in surveys. The median income, the value that divides the population into two equal halves according to their income ranking, is more stable. Given a negatively skewed income distribution, which is typical, the median income will be lower than the mean, and the corresponding relative income poverty line will be lower too. In the following analysis both measures are applied, but the median income is the one we report, for the most part. As there is a larger difference between mean and median incomes in Britain than in Germany (the income distribution being more skewed in Britain), using the median income will tend to give us a more conservative estimate of cross-national differences.

At what proportion of the mean and median income should the relative poverty line be drawn? Any one threshold may be problematic as many people may lie just above or below that threshold – for example, a large number of people may receive less than 60 per cent of the mean income, but few may receive less than 40 per cent of it. The following analysis therefore considers several relative poverty lines, based on three thresholds: 40 per cent, 50 per cent and 60 per cent of the median income.[7] In some cases the results for each line may not be presented, but they are calculated for all analyses and are presented where they give additional information.

### 4.2.3 Measuring Income

Given the choice of income as the best available measure of financial well-being, this section briefly considers some methodological issues that arise when trying to measure true income. Since our concern here is to examine how current labour force status affects household disposable income, monthly disposable net income is preferable to annual income. The annual income of the short-term unemployed may include a period when they were in employment, thus underestimating the financial impact of unemployment.[8] Another factor is that the composition of a household may change during the course of a year, which influences annual income when adjusted for household size and composition (see the discussion of equivalence scales below).

The next problem is to try to obtain income measures as close as possible to disposable income. In the measure derived from the British survey that we use, net income is measured as the sum of: cash income from all sources (income from employment and self-employment, investments and savings, private and occupational pensions, and other market income, plus cash social security and social assistance receipts) minus direct taxes (income tax, employee National Insurance contributions, and local taxes such as the Community Charge and the Council Tax).[9] For the German survey there is no computed net monthly income estimate available. The German income measure used is the reported monthly net income estimate from a household questionnaire, answered by the head of the household. The head of the household is asked to report net household income after tax and national insurance contributions, and to include regular payments such as housing benefit, child benefit and subsistence allowance. As Krause (1998), who uses this measure, points out, the question on net income is asked after a detailed section of the questionnaire on benefits, so it is expected that benefits are taken into account in the answer. Income is before housing costs in both surveys.[10]

Another concern is how income estimates are affected by the method used to collect data. While both the German and British surveys collect their data in a very similar way, difficulties remain in the collection of data, such as the exclusion of certain households from the sampling frame, differential non-response (persons not giving an interview), item non-response (not answering certain questions) and reporting error. While techniques have been developed to deal with these problems – weighting to adjust for differential non-response and imputation for item non-response and reporting error – these corrections are only ever partial.

One concern for this analysis is how the accuracy of income reporting may differ between surveys and thus affect the comparison, as the German net income measure is estimated by the head of the household and the British measure is derived from income components reported in the survey. Using the same German survey, Rendtel et al. (1998) show that the monthly income reported by the head of the household yields very similar estimates to an annual income measure they compute, for both the poverty level as well as transitions in and out of poverty. This would suggest that the difference between using a single net income measure and one using income components does not affect the results. A further concern is that while there is very little item non-response for the German reported income measure, the derived income measure for Britain has a lower response rate, and the sample differs in certain respects from the overall sample. Comparison of the total sample of the unemployed with the sample for which there is valid income data, however, reveals the differences to be minor and it is assumed here that they do not seriously bias the income measure.[11]

To summarise, the income measures used are not perfect. There is little that can be done about correcting these shortcomings but to recognise the deficiencies and assess their likely impact on estimates of poverty.

### 4.2.4 Unit of Analysis

Labour force status is conceptualised and measured at an individual level. It is important to consider, however, that only half the adult population in both Britain and Germany participate in the labour market. The rest are in home duties, retired, long-term sick, or in training or education. Therefore an analysis of welfare that focused solely on labour market participation and income from either employment or unemployment would be inadequate. Non-participants in the labour market depend on both participants and the state in a myriad of complex ways, while children are dependent on their parents. These relations of dependency have a number of implications for examining the welfare of the unemployed. Firstly, the value of benefits paid to the unemployed, and indeed of earned income from the market, depends on the number of people dependent on the income. Secondly, although the unemployment reported in official statistics may be that of individuals, the financial consequences are shared by other members of the household. Given differences between two countries in household structure, an identical rate of unemployment may have financial consequences for very different proportions of the population.

In one sense, household surveys are a flexible instrument for gauging financial welfare, as they allow us to assign a household and a group of dependants to each individual. A crucial weakness, however, is that information on how resources are shared within households is not collected. So even when we know the inputs into a household, the distribution of those inputs is a 'black box' (Jenkins 1991). This is particularly salient for the well-being of women. In particular, women who have no independent income of their own may fare much worse than our estimates, which assume equal sharing, might suggest. We may therefore underestimate poverty among those unemployed women who are not entitled to means-tested benefits because of their spouse's income from employment. The assumption that an unemployed woman's husband shares his labour income equally with her may not be correct – she may receive much less. On a household income measure of poverty such a woman may seem better off than a woman receiving insurance benefit, but the woman receiving insurance benefit may actually enjoy more disposable income. On the other hand, the problem with examining only personal income would be that many women have no personal income at all, and it would be unrealistic to assume that they do not benefit from any sharing. (For examples of work that explore the consequences of unequal sharing in households, see Davis and Joshi 1994; Hutton 1994; and Cantillon and Nolan 1998.)

Up to this point we have vaguely referred to the unit of analysis as either the family or the household. The unit of analysis refers to the group of persons whom we assume combine resources. Atkinson (1995) outlines four ways of defining the unit of analysis: common residence, the most extensive unit of analysis; common spending, where people may not be related; blood or marital ties; and dependence, i.e. parent(s) and dependent children, an 'inner family'. Jenkins (2000) notes how in the US literature on poverty, the sharing unit is typically the family rather than the household, which is more commonly used in Britain.

Which definition is chosen may depend on the way the data is collected. For this chapter the unit is defined as household of common residence where some degree of sharing occurs, either of economic resources or living accommodation, so as to preclude counting multiple households who have the same address. In the German survey that we use, households are housing or economic units, comprising of one or more individuals, and household members need not be related to each other (Wagner et al. 1993). In the British survey the household is defined as 'a group of people who either share living accommodation OR share one meal a day and have the address as their only or main residence' (Taylor et al. 1999, p. A4-4). This means that the British definition is closer to the first of Atkinson's alternatives (common residence) and the German definition closer to the second (common spending).[12] For most purposes this difference is very slight. In both cases we are assuming that a single mother who lives with both her child and her partner is not solely responsible for the child's needs. Equally in both cases we are assuming that a married couple living with two retired parents is in a different situation from a married couple living alone.

### 4.2.5 Equivalence Scales and Household Income

Since households differ in size and composition, it is necessary to adjust income to account for differences in need. If we used household income per capita we would be ignoring economies of scale in household consumption relating to size and composition. We would be assuming, for example, that a five-person household has the same needs as five one-person households. Given that a household has a certain number of fixed costs (heat, light, etc.), this seems unrealistic. Conversely, if no adjustment were made for the number of household members we would be assuming that a five-person household has the same needs as a one-person household. To avoid these unrealistic assumptions, 'equivalence scales' are used to adjust income to account for family size and composition.

Equivalence scales vary greatly in their assumptions about economies of scale, and the choice of scale is not unproblematic. Buhmann et al. (1988) demonstrate that the choice of equivalence scale can systematically affect absolute and relative levels of poverty, and therefore rankings both between countries and between different groups of the population within countries. Burkhauser, Smeeding and Merz (1996) compare relative inequality and poverty in Germany and the United States using alternative equivalence scales. They find little difference in overall estimates of poverty and inequality using a variety of national 'official' scales and 'expert' (econometric) scales for the whole population. However, the official German scale, which estimates substantially lower economies of scale than the other scales, yields quite different results with respect to the poverty levels of groups within the population, particularly older, single people. This scale is often used in German studies of poverty, for example Krause (1998) and Hauser (1995). Coulter et al. (1992) and Jenkins and Cowell (1994) argue that the McClements scale used in British official statistics 'provides lower estimates of poverty than do other scales'.

In this chapter neither the British nor the German official scales are used, but rather ones developed by economists as common international scales, representing a compromise in assumptions about economies of scale. As a precaution, two different scales are applied. In the original OECD scale the first adult has a value of 1, subsequent adults 0.7, and children under 14 have a value of 0.5 (Atkinson et al. 1993). As this scale tends to be generous to large families, Hagenaars et al. (1994) use a 'modified or new OECD scale', in which the first adult has a value of 1, but subsequent adults a value of 0.5, and children 14 and under have a value of 0.3 (Hagenaars et al. 1994; Atkinson 1998). With the old OECD scale we would expect to find more persons from multi-person households among the poor; with the new one, more single-person households.

### 4.2.6   Choice of Year and Sample of Unemployed Used

As discussed in Chapter 2, the macroeconomic highs and lows of the 1990s in Britain and Germany were somewhat different. If we look at the period 1990–96, British unemployment was highest in the early 1990s, peaking in 1993 and falling thereafter. In Germany the pattern was different: following a brief post-unification boom, recession set in. After 1991, unemployment rose rapidly, becoming a particularly serious problem in East Germany. During the period 1983–96 the highest rate of unemployment in Germany was in 1996.

In order to prevent the macroeconomic cycle unduly distorting the cross-sectional analysis in this chapter, we analyse a year of high unemployment in each country, rather than the same calendar year in both. One reason for controlling for the level of unemployment in this way is that the characteristics of the unemployed may vary with the level of unemployment. In years of low unemployment only those who are particularly disadvantaged in the labour market remain unemployed, as others enter employment. Comparing poverty among the unemployed in a year of high unemployment in one country and low unemployment in the other might result in different samples. An additional, practical advantage for analysing a year of high unemployment in each country is that the samples of the unemployed are as large as possible. The chosen years are 1993 for Britain, when the unemployment rate was 10.3 per cent of the labour force, and 1996 for Germany, when the rate was 8.8 per cent of the labour force, according to the European Labour Force Survey, which uses the International Labour Office (ILO) definition of unemployment (Eurostat 1993, 1996).

The measurement of unemployment is discussed in more detail in Chapter 2 and in the Final Appendix. There we argue that at the core of the ILO definition is the idea that the unemployed should be actively seeking work. The analysis in this chapter primarily uses a version of the ILO definition, incorporating the idea of actively seeking work, but it does not include the availability criterion. The measure includes: those who have not worked in the past week and have actively sought work in a specified period (one month for Britain; three months for Germany). According to this definition in the British survey the unemployed were 8.3 per cent of the labour force in 1993, while in the German survey the unemployed were 7.0 per cent of the labour force in 1996,[13] which is lower than the European Labour Force Survey rates described above, but consistently so for both countries. Further details of the sample and how it compares to the European Labour Force Survey sample of the unemployed are presented in the final Appendix, Section A.2.1. In the Appendix we also present results that show some implications for the analysis of poverty of using this measure of unemployment rather than other samples (Tables A.1.2 and A.1.3).

The data sources we use are the British Household Panel Study (BHPS) and the German Socio-economic Panel (GSOEP). Details of these datasets are available in the Appendix. This chapter uses all four of the samples in the GSOEP available in 1996: West Germans, foreigners living in West Germany, East Germans and immigrants to West Germany since 1984. The latter three are over-sampled relative to their proportion in the population, so appropriate weights are used to correct for over-sampling, as well as for attrition (see Appendix for details on weighting the datasets to make them cross-sectionally representative). The British data is also weighted.

## 4.3   ANALYSIS OF OUTCOMES FOR ALL THE UNEMPLOYED

The hypothesis in Section 4.1 is of a higher level of income poverty among the unemployed in Britain than in Germany. Table 4.1 presents the proportion of the unemployed falling under the 40, 50 and 60 per cent of median income poverty lines, using the new OECD equivalence scale. Our analysis does indeed reveal a much higher poverty rate in Britain than in Germany, particularly for the 40 per cent income poverty line. Using this line only 8.1 per cent of the unemployed in Germany are income poor, while in Britain the figure is 21.2 per cent. The contrast is not as marked for the higher poverty lines,

*Table 4.1* *Proportion of all unemployed individuals aged 18–64 under various median income poverty lines, Britain (1993) and Germany (1996)*

| Poverty Lines | Britain (%) | Germany (%) | West Germany (%) | East Germany (%) |
|---|---|---|---|---|
| 40% | 21.2 | 8.1 | 7.2 | 9.3 |
| 50% | 33.6 | 19.8 | 18.5 | 21.9 |
| 60% | 50.8 | 38.6 | 43.0 | 32.2 |
| No. of cases | 390 | 591 | 341 | 250 |

*Note*:   New OECD equivalence scale used for all estimates.

*Source*:   Own calculations from the BHPS and GSOEP, weighted.

particularly for the 60 per cent income poverty line. However, the proportion of the unemployed with income below the 60 per cent income poverty line is very high indeed: half of all unemployed persons in Britain, and around 40 per cent of the unemployed in Germany.[14] The findings for Britain are similar to those of Hauser and Nolan (2000) for 1994–95, using the Family Expenditure Survey.[15] The findings are also remarkably consistent, regardless of which definition of unemployment we use (see Appendix Tables A.1.2 and A.1.3).

The differences between East and West Germany are small for the 40 per cent and 50 per cent income poverty lines, with slightly lower proportions in poverty in the West. For the 60 per cent poverty line, however, there are more West German unemployed in poverty than East German unemployed.

How do we know that it is not simply the case that there are more poor in Britain, regardless of labour market status? To consider the effect of unemployment, we compare the unemployed with the employed in each country. Using logistic regression, we model the probability of being income poor, in this case under the 50 per cent median income poverty line, and compare the unemployed to the employed in each country.[16] The results are presented in Table 4.2.

If we look at the effect of unemployment on the odds of being under the 50 per cent median income poverty line, we find that the effect is strongest in Britain, as expected, and weakest in East Germany. In model 1 in Table 4.2 we find that the unemployed in Britain are 13.5 times more likely to be income poor than the employed. In models 2 and 3 we see that in West

*Table 4.2    Odds of employed and unemployed of working age falling below*
*the 50 per cent median income poverty line, Britain (1993) and*
*West and East Germany (1996) – results from a logistic*
*regression model*

|  | Britain<br>Model 1<br>Exp (B) | West Germany<br>Model 2<br>Exp (B) | East Germany<br>Model 3<br>Exp (B) |
|---|---|---|---|
| Employed | 1.00 | 1.00 | 1.00 |
| Unemployed | 13.48*** | 8.54*** | 6.09*** |
| −2 log-likelihood | 1,833.17 | 1,439.09 | 666.11 |
| Model chi-sq. | 305.81 | 100.77 | 55.43 |
| No. of cases | 4,963 | 5,073 | 2,343 |

*Note*:   *P < = 0.05; **P < = 0.01; ***P < = 0.001. New OECD equivalence scale. The exponentiated coefficients are odds ratios; scores over 1 represent an increase in the chance of being in poverty, and scores between 0 and 1 a decrease. Very different sampling probabilities for the German sample mean that the sample is only representative when weighted by the cross-sectional individual weight, so this weight is applied when running the German regression. In the interests of comparability, the British sample is also weighted for the regression analyses in this chapter.

*Sources*:   BHPS & GSOEP. Employed and unemployed aged18–64 only.

Germany the unemployed are 8.5 times more likely to be poor than those in employment, while in East Germany they are only 6.1 times more likely.

How can we account for the fact that unemployment has less of an effect in East than in West Germany? Hahn and Schön (1996) suggest a number of differences between unemployment in East and West Germany. One key point is the great heterogeneity of the unemployed in East Germany. As we noted in Chapter 2 unemployment in the 1990s in East Germany was the result of the economic transformation process and a rapid decline in employment, with a wide range of labour market groups affected. The unemployed in East Germany show much greater differentiation in terms of qualifications, work history, age and household situation than they do in West Germany. We should therefore not be surprised that their income does not differ as much from the employed population as it does in West Germany.

## 4.4 ANALYSIS OF INCOME POVERTY AMONG THE UNEMPLOYED

### 4.4.1 The Effect of Benefit Receipt

Our second group of hypotheses concerns differences in poverty rates between those receiving different types of benefit. As we saw in Chapter 3 the difference between Britain and Germany in type of benefit received is significant. Most German unemployed who receive benefit get unemployment insurance (*Arbeitslosengeld*) (Figure 3.1a in Chapter 3). In Britain we see much greater reliance on means-testing (Figure 3.2). Unemployed women are less likely to receive any benefit than men (Table 3.3). Benefit receipt as reported on the surveys used in this chapter is consistent with this picture provided by official statistics.[17]

Table 4.3 presents poverty rates among those receiving different types of benefit in Britain and in West and East Germany. The table shows the propor-

*Table 4.3*     *Percentage of unemployed under the 50 per cent income poverty line by type of benefit received, Britain (1993) and Germany (1996)*

| | Britain | Germany | West Germany | East Germany |
|---|---|---|---|---|
| No benefit (recorded) | 22.4 | 14.6 | 15.1 | 11.1 |
| Unemployment insurance | 24.1 | 11.9 | 10.0 | 13.5 |
| Unemployment assistance | N/a | 31.6 | 25.6 | 38.9 |
| Social assistance | 42.2 | 54.1 | 44.4 | 80.0 |
| No. of cases | 390 | 591 | 341 | 250 |

*Notes*:
For Britain: 'unemployment insurance' is unemployment benefit; 'social assistance' is income support or a combination of income support and unemployment benefit. For the 'no benefit recorded' category, some of these cases may be receiving benefit but have not reported it.

For Germany: 'unemployment insurance' is *Arbeitslosengeld*; 'unemployment assistance' is *Arbeitslosenhilfe*; 'social assistance' is either *Sozialhilfe* or *Sozialhilfe* combined with one other benefit.

Social assistance in Germany is recorded at the household level. To avoid counting people twice, benefit receipt is attributed to the head of household, under the assumption that it is the head of household who is most likely to receive this benefit, as is the case in Britain.

For the 'no benefit recorded' category, some of these cases may be receiving benefit but have not reported it.

*Source*:     Own calculations from the GSOEP and BHPS, weighted. 18–64-year-olds only.

tion of the unemployed under the 50 per cent median poverty line, using the new OECD equivalence scale. The findings for the three German benefits confirm our hypotheses.[18] Those on unemployment assistance (*Arbeitslosenhilfe*), who are primarily long-term unemployed, are more likely to have equivalised incomes under the 50 per cent threshold than those on unemployment insurance (*Arbeitslosengeld*). Those most at risk of income poverty are those receiving social assistance (*Sozialhilfe*): around 54 per cent fall under the 50 per cent median income poverty line, though the number of cases is small.[19] Here we find evidence of German social security provision rewarding labour market participation, and clear differences between groups of the unemployed by benefit type.

It may not be surprising that those receiving means-tested, assistance benefits (*Arbeitslosenhilfe* and *Sozialhilfe*) have higher poverty rates, as assistance benefits are only paid to those below a certain means threshold whereas unemployment insurance is paid to all who satisfy the contribution requirements. This is why it is particularly revealing that the poverty rate is much higher among social assistance recipients than unemployment assistance recipients, both of which are means-tested benefits. Most unemployment assistance recipients previously received unemployment insurance, which is earnings-related. The small number of those forced to rely on social assistance in Germany because of lack of insurance contributions are very vulnerable to income poverty, particularly in East Germany.

Comparing East and West Germany we find similar poverty rates among those receiving unemployment insurance, but higher poverty in the East for recipients of both unemployment assistance and social assistance.[20] As noted in Chapter 3, social assistance payments tend to be even lower in East Germany than in West, and one might speculate that the earnings-linked unemployment assistance payments tend to be lower there too, as earnings are lower. That said, very few East German unemployed receive social assistance (see Figure 3.1b in Chapter 3).

A similar pattern emerges in Britain: those receiving unemployment insurance (unemployment benefit) are much less likely to have equivalised incomes below the 50 per cent income poverty line than those receiving means-tested social assistance (income support). This too is consistent with our hypotheses. There is not much difference in rates of payment for unemployment insurance and social assistance in Britain, but recipients of social assistance are more likely to be living in poor households than recipients of unemployment insurance. To qualify for social assistance a household's income must fall below a certain threshold, whereas unemployment insurance is given regardless of income.

While our findings show a difference in the incidence of poverty between recipients of different types of benefit in Britain, the difference is not as marked as in Germany. Our findings confirm the 'hierarchical' nature of the benefit system in Germany, as hypothesised at the beginning of the chapter. The unemployed in Germany who have good continuous employment records are well served by insurance benefits, which cannot be said for social assistance.

### 4.4.2 The Role of Gender

Our third group of hypotheses concerns the impact of welfare benefits on gender differences in income poverty among the unemployed. From Lewis and Ostner (1994) we derive the hypothesis that unemployed women suffer less income poverty than unemployed men in both countries. Daly's model (1996) suggests that gender differences in individual poverty are greater in Germany than in Britain.

Table 4.4 presents median income poverty rates among the unemployed in Britain and in East and West Germany by gender. Of the sample with valid income data, women account for 37 per cent of the British unemployed and 54 per cent of the German unemployed. The unemployed women in the sample are much less likely to be income poor than the unemployed men in both Britain and Germany, for all three poverty lines. Our findings support the hypothesis that women do not suffer as much from the income consequences of unemployment as men. However, the findings do not clearly support the predictions derived from Daly's characterisation of Britain and Germany, as the gender differences in poverty among the unemployed in Britain and Germany are similar, as shown by the ratios of men's to women's poverty rates, in columns (3), (6) and (9).[21]

Regarding East–West differences within Germany, in Chapter 2 we noted that there is a much higher proportion of dual breadwinner households in East Germany (Table 2.6), which might lead us to expect that gender differences in poverty in East Germany would be less than in the West. While we do see a smaller gender difference in East Germany for the 50 per cent poverty line, this is not true of the other poverty lines in Table 4.4. One explanation is that particularly high unemployment in the 1990s among East German women, who have been harder hit than men by economic restructuring, has led to many more 'traditional' households, in which the man works and supports the unemployed woman (Berger, 1999).

It is important to note that these estimates are of individual poverty based on equivalised income and assume that resources are shared equally within the household, which may not be the case. Poverty among women may thus be underestimated. As Chapter 3 shows, many more unemployed women than men – especially in Britain – do not receive benefits themselves and therefore have to rely on the income of others in the household. The fact that this is particularly the case in Britain further weakens the evidence for the hypoth-

*Table 4.4  Percentage of unemployed under 40, 50 and 60 per cent median income poverty lines by gender, Britain (1993), West and East Germany (1996) (new equivalence scale)*

| | Britain | | | West Germany | | | East Germany | | |
|---|---|---|---|---|---|---|---|---|---|
| | Men | Women | Ratio men to women | Men | Women | Ratio men to women | Men | Women | Ratio men to women |
| | (1) | (2) | (3) | (4) | (5) | (6) | (7) | (8) | (9) |
| 40% median | 26.2 | 12.0 | 2.18 | 9.2 | 5.0 | 1.84 | 15.1 | 4.8 | 3.14 |
| 50% median | 39.3 | 23.5 | 1.67 | 26.3 | 11.5 | 2.28 | 28.8 | 17.1 | 1.68 |
| 60% median | 55.8 | 42.1 | 1.33 | 48.7 | 38.1 | 1.27 | 40.5 | 26.0 | 1.55 |
| No. of cases | 245 | 145 | | 175 | 166 | | 97 | 153 | |

*Source:*  Own calculations from the BHPS and GSOEP, weighted.

esis derived from Daly that unemployed women are better off in the means-tested system than the insurance-based system.

### 4.4.3 The Effect of Household Type

In our hypotheses we also suggest that different welfare states prioritise different household types. One hypothesis is that both Britain and Germany prioritise male breadwinner households (Lewis and Ostner 1994), another that Germany favours male breadwinner households more (Daly 2000). In this section we consider differences in poverty rates by household type.

Table 4.5 presents the household situation of unemployed men and women in Britain and Germany. The table incorporates both household composition and the employment status of others in the household, giving five categories of household type: an unemployed person living alone; an unemployed person living with one or more adults, none of whom are working ('multi-adult workless household'); an unemployed person living with dependent children and with one or more adults, at least one of whom is working; an unemployed person living without dependent children but with one or more adults, at least

*Table 4.5    Unemployed men and women by household type, Britain (1993) and West and East Germany (1996)*

| Household Type | Britain (1993) | | West Germany (1996) | | East Germany (1996) | |
|---|---|---|---|---|---|---|
| | Men (%) | Women (%) | Men (%) | Women (%) | Men (%) | Women (%) |
| Unemployed living alone[23] | 12.4 | 7.8 | 17.1 | 21.0 | 33.3 | [5.6] |
| Multi-adult workless household | 40.7 | 19.9 | 29.3 | 18.5 | 24.1 | 22.2 |
| 2 or more adults, 1 or more working, dependent child(ren) | 19.6 | 28.3 | 18.6 | 35.7 | 19.5 | 40.7 |
| 2 or more adults, 1 or more working, no children | 26.7 | 30.7 | 33.6 | 20.4 | 23.0 | 25.0 |
| 1 adult with dependent child(ren) | [0.4] | 13.3 | [1.4] | [4.5] | 0 | [6.5] |

*Note*:    [ ] = N less than 10.

*Source*:    Own calculations from the GSOEP and the BHPS.

one of whom is working; and finally, an unemployed person living alone with dependent children.[22]

In this classification it is the household situation of the unemployed person that is crucial, not their marital status. The emphasis on household situation has some disadvantages. Most notably we cannot distinguish lone mothers as a separate group. This classification method is consistent with our strong assumption of household sharing: that lone mothers living in households with other earners (their parents or a cohabiting partner, for example) are expected to benefit from the income of the other earners.[24]

Of note in Table 4.5 are cross-national and gender differences in the proportion of unemployed people living in multi-adult workless households. All cases of traditional male breadwinner households in which the breadwinner becomes unemployed fall into this category.[25] In Britain, two in five unemployed men live in multi-adult workless households (40.7 per cent); only one in five unemployed women. In Germany the gender difference is not so marked, though still around 30 per cent of West German men live in such a household. In Germany there are more unemployed living alone than in Britain.[26] In both countries a greater proportion of women live in a household with two or more adults, one or more of whom is working, and with dependent children. In East Germany the proportion of the unemployed living in multi-adult workless households is rather similar for men and women, possibly in many such cases with both partners unemployed, which is more common there than in either West Germany or Britain (see Table 2.6 in Chapter 2).

We compare income poverty among different household types by estimating logistic regression models. This technique allows us to take into account the sample size when assessing the reliability of our estimates.[27] Table 4.6 presents the odds that the unemployed in different household types will fall under the 50 per cent median poverty line. We also apply a significance of difference test to compare the model estimates for Britain and Germany. This test uses information about the differences in the coefficients for Britain and Germany and their standard error to provide an indication of the significance of the difference in the two coefficients.[28] The equivalence scale used in these models is the new OECD equivalence scale. As assumptions about how household income is shared are implicit in equivalence scales, models were also estimated using the old equivalence scales, discussed below. Because of the small number of cases for some household types, women and men are combined for this analysis.

We first compare odds for Britain and Germany in columns (1) and (2). The table shows that in both countries the unemployed living in households with another earner (the reference category) are much less likely to be income poor than the unemployed living in any other household type. Compared to this reference category, the unemployed who live alone are

*Table 4.6*  *Odds of unemployed individuals falling below the 50 per cent median income poverty line, Britain (1993) and East and West Germany (1996)*

| Household Situation of the Unemployed | Britain (1) | Germany (2) | T. Stat of Difference (3) | West Germany (4) | East Germany (5) |
|---|---|---|---|---|---|
| *REF: 1 or more others working; no children under 18* | | | | | |
| Female | 0.6* | 0.4** | 0.77 | 0.4** | 0.7 |
| Living alone (1) | 16.7*** | 5.4*** | 1.92 | 4.7* | 8.8*** |
| Multi-adult workless household | 5.5*** | 2.7** | 1.65 | 3.1** | 1.8 |
| Children under 18 in household | 2.9*** | 2.0* | 0.91 | 5.5*** | 0.5 |
| Lone parent (2) | 2.9* | 13.0*** | −1.86 | 8.2** | 27.6*** |
| −2 log-likelihood | 383.87 | 381.98 | | 203.24 | 151.06 |
| Model chi-sq. | 83.38 | 52.60 | | 43.37 | 36.13 |
| No. of cases | 390 | 591 | | 341 | 250 |

*Notes*:
*P < = 0.05; **P < = 0.01; ***P < = 0.001. New OECD equivalence scale.
The number of single unemployed people with valid income data in the samples is low (36 in Britain, 44 in Germany). The number of adults living alone with dependent children in the samples ('lone parent') is very low indeed (19 in Britain, 15 in Germany). Note that this group does not include those lone parents who live in the same household as other adults.

*Sources*:  Own calculations from the BHPS and GSOEP. All analysis weighted by cross-sectional individual weights.

much more likely to be income poor in both countries, especially in Britain. In both countries, an unemployed person living in a multi-adult workless household is more likely to be in poverty, especially in Britain again. In Germany the effect of living alone with dependent children is very marked; in Britain this effect is not significant once we control for the presence of children, among other factors. In general, the household type, in particular having an earner in the household, has more of an impact in Britain than in Germany. This is confirmed by the findings of the significance of difference test in column (3). In Britain, benefit payments are so low that those households without another source of income are very likely to be under the 50 per cent median income poverty line.[29] The one exception to this finding is unemployed lone parents who do not live with other adults. Those

German unemployed lone parents who do not live with other adults are at much higher risk of poverty relative to households with an earner than are their British equivalents.

Our findings here do not support the hypothesis that these welfare systems favour single breadwinner households by protecting them from the consequences of unemployment. Single breadwinner households fare very badly in both systems when the breadwinner becomes unemployed. Those who fare best are in dual-earner households. On whatever principle the compensation systems are organised – and it may well be with the male breadwinner model in mind – in practice, dual breadwinner households are much better protected from the income risk of unemployment. And significantly, as seen in Table 4.5, about one-third of the unemployed in Britain (including about 40 per cent of unemployed men) live in multi-adult workless households. The single unemployed are also at a high risk of falling under the 50 per cent income poverty line. When unemployment compensation (and related transfers) is the only source of income, it is insufficient to prevent a significant number of the unemployed having equivalised incomes below the 50 per cent income poverty line.[30] While the traditional male breadwinner household fares badly when the breadwinner becomes unemployed in both countries, the fact that they are less disadvantaged relative to former dual-earner households in Germany does lend some support to Daly's (1996) typology. The insurance system pays high benefits to the former earner, thus protecting the family from poverty – or at least to a greater extent, relative to other households, than in Britain.

Comparing East and West Germany in columns (4) and (5) in Table 4.6, two differences are particularly interesting. The first is that in East Germany the unemployed living in multi-adult workless households do not seem to be as vulnerable to poverty, relative to those living with another earner, as do their equivalents in West Germany. This may be because in East Germany such households are more likely to be made up of two or more unemployed, both potentially receiving unemployment insurance, whereas in West Germany such households are more likely to include only one unemployed person, with one non-earner (see Table 2.6 in Chapter 2, and Holst and Schupp 1996). The second East–West difference is that the albeit very small group of unemployed lone mothers in East Germany are much more likely to be income poor than the unemployed in East Germany who live with another earner, and to a much greater extent than their counterparts in West Germany.

The risk of poverty among lone mothers is an important issue for our gender-sensitive typologies. However, the finding that lone mothers in Germany are more at risk of income poverty than in Britain is tentative as the number of cases is small and because, as noted above, unemployed lone mothers are not assessed separately if they are living with a partner or their parents. Notwithstanding the data limitations, these findings do support the analysis of Daly (2000) who argues, comparing Britain and Germany, that 'lone mothers are less marginalized in a minimum-income welfare state model than they are in Germany's hierarchical social insurance model, where no specific provision exists for them and so they have to claim through the stigma-ridden safety-net program' (i.e. *Sozialhilfe*) (Daly 2000, p. 216).

The disadvantage suffered by German unemployed lone mothers leads us to reflect that our focus here is on the income risk of unemployment only, while there are other important income risks that welfare states affect, a key one being the financial consequences of marital disruption. Overall poverty rates for German women may be much lower than for British women (see Table 4.4), but, as Ruspini (1998) finds, marital disruption is a high risk factor for poverty among German women, while British female poverty is more strongly related to unemployment.[31] How the countries compare in terms of gender differences depends on the risk being investigated.

## 4.5 INCOME CHANGES AND LABOUR MARKET TRANSITIONS

Up to this point our comparison is of poverty rates among the unemployed in two specific years, 1993 for Britain and 1996 for Germany. One of the limitations of this approach is that we still do not know whether the unemployed were already income poor before they became unemployed. Can we attribute their poverty to their labour market status? The reason for the higher rate of poverty among the unemployed in Britain might be that the unemployed are disproportionately drawn from the ranks of the poor in Britain, but not in Germany. Indeed, Gosling et al. (1997), in their study of the dynamics of low pay and unemployment in early 1990s' Britain, find that people on low incomes are more likely to become unemployed than those on higher incomes. To resolve this uncertainty, we need to look at the change in financial situation experienced by individuals who are employed one year and unemployed the next. This section is a preliminary foray into the dynamics of income and unemployment.

We look here at the change in income for all of those who moved into unemployment, not just those who became poor. The non-poor unemployed may also have experienced a fall in income, and they are therefore included in the analysis.[32] On the other hand because we are interested in the income effects of losing a job, we exclude those who were not previously employed, e.g. those who were in education, and women returning to work after an absence from the labour market. This may mean that our sample will include fewer young people and fewer women than a normal sample of the unemployed. In sum we consider the income change of all those who were employed in year *t* and unemployed in year *t* + 1.

Table 4.7 compares the equivalised income change of these 'negative movers' within the labour market with the income change both of 'positive movers', who move in the opposite direction (from unemployment to employment), and of those who were employed in both years ('employed stayers'). The table also presents the change in equivalised income for the whole sample for whom we have data on labour market status. The table compares income changes over three two-year periods, and focuses on percentage change in mean incomes as an attempt to account for the large variance in initial income.[33] It is important to bear in mind that this is merely a summary statistic; while mean income may fall for a whole group, it may rise for certain individuals.

*Table 4.7*   *Percentage change in mean of monthly equivalised income for different groups, Britain and West and East Germany*

|  |  | All: 18–64 (1) | 'Employed Stayers' (2) | 'Negative Movers' (3) | 'Positive Movers' (4) |
|---|---|---|---|---|---|
| Britain | 1991–92 | +6 | +6 | −34 | +59 |
|  | 1992–93 | +2 | +2 | −31 | +52 |
|  | 1993–94 | +3 | +5 | −26 | +43 |
| West Germany | 1994–95 | +2 | +3 | −24 | +29 |
|  | 1995–96 | 0 | +2 | −21 | +26 |
|  | 1996–97 | 0 | +1 | −17 | +25 |
| East Germany | 1994–95 | +5 | +6 | −11 | +29 |
|  | 1995–96 | +3 | +4 | −12 | +22 |
|  | 1996–97 | +2 | +3 | −16 | +18 |

*Note*:   Weighted by relevant cross-sectional weight for destination year (*t* + 1). Income equivalised using new OECD equivalence scale.

*Source*:   Own calculations from the BHPS and GSOEP. Working-age population.

The overall picture of change in equivalised income shown in Table 4.7 is as expected. For the working population as a whole, and for those who stay in employment, there is a slight increase in equivalised income from one year to the next. In general the increase is slightly more for 'employed stayers' than for the population as a whole. For 'positive movers' there is a significant and substantial rise in equivalised income. By contrast for 'negative movers', the group we are most interested in, there is a fall in mean income in both countries in each year.

The between-country differences are interesting, most specifically for the 'movers'. For 'negative movers' the fall in mean income in West Germany is less than in Britain. In East Germany the fall in income following a transition to unemployment is much less than in either Britain or West Germany, with the exception of 1996–97 in West Germany. For 'positive movers' whereas Germans experience an average rise of between 20 and 30 per cent in mean income when they get a job, British respondents experience an average increase in the region of 50 per cent. Some year-to-year fluctuations may be accounted for by small sample sizes.

In summary this preliminary analysis of yearly transitions supports our earlier findings about the income changes associated with unemployment. Those who become unemployed in Germany tend to experience less of a fall in income than those who become unemployed in Britain.

## 4.6  CONCLUSION

In this chapter we draw on a number of typologies to develop hypotheses regarding income poverty among the unemployed in Britain and Germany. We test these hypotheses by analysing income poverty rates in the two countries.

Our first general hypothesis is that income poverty among the unemployed is higher in Britain than in Germany. This hypothesis is endorsed, in line with Gallie and Paugam (2000), who predict greater rates of poverty among the British unemployed, and with Schmid and Reissert (1996), who argue that means-testing is less effective at protecting the unemployed from poverty than insurance-based schemes. When we check the robustness of these findings by looking at income change following a move from employment to unemployment, we find a greater drop in income on average in Britain than in Germany.

Our second major hypothesis is that the type of benefit received makes a greater difference to poverty rates among the unemployed in Germany than it does in Britain. This hypothesis is also endorsed. In Germany, the unemployed receiving unemployment assistance and social assistance are more vulnerable to poverty than those who receive unemployment insurance, with social assistance recipients particularly vulnerable to poverty. This supports one of the criticisms of the insurance-based system we discussed in Chapter 1, that the system protects some groups well – specifically those who qualify for unemployment insurance – but not those who need to rely on social assistance. Those who rely on social assistance in Germany are those without a continuous employment record, often lone mothers and young single unemployed people. In Germany, overall poverty rates are lower, but this is due to the unemployment insurance system, not to social assistance. This finding is in keeping with the conclusions of Behrendt (2000). In Britain, there are higher rates of poverty overall, but not such a large difference between types of benefit.

Our third group of hypotheses concerns gender and household type. One hypothesis is that there are lower income poverty rates among unemployed women than among unemployed men. Our findings confirm this hypothesis, and there is little difference between the countries in this regard. This latter finding goes somewhat against Daly's (1996) prediction that in Germany gender differences in poverty rates will be considerably less than in Britain, at least in the sphere of unemployment. However, in asserting that poverty rates are lower among unemployed women than unemployed men, the following caveat should be borne in mind: our finding rests on the assumption that income is shared equally among household members, which may not be the case. Testing this assumption is beyond the scope of this book.

What emerges strongly from our findings is the vulnerability to poverty of those households without a second earner, particularly in Britain. Some authors argue that both Britain and Germany favour the male breadwinner household (Lewis and Ostner 1994), but if the male breadwinner becomes unemployed the individuals in that family – especially in Britain – are at high risk of income poverty. Transfers paid to the unemployed are so low in Britain that the benefit system alone is not enough to protect many of the unemployed from poverty. Differences in poverty rates by household type among the unemployed are not as great in Germany, suggesting that the German benefit system is more likely to protect from poverty single unemployed persons or those living in multi-adult workless households. However, an important exception to this is unemployed lone parents living alone in Germany, who in our limited analysis we find to be much more vulnerable to income poverty than their equivalents in Britain. The very poor protection of unemployed lone parents in Germany, combined with somewhat greater protection of the former male breadwinner households, the multi-adult workless households, at least compared to Britain, tends to support Daly's (1996) predictions about the two welfare states. Daly's typology is thus given some support when we compare poverty outcomes among different household types, though not when comparing overall gender differences in poverty rates in Britain and Germany.

In East Germany we find the hierarchical nature of the German unemployment compensation system to be even more exaggerated: marginal groups are even more disadvantaged than in West Germany. Very few East German unemployed receive unemployment assistance, and even fewer receive social assistance, but those who do are very vulnerable indeed to income poverty, as are lone mothers in East Germany. On the more positive side, a much smaller proportion of the East German unemployed live in multi-adult workless households, and when they do they are not as vulnerable to poverty, relative to other unemployed people, as are their equivalents in West Germany (or in Britain). This we attribute to the much higher incidence of dual-earner households in East Germany; when an individual becomes unemployed in East Germany, it is more likely that his or her spouse is working, and workless households are more likely to be made up of two unemployed people, both potentially receiving unemployment insurance.

What needs to be reiterated at this point is the limitations of the income data and the samples of the unemployed used. In the final Appendix, Section A.2.1, we suggest that the sample of the unemployed used in this chapter includes a greater proportion of women and young people than the sample in the European Labour Force Survey, and that it is a somewhat smaller proportion of the labour force than would be expected. If anything, we are therefore underestimating the differences between Britain and Germany if we use a sample of the unemployed who are younger and less likely to receive insurance benefits. Looking specifically at the British data, there is a slight tendency in the British Household Panel Survey to underestimate income poverty when compared to the Family Expenditure Survey, as noted in the Appendix, Section A.1.6. In addition we report median income poverty lines, which tend to understate cross-national differences. All these limitations suggest that we underestimate cross-national differences in poverty among the unemployed.

Finally, in this chapter we have taken household structure as given, as not influenced by the system of unemployment compensation. However, it may not be true that household structure and household employment are independent of the social welfare system; when one member of a household becomes unemployed others may alter their behaviour. This type of effect is considered in Chapter 6 where we look particularly at the impact of a husband's unemployment and benefit status on his wife's transitions into and out of the labour force. Given the high poverty rates among workless households, as shown in this chapter, the effect of unemployment on the labour market status of others in the same household is particularly important.

## NOTES

1. In particular, the purpose of active labour market policies and programmes is primarily to place participants in employment, not replace their income. The effect of active labour market programmes is beyond the scope of this chapter: here our focus is on financial deprivation.

2. We expect those receiving means-tested benefit in both countries to be more at risk of income poverty than those receiving insurance benefit, by virtue of the fact that the former group is limited to households falling below a certain income level and the latter receive benefits regardless of their income.

3. However, some women, such as lone mothers, will need to provide for dependants.

4. In Chapter 3 we saw that both British and German women are disadvantaged relative to men in the receipt of benefits, which might suggest an alternative hypothesis that unemployed women experience higher rates of income poverty than men. However, such a hypothesis would assume that households do not share resources and would require us to look at the woman's income only, not the income of the household.

5. The definition of lone mothers is discussed later in the chapter.

6. For example, we use OECD equivalence scales, not national ones.

7. Another method of assessing 'depth' of poverty is to use the poverty gap statistic, which is based on the income shortfall of those below the poverty line. The advantage of this measure is its sensitivity to the mean level of income of the poor relative to the poverty line.

8. In many studies of poverty, annual income is the preferred measure. In these studies the emphasis is on well-being from a longer-term perspective, as opposed to well-being related to current labour market status.

9. The British Household Panel Survey (BHPS) net monthly income measure is derived by Jarvis and Jenkins (1995). Jarvis and Jenkins use BHPS data in conjunction with a simulation model of the tax and benefit system, deriving estimates of income tax, national insurance contributions and local tax liabilities for all persons in the survey. By deducting these liabilities from gross income, an estimate of net income before housing costs is provided (Jarvis and Jenkins 1995). The measure of net income is designed to be as close as possible to the Department of Social Security's 'before housing costs' measure used in the *Households Below Average Income* series (e.g. Department of Social Security 1995).

10. Neither the British nor the German measure includes bonus income, private transfers to persons outside the household, or imputed rental income for owner-occupiers.

11. For details of how the sample with valid income data differs from the overall BHPS sample, see Jarvis and Jenkins (1995).

12. Note that in neither case is the definition of the household the same as the benefit unit, which is the nationally-defined 'household' for the purpose of calculating benefit entitlement.

13. The German estimate is based on the whole labour force, that is, the unemployed as a percentage of the unemployed, self-employed and employees, including apprentices.

14. We also tested the sensitivity of our results to the definition of unemployment used. Overall, the poverty rates are very similar to those reported in Table 4.1. We find slightly higher poverty rates in Britain for the self-defined unemployed. For Germany, although the samples are different in size, the poverty rates for the registered unemployed are very similar to those reported in Table 4.1.

15. It is difficult to compare Hauser and Nolan's findings for Germany, as their estimates are based on West Germany alone, using a poverty line that is specific to West Germany. The effect of applying separate relative poverty lines to East and West Germany is that East German poverty appears lower and West German poverty higher.

16. Given that the primary focus of this chapter has been the probability of individuals falling under different income poverty thresholds, it seems consistent to conceive of poverty as a binary 'choice', which has a value of one for being under a specific poverty line, otherwise zero. For a binary dependent variable, logistic regression modelling is one appropriate method (Menard 1995). The obvious disadvantage of this strategy is that the result will be highly dependent on the poverty measure we choose. For this reason, sensitivity analysis is carried out, using a different measure of central tendency and a different equivalence scale, as has been the strategy throughout the chapter. Where the findings of this analysis is different to that presented this is noted in the text.

17. For Germany the 1996 European Labour Force Survey shows 74 per cent of ILO unemployed in receipt of benefits, compared to 69 per cent for the sample of the

unemployed in the GSOEP used in this chapter. Some of the difference is accounted for by the fact that the samples are defined differently; when we apply the full ILO definition to our German data we find a larger proportion of the unemployed in receipt of benefit (71.5 per cent). For Britain the 1993 European Labour Force Survey does not show the proportion of ILO unemployed in receipt of benefit. Estimates from the *Employment Gazette* for that year show 65.7 per cent of ILO unemployed in receipt of benefits, which is very close to the 65.4 per cent of the pseudo-ILO reported in the BHPS sample used here.

18. Mean income poverty lines were also applied. With mean income as the comparison, higher proportions are in poverty than with median income, though the overall story is very similar, the only notable differences being for social assistance in Germany (discussed below).

19. Though the number of social assistance recipients in the unemployed sample is relatively small (36), they have similar poverty rates to other social assistance recipients in the full GSOEP sample, suggesting that they are not a particularly select group.

20. However, as noted above, the number of social assistance recipients in the German sample is small, especially in East Germany. What is more, if we apply the 50 per cent *mean* income poverty line, poverty among West German social assistance recipients is also very high (75 per cent).

21. However, if we repeat the analysis excluding lone mothers, we do indeed find somewhat greater gender differences in income poverty among the unemployed in Germany, particularly in West Germany, more in support of Daly (1996). See the discussion on lone mothers in Section 4.5.3.

22. Dependent children are defined as those aged 18 or under who are not participating in the labour market; conversely adults are all those over 18, plus 16–18-year-olds who are participating in the labour market.

23. The small number of single unemployed people in Britain is partly due to the definition of the household, as single unrelated adults living together fall into one of the 'two or more adults' categories, on the assumption that they share resources.

24. Some unemployed lone mothers are separately identified in the 'one adult (woman) with dependent children' category. But some others fall into other categories: if they are living with other earners they fall into the 'two or more adults, one or more working, dependent children' category; if they are living with non-earners they fall into the 'multi-adult workless household' category. In addition, the number of cases in the category 'one adult with dependent children' is very small indeed.

25. Another situation that could give rise to this category of household is a dual breadwinner household in which both breadwinners become unemployed at the same time.

26. The small number of single unemployed in Britain may be partly due to the definition of the household, as single unrelated adults living together fall into one of the 'two or more adults' categories, on the assumption that they share resources.

27. For further details of why logistic regression is used see note 16 above.

28. The *t*-statistic is calculated using the following formula:

$$t = \hat{\beta}_G - \hat{\beta}_B / \sqrt{(\hat{\sigma}_{\hat{\beta}_G})^2 - (\hat{\sigma}_{\hat{\beta}_B})^2}$$

where $\hat{\beta}_G$ is the coefficient for Germany, $\hat{\beta}_B$ the coefficient for Britain, and $\hat{\sigma}$ the relevant standard error.

29. To test the sensitivity of these findings to the equivalence scale chosen, the model was repeated using the old OECD equivalence scale. The old OECD equivalence scale gives more weight to dependants (both other adults and children), and should therefore result in more multi-person households falling under the poverty line. This was found to be the case, but the results do not distort the overall picture, that there is a high risk of poverty in households where no one is working.

30. The finding that the unemployed in dual-earner households are better protected from poverty is consistent with the findings of Gallie et al. (2000).

31. DiPrete and McManus (2000) also find that German welfare policies provide better protection from the financial consequences of unemployment than of partner loss.
32. Considering only those who were employed and non-poor one year and unemployed and poor the next would also entail a reduction in sample sizes.
33. Change in median income was also calculated, though not presented here. The differences between mean and median income changes were found to be negligible.

# 5. Comparing durations of unemployment

In Chapter 1 we noted how Esping-Andersen (1990, 1999) writes about the insider/outsider tendency in conservative, insurance-based welfare regimes, of which Germany is one. This tendency is for core workers – those with full-time, continuous employment histories – to be given priority over others. Gallie and Paugam (2000) and Schmid and Reissert (1996) note how insurance systems (like the German one) tend to protect well the incomes of core workers but neglect marginal workers. This claim is confirmed by the analysis in Chapter 4: in Germany those who have been core workers are not as vulnerable to income poverty as those who have previously not worked. In Britain, we do not detect such a strong distinction.

In this chapter, in which we look at the duration of unemployment, we widen the idea of the institutional regulation of unemployment beyond the benefit system. We consider the market more carefully, and market differences between Britain and Germany. As we discussed in Chapter 1, one issue prominent in the discussion on the causes of unemployment has been the institutional regulation of the labour market and how it affects labour market clearing (Grubb and Wells 1993; OECD 1994; Siebert 1997). One of our typologies divided countries into those with high levels of labour market regulation and those with lower levels. But how does labour market regulation affect unemployment? In spite of much research, no conclusive findings have emerged. In particular, no simple relationship has been established between labour market regulation and the overall level of unemployment. However, it has been shown that labour market regulation affects the structure of unemployment (Esping-Andersen 1998; OECD 1999): the regulatory structure produces a higher level of unemployment among some socio-economic groups than among others. Esping-Andersen argues that, in labour markets with stronger regulation, among the weakest groups in the labour market we should expect high, persistent and long-term unemployment, with low chances of mobility into jobs. He identifies the weakest labour market groups as women, the low-skilled and young people. The expected effect is not on job-to-job mobility – this may be the same in labour markets with low level of regulation – but on the transition between unemployment and jobs (or vice versa).

One way of exploring the link between labour market regulation and the structure of unemployment then is to look at the transition from unemployment to employment. Which groups find this transition most difficult? Is it the case that in Germany – and not in Britain –we find a contrast between 'insiders' and 'outsiders', between core workers with relatively short durations of unemployment, and others more marginalised in the labour market who find it more difficult to re-enter employment? The primary focus of this chapter is a comparison of the extent to which durations of unemployment are longer for outsiders – women, the low-skilled and young people – in the two countries.

Though the main focus is on insiders and outsiders, we also need to consider other institutional differences and how they affect unemployment duration. We look at the family and examine how differences in the responsibility for children explain many of the gender differences in employment and unemployment. We consider differences in the education systems and how these particularly affect the transition from unemployment to employment for young people. In addition, we consider the welfare systems and how receipt of benefit may affect durations. Finally, we also consider the effect of benefit receipt on durations, though our findings are tentative, given the methods used and data available.

A valuable reason for examining the duration of unemployment is the debate on social exclusion discussed in Chapter 1 and the idea that unemployment may be an exclusionary *process*, whereby those who are unemployed the longest become increasingly marginalized from society. In societies where work is seen as a primary form of identity, those without work may come to feel more and more excluded as their identity as a member of society is somehow threatened. In addition, there is the problem of depreciation of skills, which makes the transition back into the world of work even more difficult. These concerns prompt us to ask the question: which individuals or groups stay unemployed the longest?

We argued in Chapter 1 that we need to focus on micro-level outcomes to understand what is going on at the level of aggregate unemployment. We also stressed the need to understand unemployment as a process, rather than a state. In this chapter we put these principles into practice. We use longitudinal data rather than simply comparing durations of unemployment across countries. We compare the process of exit of individuals from unemployment in Britain and West Germany and reveal systematic differences in micro-level outcomes.[1] We use a statistical model – an event history model – that was specifically developed to examine the timing of events. This model is excellently suited to our substantive concerns.

In Section 5.1 we consider some relevant institutional differences and how these relate to the insider/outsider hypothesis. Using these institutional differences, in Section 5.2 we build hypotheses about which individuals we would expect should find a job most quickly in Britain and West Germany. In

Section 5.3 we describe the statistical model, and in Section 5.4 we discuss the data and how we measure unemployment and the independent variables. In Section 5.5 we present a descriptive profile of escape from unemployment and then model outcomes to examine the process in more detail. The findings of these models are presented in Section 5.6. In Section 5.7 we conclude by reflecting on the implications of the results for the insider/outsider hypothesis.

## 5.1 INSTITUTIONAL DIFFERENCES BETWEEN BRITAIN AND GERMANY

In this section we consider briefly some institutional differences between Britain and Germany relevant to the duration of unemployment. We are particularly concerned with how these differences might affect outsiders, or weaker labour market groups (young people, the low-skilled and women), in a different way from insiders. We consider differences in the labour markets and labour market regulation; welfare benefits for the unemployed; the education systems; and the family.

### 5.1.1 Labour Market Structure

Labour market 'rigidities' is a term often applied to measures such as generous unemployment benefits (discussed in more detail below), employment protection measures, a high minimum wage, and high overall taxes impinging on labour. The British labour market is generally regarded as considerably less 'rigid' than the German labour market, sharing many of the features of the US labour market, particularly in the light of reforms during the 1980s (Grubb and Wells 1993; Siebert 1997; Nickell 1997).

Employment protection usually refers to the difficulty in firing people and is measured as a combination index of firing costs (such as severance pay), notification period, priority rules (such as seniority) and procedural obstacles. Employment protection can affect both the strategy and speed of labour adjustment. In terms of strategy, high dismissal costs encourage employers to adjust using earnings rather than personnel (Büchtemann 1993). In terms of speed, rigid protection generally leads to slower turnover of employees. The net effect is less mobility and rotation of jobs, tending to exclude weaker groups and protect insiders. However, employment protection is notoriously difficult to measure, particularly because the rules that govern workers' rights are a combination of legal, contractual and informal rules and norms (Büchtemann and Walwei 1996; Esping-Andersen 1998). Notwithstanding reservations about measurement, German legislation and practice is more restrictive than British, as seen in a wide range of measures from legislation through to employer attitude surveys (Bentolila and Bertola 1990; Grubb and Wells 1993; OECD 1994). Though these measures may be rather narrowly defined, the indices are fairly consistent (Büchtemann and Walwei 1996; Esping-Andersen 1998).

A high minimum wage and compressed wages may limit the creation of both low-wage and part-time jobs, pricing out the less desirable workers, such as young people and the low-skilled (Dolado et al. 1996; Esping-Andersen 1999). The wage structure is more compressed in Germany than in Britain; total earnings dispersion in 1993 was around 2.25 in Germany and 3.25 in Britain (OECD, 1996a).[2] In addition, the minimum wage in Britain, at 40 per cent of the average industrial wage, is considerably lower than in Germany, where it is 55 per cent of the average industrial wage (OECD 1994; Dolado et al. 1996). Some authors argue that in Germany it is unfeasible for employers to pay such wages for some low-wage, service sector jobs, so the jobs simply do not exist (Appelbaum and Schettkat 1990).

It has been argued that a large tax wedge – the gap between real labour costs and take-home pay – may have a similar effect. Nickell (1997) estimates the overall tax on labour, which includes the sum of average payroll income tax and consumption tax rates, to be substantially higher in Germany (53 per cent) than Britain (41 per cent). These taxes may affect not only low-skilled employment but also part-time work.[3] Smith et al. (1998, p. 49) note how, although part-timers who work fewer than eight hours per week are excluded from social protection in Germany, many part-timers – particularly those working 15 hours or more – are now entitled to the same rights on a pro rata basis as full-timers. Paradoxically the move to greater rights for part-time work has made it more expensive to hire part-time workers.

### 5.1.2    State Benefits for the Unemployed

While labour market legislation and family structure play an important role in determining unemployment durations, a particular issue that has received much critical attention among both academics and politicians in recent years is welfare payments for the unemployed. As discussed in Chapter 3, in Germany the level and duration of benefits is often (though not always) linked to previous earnings, and may be as much as two-thirds of previous earnings. In Britain, a flat-rate, minimalist system of unemployment compensation operates – the amount of benefit is not linked to previous earnings and the level of benefits is usually low. There is greater equality of provision in the British system, which, unlike the Germany system, does not especially favour insiders.

We also noted in Chapter 3 a certain 'polarisation' of benefits in both countries during the 1980s. In Britain, the 1980s saw a series of changes in welfare provision for the unemployed in response to the perceived disincentive effect of benefits. Insurance benefits were scaled back and the level of compensation fell dramatically relative to earnings. In Germany, by contrast, a number of measures were introduced that strengthened the insurance principle and further improved the position of insiders. A series of laws were passed lengthening the duration of benefit for unemployed individuals aged 42 and over.[4] Furthermore, there were special provisions for the long-term unemployed aged 60 and over to pass directly from unemployment to retirement pensions (see Section 2.3.3 in Chapter 2 for details).

### 5.1.3 Education and Training Systems

As discussed in Chapter 2 the systems of education and training play an important role in unemployment. Those with lower qualifications do worse in the competition for jobs, receive lower wages and are more vulnerable to unemployment (Becker 1993). In addition, once an individual does become unemployed, the level of education may affect the duration of unemployment. In the queue for jobs, those with better qualifications are taken first.

However, education systems may differ substantially in how they match their outputs with labour market demand. In particular, the extent and nature of vocational training is thought to be salient in determining the matching process in the labour market. As noted in Chapter 2, Britain lacks a standardised and widespread system of vocational training, and there is a much stronger vocational orientation in Germany, with segmentation along occupational lines (Müller et al. 1998). Youth unemployment has been consistently lower in Germany than in Britain, and much of this difference is attributed to the role of the German apprenticeship system in facilitating the transition from school to work (OECD 1998; Brauns et al. 1999). In Britain, apprenticeships are limited to a specific number of (mostly manual) occupations, and in recent decades apprenticeship training has been further devalued. As Bernardi et al. (2000) note, attending a vocational course instead of a more regular school course is often thought to be a sign of educational failure in Britain.

While outcomes may be positive in Germany for those who succeed in the vocational training system, there are some individuals for whom the system is not so advantageous. One example is the very small number who receive no vocational training in Germany. This is a select group, and they are very vulnerable to unemployment (Brauns et al. 1999). Another group who may suffer is the older unemployed. A vocational training system stratified by occupation, as in Germany, may lead to clear and stable occupations for those in employment and to quick re-employment for those who become unemployed, if there are jobs in their occupation. If there are no new jobs in their occupation, because of economic restructuring for example, it might be very difficult – particularly for the older unemployed – to re-enter employment. In Britain, where qualifications are not so highly formalised, it may be easier for the older unemployed to re-enter employment.

### 5.1.4   The Family

The role of the family is prominent in the feminist typologies of the labour market we discussed in Chapter 1 (Lewis 1992; Orloff 1993; Sainsbury 1994; Daly 1996). The role of the welfare state in the construction of family models, and the implications of this for inequalities between men and women, are central concerns. While these typologies are perhaps most relevant for considering labour market participation, we argued in Chapter 1 they offer useful insights for analysis of gender differences in unemployment. However, we do also need to bear in mind that differences in labour market participation will affect who is counted as unemployed, and that labour market participation is affected by the welfare systems.

What we take from these typologies is the importance of family situation in understanding employment and unemployment for women; many labour market differences between men and women may be a result of differences in their current family situation or of differences in their past family situation, which may have influenced the woman's work history. Young single women with continuous work histories may not differ substantially in their employment patterns from men. By contrast, unemployed women with young children may be more restricted in the kind of work they can take up, and women returning to the labour market after a break for childcare may find they are disadvantaged in the search for jobs. Being married with young children may mean constraints on the kind of work women may take up if they are unemployed – both in terms of the hours worked, if they do not have childcare facilities available, or the wage rate, if working means paying for childcare privately (Connelly 1992).

Family situation is particularly important in welfare states like the British and German, which treat women as wives and mothers (Lewis and Ostner 1994). Daly (2000) might argue that family situation would have even more of an impact on women's unemployment in Germany than in Britain, as the German state favours the male breadwinner model more. We found in Chapter 2 that in neither country do women with small children receive much support for working. In Section 2.3.4 we noted that overall levels of state childcare provision in both countries are rather low, although the school day in Britain is more compatible with mothers working part-time. The labour market participation of women is higher in Britain, where much of it is part-time. The German labour market structure favours full-time jobs, and there is a lower rate of women's labour market participation. The difference in the prevalence of part-time work may be particularly important for those unemployed women with family commitments.

## 5.2   HYPOTHESES IN THE COMPARATIVE FRAMEWORK

Given the greater extent of labour market regulation in Germany than in Britain, we hypothesise that, in general, labour market outsiders will find it more difficult to get a job in Germany than insiders. In Britain, differences between insiders and outsiders will not be as great. More specifically we expect young unemployed individuals, women and the low-skilled to find it more difficult to get a job in Germany relative to prime-age or older, highly-skilled men (Esping-Andersen 1998).

However, this general hypothesis may be qualified by some of the institutional differences described above. In particular, previous research has stressed the role of the German education and training system in facilitating the first transition to employment for young people (OECD 1998; Brauns et al. 1999). While labour market outsiders in general may be at a disadvantage in finding a job in Germany, this may not be true of young people seeking their first job. Although our overall hypothesis is not restricted to first-time labour market entrants, we expect many young unemployed persons to be seeking their first job. If the German education system does facilitate youth transitions in this way, Germany would be in sharp contrast to other insider/outsider labour markets such as Spain and Italy, where young people find it very difficult to find a job. As regards the contrast between Britain and Germany, the difference in the difficulty of transition for young people may depend on which prevails in Germany – the insider/outsider effect or the education and training system.

As regards the effect of education and training more generally, if we take educational qualifications as a rough proxy for skill level, according to the insider/outsider dichotomy we might expect the low-skilled, as outsiders, to fare worse in the German labour market, where there are fewer opportunities for low-skilled, service sector employment. Alternatively, the human capital approach might lead us to expect a similar effect of education on durations of unemployment in both countries – those with lower qualifications would have higher unemployment rates, and find it more difficult to get a job once they become unemployed, in both Britain and Germany.

For women, the insider/outsider hypothesis leads us to expect that women in Germany will have longer durations of unemployment relative to men than will British women. As paid employment of mothers is not well supported in either country, we expect longer durations of unemployment for women with young children, whether married or lone mothers. We also expect the age of the youngest child to be important when considering women's labour market behaviour. Children under five require the most intensive care, given the school starting age and the low level of public childcare. In general, we might expect particularly long durations of unemployment for women with children in Germany, where there are fewer opportunities for part-time work. This would be in keeping with Daly (1996) who maintains that the employment of mothers is given even less state support in Germany than in Britain.

As regards the effect of unemployment compensation on the duration of unemployment, the rigid/flexible labour market typology would lead us to expect that the higher the level of unemployment compensation – and the longer benefits are given – the less the incentive to find a job. If this view is correct, we would expect longer durations of unemployment in Germany, given the higher replacement rates and longer durations of benefits. Schmid and Reissert (1996) make the same prediction. We would expect to find particularly long durations of unemployment for some older unemployed people in Germany, for whom, as discussed in Chapter 3, special regulations are in place regarding the transition to early retirement and conditions of benefit receipt. Against this hypothesis, in a recent review of the state of research, Spiezia (2000) concluded that studies have found either no effect, or a very small effect of benefits on the duration of unemployment.

## 5.3   MODELLING STRATEGY

The model employed in this chapter belongs to a family of models known as event history models. These models are so called because they are used to describe the occurrence of an event, more specifically the duration of elapsed time until the event occurs. They are particularly useful for studying processes, social change and transitions. Using longitudinal data we can not only examine the exact duration of events and their sequence of occurrence, but also variables that individually, or in combination, influence the timing of an event. Another positive feature of these models is their ability to cope with 'right censoring'. Right censoring occurs when the event of interest has not happened before the end of the observation period – if, for example, in a study looking at the duration of exit from unemployment, the person is still unemployed at the last recorded point. The ability to cope with right censoring is useful given the sometimes arbitrary length of observation periods.

The concept that allows us to describe the development of a process at every point in time is known as the 'transition rate' or 'hazard rate'. We can interpret the transition rate as the propensity to change state given that the change has not already occurred (Blossfeld and Rohwer 1995). Different kinds of models make different assumptions about the distribution of durations, and thus about the transition rate.[5] In the case of unemployment durations, though it seems unrealistic to assume a constant transition rate, we do not have strong prior assumptions about how the rate varies, so we choose a piecewise constant model. In this model we split the time axis into 'pieces' of time, allowing the transition rate to vary between pieces, but not within them. Thus we can control for time-dependence, without specifying the shape of that dependence.

For the duration of unemployment the 'pieces' or periods of time we use are: less than three months; three to six months; six to 12 months; 12 to 24 months; and greater than 24 months. The transition rate in the basic model is:

$$r_{jk}(t) = \exp\{\overline{\alpha}_l^{(jk)} + A^{(jk)}\alpha^{(jk)}\} \text{ if } t \in i_l$$

For each transition $(j, k)$: $\overline{\alpha}_l^{(jk)}$ is a constant coefficient associated with the $l$th time period. $A^{(jk)}$ is a vector of covariates, and $\alpha^{(jk)}$ is an associated vector of coefficients assumed not to vary across time periods (Blossfeld and Rohwer 1995). The model is estimated using maximum likelihood estimation.[6] In order to account for change over time of all the covariates, where possible we model covariates as time-varying covariates. We introduce time-varying covariates through external 'episode splitting', as described in Blossfeld et al. (1989) and Blossfeld and Rohwer (1995).

We can estimate the model either for a single transition to a single destination state or for transitions to multiple destination states, known as a 'competing risks model'. As the substantive focus of this chapter is specifically the transition from unemployment to employment, we wish to distinguish the transition to employment from the transition out of the labour force and we therefore estimate a competing risks model. The assumption here is that the transitions to each destination are independent.[7] For the analysis of exit to employment, labour market exits are treated as censored. Likewise, for exit from the labour market, employment exits are treated as censored.

## 5.4 DATA SOURCES AND MEASUREMENT ISSUES

### 5.4.1 Data Sources and Measuring Unemployment

In this chapter we use as much longitudinal data as is available for our purposes, to maximize the sample size, though we also test whether the fact that we use a longer time period for Germany than for Britain affects the results. The analysis for Germany is based on data from the German Socio-economic Panel (GSOEP).[8] For the survival curves we use waves 1–14 of the survey, selecting only West German households; foreigners and later extensions of the survey are excluded. The reason for examining only West Germany in this chapter is further discussed in Chapter 1. For the models we use waves 1–11 of the GSOEP, as information about the receipt of unemployment benefit is only recorded until December 1993. The analysis for Britain is based on data from the British Household Panel Study (BHPS). In this chapter we use waves 1–6 of the BHPS, selecting only non-ethnic minority households, for compatibility with the German sample.[9]

One issue related to reporting unemployment that has been noted by researchers working on German data (Hunt 1995; Fehlker and Purfield 1998) is that the most common month given by survey respondents for the end of a spell of unemployment is December. However, in aggregate data, unemployment actually increases from November to December. For this reason we group months into four seasons when timing the end of a spell of unemployment.[10] Given seasonal fluctuations in both hiring and becoming unemployed, the difficulty of finding a job may depend on the time of year.

Labour force statuses recorded in the monthly calendar are aggregated from detailed categories into the following possibilities:

1.   employment;
2.   unemployment;
3.   out of the labour force.

Employment includes full-time, part-time and temporary employment, as well as those on active labour market programmes (e.g. ABM)[11] and in Germany the separately defined apprenticeship category.[12] The 'out of the labour force' category comprises the retired, those in full-time education, those on military service (Germany only), those in home duties and 'others'. For the unemployment category there is a difference in definition between the surveys, which is discussed in more detail in the Appendix at the end of the book. Where multiple statuses are reported in the German survey, a hierarchy of statuses was introduced as follows: employment, education, unemployment, other (including retired and those in home duties). Thus for a person reporting part-time work and home duties, priority is given to part-time work.[13]

Completed durations of individual unemployment spells are derived from information on the date of entry into unemployment and the date of the transition either into employment or out of the labour force.[14] Unemployment spells beginning before the first month of the calendar (January 1983 for Germany and September 1990 for Britain) are treated as left censored and excluded from the analysis. For this analysis the population is defined as those who were 18–64 (inclusive) at the start of the spell. This gives a total of 3,138 spells for Britain, of which there are 1,929 exits to employment, 555 labour market exits and 654 right censored observations.[15] For Germany the total number of spells is 3,585, of which there are 2,387 exits to employment, 741 labour market exits and 457 right censored observations.[16] These are the observations used for the survival curves. When we restrict spells to those with no missing data on any of our covariates, the number of spells is reduced to a total of 2,953 observations in Britain and 2,461 in Germany.[17]

### 5.4.2 Measuring the Independent Variables

There are two kinds of independent variable: time-constant and time-varying. Time-varying variables can change their state within the spell of unemployment. Gender and age are time-constant within the spell as age is measured in months at the start of the spell and then divided into age groups: 18–24 years; 25–39 years; 40–54 years; and 55–64 years. As previous work history has been shown to have a significant impact on both risk of and exit from unemployment (see for example numerous chapters in the edited volume by Gallie and Paugam, 2000), we include a measure of the proportion of time previously employed. This variable is also time-constant, and is measured as the proportion of time spent employed since entering the labour market before the unemployment spell began. The information is taken from the long-term work history data on both the surveys.[18]

To measure the influence of the family on exit from unemployment we use time-varying covariates indicating marital status and the presence of children. Marital status is constructed from monthly marital biography data in the surveys. Two covariates, constructed from childbirth biographies, are used to measure the presence of children. They refer to the age of the child during the unemployment spell: any child under five; and any child between five and 18. Educational qualifications are also time-varying, and are coded according to a variant of the 'casmin' schema (see Appendix, Section A.2.2 for further details).[19]

For receipt of unemployment benefits, both surveys record receipt and type of benefits in monthly calendars. This information is matched to information about unemployment spells. In this way we only consider an unemployed person to have received benefit if they actually report receiving it.[20] Ideally we would separate the effect of receiving insurance benefits from receiving assistance benefits. However, people receiving assistance benefits often do so after a period of receiving unemployment insurance, so their durations of unemployment will by definition be longer. We therefore do not attempt to look at the impact of the type of benefit on the duration of unemployment, and simply compare those in receipt of any benefit with those who receive no benefit. For Germany, social assistance (*Sozialhilfe*) is not reported in the monthly calendars as benefit receipt at all. While only a minority of the unemployed receive social assistance, the lack of information on it is a disadvantage. As we might expect special benefit regulations to lead to even longer unemployment durations for the unemployed over 57 in Germany, we introduce an interaction term for those receiving benefit and over 57. To keep the models consistent we also include this term in the British model.

We also expect macroeconomic fluctuations to affect the escape from unemployment. As a crude indicator of the relative difficulty of finding a job, we use the percentage change in total employment in the year the spell of unemployment started. However, given that there are costs associated with moving, we also expect to find regional variation in unemployment durations in each country. To account for this we estimate another model using regional unemployment rates instead of the percentage change in total employment.[21] As we also expect health problems to influence exit from unemployment, we include a measure of health status in our models. If the unemployed respondent reported any health problems at the time of the survey, we attach this information to the spell.

## 5.5    UNEMPLOYMENT EXIT – A DESCRIPTIVE PROFILE

As a prelude to our modelling later in the chapter, we first compare the duration of unemployment in Britain and Germany using Kaplan-Meier estimation. Kaplan-Meier estimation is useful for presenting descriptive statistics in situations where there are censored cases, enabling the calculation of nonparametric estimates of the survivor function (Blossfeld and Rohwer 1995). In this case the 'survivor function' estimates the proportion of respondents who remain unemployed in each month after becoming unemployed. In Figure 5.1 we present survivor functions for exit to employment, in Figure 5.2 for exit out of the labour market. The horizontal axis is the month within the spell of unemployment and the vertical axis is the proportion of respondents who remain unemployed in each month. The estimates are presented separately for men and women in each country.

Figure 5.1 shows that in both countries there is fairly rapid exit from unemployment in the first 12 months, by which point it is estimated that less than 40 per cent of both men and women are still unemployed. In West Germany the median duration of unemployment (around six months) is a little shorter than in Britain (approximately seven months), somewhat contrary to expectations. What is striking in the figure is the contrast between the countries in the difference between men and women. In Germany, women find a job more slowly than men, and a greater proportion of women are still unemployed at 48 months. In

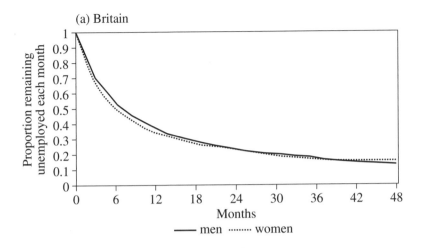

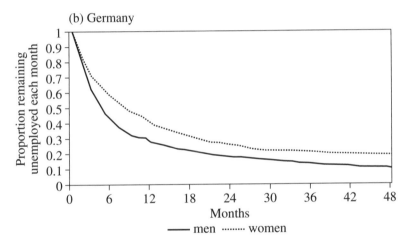

*Note*: Kaplan-Meier estimations of spells of whites (Britain) and native West Germans only. Only those aged 18–65 at start of spell are included.

*Sources*: BHPS 1991–96; GSOEP 1984–97.

*Figure 5.1 The transition to employment – survivor functions*

Britain the survival curves are very similar for men and women, though if anything, women's exit to employment is quicker than men's. This finding seems to support our hypothesis that women in Germany, as a relatively weak labour market group, would have longer durations of unemployment.

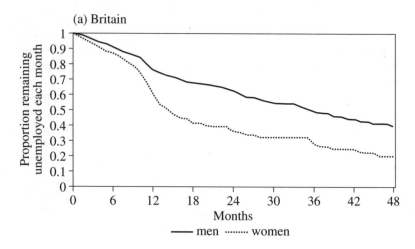

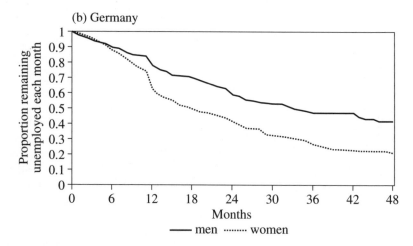

*Note*:   Kaplan-Meier estimations of spells of whites (Britain) and native West Germans only. Only those aged 18–65 at start of spell are included.

*Sources*:   BHPS 1991–96; GSOEP 1984–97.

*Figure 5.2    The transition out of the labour market – survivor functions*

Figure 5.2 shows exits out of the labour market. The timing of labour market exit is rather different from exit to employment, though it is similar in both countries. Firstly, exit out of the labour market is much slower than exit to employment in both countries. Secondly, in both countries a greater proportion of women exit the labour market than men, and they do so more quickly. This is particularly true in Britain, where we estimate that after 12 months of unemployment, around 40 per cent of women have left the labour market. Women in both countries are presumably much more likely than men to leave the labour market for family reasons.

Because our observation period for Germany (168 months) is much longer than for Britain (76 months), we might expect German durations to be longer than British. As a check we repeat the estimations for a similar (shorter) period in the economic cycle for both countries. We limit spells to those beginning and ending between September 1990 and September 1993 for Britain, and between September 1991 and September 1994 for Germany (see Figure 2.7 in Chapter 2 for why we choose these periods). Using these time periods the median duration is around 25 per cent shorter in both countries, but the difference (in comparison with the estimates presented above) is actually greater for Britain, which does not suggest that the estimates for Germany presented above are unduly long because of the longer observation period.

Figures 5.1 and 5.2 give a general idea of unemployment durations in Britain and Germany. However, in order to disentangle the influences of characteristics we discussed earlier – age, gender, education, family situation and unemployment compensation – on the process of exit from unemployment, we now turn to the event history model.

## 5.6 MODELLING THE TRANSITION FROM UNEMPLOYMENT TO EMPLOYMENT

### 5.6.1 The Transition from Unemployment to Employment, for all the Unemployed

To investigate the impact of individual characteristics on exit from unemployment we estimate separate piecewise constant exponential models, as described above, for Britain and West Germany. The results are presented in Table 5.1. Columns (1) to (3) present results for the transition to employment, which is the main focus of this chapter, while columns (4) to (6) present the transition out of the labour market. Covariates included in these models are gender, age category, educational level (as measured using the casmin schema), variables for family situation, receipt of unemployment benefit, previous labour market history, health status and current labour market situation. For each transition coefficient estimates are presented for Britain and Germany, and then the significance of difference test for each coefficient. The latter test uses information about the differences in the coefficients for Britain and

Table 5.1  Competing risks piecewise constant exponential model for Britain and West Germany

|  | Transition to Employment | | | Transition out of Labour Market | | |
|---|---|---|---|---|---|---|
|  | Britain | Germany | T-stat. of diff. | Britain | Germany | T-stat. of diff. |
|  | (1) | (2) | (3) | (4) | (5) | (6) |
| Baseline hazard: |  |  |  |  |  |  |
| Duration <3 mths | -2.79*** | -1.80*** | -5.02 | -5.52*** | -4.60*** | -2.44 |
| Duration 3–6 mths | -2.28*** | -1.24*** | -5.18 | -4.93*** | -4.49*** | -1.13 |
| Duration 6–12 mths | -2.58*** | -1.67*** | -4.34 | -4.54*** | -4.06*** | -1.24 |
| Duration 12–24 mths | -2.80*** | -2.02*** | -3.00 | -4.37*** | -3.27*** | -2.74 |
| Duration >24 mths | -3.19*** | -3.07*** | -0.22 | -5.06*** | -3.94*** | -1.79 |
| Ref: age 25–39 |  |  |  |  |  |  |
| Age: 18–25 | 0.13* | 0.29 | -1.83 | 0.11 | 0.03 | 0.51 |
| Age: 40–54 | -0.36*** | -0.29*** | -0.81 | 0.10 | -0.32** | 2.41 |
| Age: 55–64 | -0.45** | -1.69*** | 5.34 | 0.68*** | 0.91*** | -1.06 |
| Ref: incomplete or lower secondary education (1ab) |  |  |  |  |  |  |
| Basic vocational (1c) | 0.20* | 0.14* | 0.58 | -0.02 | 0.05 | -0.35 |
| Secondary voc. (2ac) | -0.22** | 0.25*** | -4.25 | -0.38* | 0.34** | -3.77 |
| Secondary gen. (2bc) | 0.38*** | 0.21* | 1.40 | 0.50*** | 0.72*** | -1.10 |
| Tertiary (3ab) | 0.50*** | 0.51*** | -0.09 | 0.50*** | -0.23 | 3.42 |
| Prop. of time emp. | 0.48*** | 0.44*** | 0.36 | -0.18 | -0.38** | 1.00 |

| | | | | | | |
|---|---|---|---|---|---|---|
| Ref: single | | | | | | |
| Married | 0.15** | 0.09 | 0.73 | 0.09 | 0.58*** | -3.68 |
| Ref: no. of children | | | | | | |
| Children under 5 | -0.42*** | -0.52*** | 1.06 | 0.02 | 0.34*** | -2.01 |
| Children 5-18 | -0.01 | -0.02 | 0.18 | -0.09 | -0.22* | 0.83 |
| Ref: no benefit recorded | | | | | | |
| Benefit received | -0.57*** | 0.10 | -9.14 | -0.03 | 0.14 | -1.32 |
| Benefit × over 57 | -0.55 | -1.00** | 0.94 | -0.23 | 0.56*** | -2.58 |
| % change in total emp. | 0.12*** | 0.10*** | 0.65 | -0.01 | 0.11*** | -2.92 |
| Health | -0.22*** | -0.34*** | 1.83 | -0.07 | 0.02 | -1.05 |
| Observations (spells) | 2,953 | 2,461 | | 2,943 | 2,461 | |

Notes:
*P <= 0.05; **P <= 0.01; ***P <= 0.001. Spells of whites (Britain) and native West Germans only. Only includes those aged 18–65 at start of spell and with no missing values for any of the covariates.

A 'model chi-square' statistic is calculated for each of the models by taking the difference between the initial −2 log-likelihood of the model (i.e. without any covariates) and the final −2 log-likelihood for the full model. The model chi-square for the models are the following: Britain 521.09; Germany 939.18. Additional covariates are included for season of the year.

Sources: BHPS 1991–96; GSOEP 1984–93.

Germany and their standard error to provide an indication of the significance of the difference in the two coefficients. It is a rather conservative test; it makes it difficult to prove difference between the coefficients, but means that where we do have evidence of difference then the evidence is strong (see Chapter 4, endnote 28 for more details of this test).

Our general hypothesis in this chapter is that certain weaker labour market groups will have longer durations of unemployment, relative to insiders, in Germany than in Britain. Our first finding, regarding gender differences in unemployment in the two countries, supports this hypothesis. In Germany, women have significantly longer unemployment durations than men. In Britain, this is not the case: women's unemployment durations are rather similar to those of men. As we can see from column (3), the significance test shows the difference between the coefficients to be significant. We expect women's labour market outcomes to be strongly related to family commitments. To investigate which groups of women have the longest durations of unemployment, and, in particular, to investigate the effect of family situation, we model the transitions of men and women separately: this is the subject of Section 5.6.2 below.

Another implication of our general hypothesis is that young unemployed people may find it more difficult to find a job than their older counterparts in the more regulated German labour market. However, we also noted an opposing hypothesis that the German system of education and training works to ensure a smooth transition to employment for all but a few young Germans. To test these hypotheses we compare transitions of young unemployed people in the two countries with transitions of 'prime age' workers (25–39). Our findings tend to support the second hypothesis. In Germany, young people exit unemployment more quickly than the prime age group – see column (2). This finding supports the conclusion of Brauns et al. that in Germany tight selection at entry implies a smooth and, in terms of job allocation, 'structured' transition into employment – 'for those who are endowed with the critical entry tickets' (1999, p. 27).

Where we find a more dramatic difference between the countries is in the oldest age group. The 40–55 age group have longer durations than the reference category, but the overall effect is rather similar in both countries. The big difference comes in the 55–65 category, where Germans have much longer durations of unemployment relative to 25–40-year-olds than do people of this age in Britain, and this difference is significant – see column (3). This effect may be related to the measures introduced for unemployed people over 59 in Germany, which allow them to go into early retirement if they remain unemployed for one year, though some of those measures are picked up by the interaction term for receiving benefit and being over 57 (Casey 1996; Kruppe et al. 1999).[22] It could also be that some of the older long-term unemployed who view their chances of getting a job as poor and have health problems, withdraw from the labour market to long-term sickness benefit, especially in Britain (see Section 2.3.3 in Chapter 2). Finally, as noted in Section 5.1.3 above, it could be that the German vocational training system leads to longer durations of unemployment for older individuals, because of the difficulty of making transitions between occupations where qualifications are highly formalised.

A third implication of our general hypothesis concerns skill level. We expect the low-skilled to be most disadvantaged in Germany. We measure skill level in this chapter as educational level, while noting that this is not ideal. Our findings from the models are that education clearly matters: by and large those with a higher level of education have shorter unemployment durations. If we take the group (1ab), i.e. those with incomplete and lower secondary education, as our low-skilled group, as we do for the model presented in Table 5.1, our findings do not support the insider/outsider hypothesis. The differences between the (low-skilled) reference category and groups with higher qualifications are of a similar magnitude in both countries.[23] This finding is more supportive of human capital theory than of the insider/outsider hypothesis.

However, if we repeat the model, selecting the small group with no qualifications (1a) as our reference category, the effect of education is somewhat different in the two countries. Note that this group is rather small, especially in Germany (amounting to around 2 per cent of all spells of unemployment). These are the unemployed who have neither finished compulsory education nor entered the vocational training scheme. In this model the difference in durations of unemployment between the lowest group and all other educational levels is greater in Germany, and this difference is significant in our difference test at all levels. This finding is consistent with Müller and Shavit (1998) who find that in Germany the crucial distinction is between those who have any qualification and those who do not. So we find a specific small group in Germany with no qualifications who are very disadvantaged. In this sense they are the outsiders in the system. But for the most part we cannot say that the low-skilled are more disadvantaged in Germany than in Britain.

Regarding the effect of benefit receipt, we follow the strategy of previous research in this area by introducing dummy variables for receipt of benefit. Note that using this method our results are 'only as good as the reference category', as we simply compare those who received benefit with those who did not. To the extent that this is a select group (with a poor previous employment record and recourse to other earnings), we need to be cautious in interpreting our results. For an experiment that properly tests the disincentive effect of benefits, we would need to randomly assign benefits to the unemployed and then compare durations of unemployment.

In Germany, those under 57 who receive either *Arbeitslosengeld* or *Arbeitslosenhilfe* do not have longer durations of unemployment than those who do not. This finding is largely consistent with previous work on the German data that measures receipt of benefit in this way (Hujer and Schneider 1995; Fehlker and Purfield 1998) – though not with work using alternative measures of benefit receipt.[24] British unemployed persons in receipt of benefit have longer durations than those who do not receive benefit and this effect is statistically significant. This difference in the effect of benefit receipt across countries is statistically significant – see column (3). If we repeat this analysis restricting the sample to those unemployed who were previously in employment (i.e. displaced workers), the coefficients are almost identical to those presented in Table 5.1; this is also the case if we exclude the interaction term for being both in receipt of benefits and over 57. In so far as tested here, there is no indication that unemployment compensation is associated with longer durations of unemployment in Germany than in Britain. Indeed for most of the unemployed there is a much greater difference in durations between those who do and do not receive benefits in Britain than in Germany. The exception to this is the unemployed over 57. We find that in Germany over-57-year-olds who receive benefit have much longer durations of unemployment than those who do not. In Britain the duration of unemployment for those receiving benefits is longer for over 57s than for those 57 and under, though the difference between the age groups is only marginally significant. It is in Germany, where the special benefit provisions for older unemployed people exist, that the contrast is most marked.

As our hypotheses for the effect of family circumstances were mainly based on the effects for women, we postpone our discussion of them to the gender-specific models in Section 5.6.2 below. Suffice to say here that the overall effect of family situation is rather similar in both countries. In particular, there are longer durations for those with children under five, an age group where childcare provision in the two countries is particularly low. Turning to the other effects we measure, in both countries there is a negative and rather similar effect of health on durations of unemployment – those with health problems find it more difficult to find a job – while those who have spent a greater proportion of time in employment since entering the labour market have shorter durations of unemployment. In addition, the overall measure of labour market demand has a similar effect on durations of unemployment in both countries: in years of greater employment growth people have shorter durations.[25] In further modelling we discover that having been out of the labour market immediately prior to the spell of unemployment substantially lengthens the duration of unemployment, though we do not distinguish first-time jobseekers from women returning to the labour market.[26] There is no difference between the countries in this respect.

Looking briefly at the transition out of the labour market, we see firstly from the estimates of the baseline hazard in Table 5.1 that the rate of exit is much lower than for the exit to employment. For the transition to employment we see that in both countries the estimated parameters for the baseline hazard increase at first and then decrease, indicating that the rate of exit to employment tends to be highest between three and 12 months. For the transition out of the labour market the rate of exit is much slower (as seen in Figure 5.2) in both countries, and is highest between 12 and 24 months in both countries.

Unemployed women and those over 55 leave the labour market more quickly in both countries, though one might suspect for rather different reasons.[27] Being over 57 and receiving benefit in Germany also increases the rate of labour market exit, supporting the idea that these unemployed people receive the special retirement pension for the long-term unemployed. In other respects benefit receipt does not have any significant effect on labour market exit.

### 5.6.2   The Transition from Unemployment to Employment, by Gender

We noted in Section 5.5 how the gender differences in the duration of unemployment seem to support the hypothesis that weaker labour market groups find it more difficult to exit from unemployment in Germany than in Britain. To investigate gender differences in more depth, in this section we present the findings of separate models for men and women, shown in Table 5.2. Columns (1) to (3) present results for the transition from unemployment to employment for British men and women, columns (4) and (6) present results for German men and women. In general, for Britain we find very similar findings to Bernardi et al. (2000), whose methodology we follow.[28]

Overall, gender differences in the effect of family circumstances tend to be greater in Germany than in Britain. As hypothesised we find that women with small children (aged under five) have longer durations of unemployment than women without children, in both countries. Once we account for the presence of children, in Britain, the effect of being married on the duration of unemployment is small, and not very different for men and women. And though we notice a strong effect on unemployment durations for British women who have children under five, we also notice a (somewhat weaker) effect for British men. In Germany, by contrast, married women have longer durations of unemployment than married men. What is more, in Germany there is a rather large difference between men and women with young children, and this effect is significant in our significance of difference test. These findings support the overall message from the gender-sensitive typologies of welfare, namely that it is important to consider the family situation of women in

Table 5.2   *Competing risks piecewise constant exponential model for British and West German men and women: transition from unemployment to employment*

| | British Men | British Women | T-stat. of Diff. | German Men | German Women | T-stat. of Diff. |
|---|---|---|---|---|---|---|
| | (1) | (2) | (3) | (4) | (5) | (6) |
| Baseline hazard: | | | | | | |
| Duration <3 mths | −2.65*** | −2.69*** | −0.31 | −2.14*** | −2.60*** | 1.79 |
| Duration 3–6 mths | −2.17*** | −2.10*** | 0.44 | −1.42*** | −2.16*** | 2.72 |
| Duration 6–12 mths | −2.38*** | −2.54*** | 0.09 | −2.00*** | −2.35*** | 1.30 |
| Duration 12–24 mths | −2.66*** | −2.61*** | 0.00 | −2.43*** | −2.68*** | 0.51 |
| Duration >24 mths | −3.00*** | −3.05*** | 0.73 | −3.16*** | −3.98*** | 0.38 |
| *Ref: age 25–39* | | | | | | |
| Age: 18–25 | 0.20* | 0.08 | 0.14 | 0.20** | 0.43*** | −1.60 |
| Age: 40–54 | −0.31*** | −0.41*** | 0.93 | −0.36*** | −0.23* | −0.49 |
| Age: 55–64 | −0.61** | −0.13 | −1.03 | −1.57*** | −2.41*** | −1.20 |
| *Ref: incomplete or lower secondary education (1ab)* | | | | | | |
| Basic vocational (1c) | 0.16 | 0.27 | −0.47 | 0.25*** | 0.13 | 1.51 |
| Secondary voc. (2ac) | −0.04 | −0.50*** | 2.63 | 0.28* | 0.32** | 0.11 |
| Secondary gen. (2bc) | 0.28** | 0.57*** | −1.92 | 0.09 | 0.24 | −1.24 |
| Tertiary (3ab) | 0.44*** | 0.65*** | −0.72 | 0.74*** | 0.34* | 0.50 |
| Prop. of time emp. | 0.52*** | 0.59*** | −0.86 | 0.52*** | 0.35** | 0.41 |

| | | | | | |
|---|---|---|---|---|---|
| *Ref: single* | | | | | |
| Married | 0.14 | 0.18* | 0.35 | 0.30*** | -0.08 | 3.19 |
| *Ref: no. of children* | | | | | |
| Children under 5 | -0.34*** | -0.60*** | 1.99 | -0.15 | -1.02*** | 5.74 |
| Children 5–18 | -0.10 | 0.21 | -1.74 | -0.24** | 0.04 | -0.82 |
| *Ref: no benefit recorded*\* | | | | | |
| Insurance benefit | -0.57*** | -0.55*** | -0.55 | -0.06 | 0.22** | -0.85 |
| Benefit × over 57 | -0.31 | -8.88 | -0.43 | -2.18*** | 0.93 | -0.42 |
| % change in total emp. | 0.14*** | 0.07* | 1.49 | 0.14*** | 0.07** | 1.75 |
| Health | -0.22*** | -0.23*** | 0.06 | -0.42*** | -0.30*** | 0.40 |
| Observations | 1,851 | 1,102 | | 1,343 | 1,118 | |
| Model chi-square (for full model) | 307.65 | 231.29 | | 655.91 | 461.50 | |

*Notes:*
*$P <= 0.05$; **$P <= 0.01$; ***$P <= 0.001$.
Spells of whites (Britain) and native West Germans only. Only includes those aged 18–65 at start of spell and with no missing values for any of the covariates. Additional covariates are included for season of the year.

*Sources:* BHPS 1991–96; GSOEP 1984–93.

considering employment and unemployment. We also find support for the idea from Daly (1996) that family situation has a greater impact in Germany than in Britain.[29]

An interesting effect regarding the age of children in both countries is that women who have children of school-going age, between five and 18, do not have longer durations of unemployment than those with no children. One explanation for this is that these women are seeking part-time work.[30] In Britain, women with children of school-going age actually have shorter durations of unemployment than those without, which supports the idea that the part-time work opportunities available in the British labour market make it easier to combine work and family life, even though there is little public provision of childcare. This finding suggests that, when considering the employment and unemployment of mothers in a gender-sensitive typology of welfare, it is important to distinguish between school-age and younger children. Turning to gender differences in age, we note that young German women tend to exit unemployment faster than prime-age women, relative to German men, though the effects for men and women are not significantly different. Longer durations among German women are particularly found among those aged over 25, and especially those over 55. But, confirming our findings from the previous model, in general we find no evidence that young people in Germany have particularly long durations relative to either the prime age unemployed in Germany, or to the young British unemployed. It is older German unemployed people who have long durations of unemployment. As regards the effect of benefit receipt, we find not so much difference between British men and women, and the effects are similar to those discussed in the previous section. For Germany, by contrast, women who receive unemployment benefit actually have shorter durations of unemployment than those who do not. This is even true of women over 57 who receive benefit. A plausible explanation is that women who receive benefits have a better recent employment record than those who do not, which helps them find work more quickly.[31] For German men 57 and under there is no difference between those who receive benefit and those who do not, but for men over 57 durations of unemployment are longer for men receiving benefits. If there is an effect of the special benefit regulations in Germany, as suggested above, it operates for men, not for women.[32]

In summary, the German women who have longer durations of unemployment are not the young or those receiving benefit, but those over 55 and those married with very young children. The latter two groups are also the women who leave the labour market most quickly.[33] As a word of caution, however, we note that the samples of the unemployed that we derive from the work histories are somewhat different in each country – self-defined in Britain, registered in Germany.[34] Compared to an ILO sample, women are under-represented in the self-defined sample of the unemployed used in this chapter for Britain. We might expect that it is women with very young children (aged under five) who may not define themselves as unemployed even though they are seeking work, thus excluding themselves from the British sample. It is precisely those women who find it most difficult to find a job in both countries.[35] This problem does not arise in Germany, because there we use the registered definition of unemployment. Therefore, the longer durations of unemployment for German women may in part result from the somewhat different samples of the unemployed.

## 5.7 CONCLUSION

The purpose of this chapter was to compare unemployment durations in Britain and Germany, and relate these durations to the labour markets, labour market regulation, the family, the education and training system, and the welfare system. Our guiding hypothesis was that in Germany's more regulated labour market we would find more significant differences between labour market insiders and labour market outsiders.

For women this hypothesis is supported. We find that in Germany women have longer durations of unemployment than men, while in Britain, men have longer durations than women. When we investigate the effect of different characteristics in our models, we note the importance of family situation, particularly for women. This is consistent with the expectations derived from the gender-sensitive typologies of welfare. For German women, both being married and having small children tends to lengthen the duration of unemployment until exit to employment. In Britain, having small children also increases the duration of unemployment until finding a job, but being married has a negligible effect. The stronger effect of family situation in Germany lends some credence to Daly's (1996) argument that there is even less support for the employment of mothers in Germany than in Britain.

The hypothesis that the young unemployed in Germany, as labour market outsiders, would have longer durations of unemployment, is not borne out. The opposite is true: young German unemployed find employment more quickly than core workers. However, we argue, as do Brauns et al. (1999), that while on average young Germans have short durations, there is a specific small group of those who miss out on vocational training who are particularly disadvantaged in the German system. Not everyone benefits.

Contrary to the insider/outsider hypothesis, older age groups have particularly long durations of unemployment in Germany. We propose three explanations. Firstly, there are special benefit regulations for those unemployed over 57 in Germany. Secondly, in Britain we speculate that some of those who might otherwise have had long durations of unemployment are receiving disability benefits, thus shortening the overall duration of unemployment in Britain for this age group. Insofar as this is true the state in both countries is supporting a group of older workers out of employment; it is just that the manner in which they do this differs. Finally it could be that the German vocational training system leads to longer durations of unemployment for older individuals due to the difficulty of making transitions between different occupations where qualifications are highly formalised.

Our third hypothesis was that the low-skilled would be more disadvantaged in Germany. Using education as a measure of skill – which we note is not an ideal measure – we find education to have a strong effect on labour market outcomes in both Britain and Germany. Our findings for the most part support human capital theory, according to which the unemployed are ranked according to qualifications, and those with fewer formal qualifications are disadvantaged.

Our overall findings then, while supporting the insider/outsider hypothesis for women, lead us to qualify it somewhat for the two other groups to reflect on a weakness of the insider/outsider hypothesis. For example, our findings on youth unemployment lend more credence to the idea that the German system of education and training plays a crucial and integrative role in transitions for most young people. In this way the German labour market stands in contrast to Spain and Italy, which have high levels of labour market regulation but also high levels of youth unemployment. This suggests that in considering the duration of unemployment it is very important to look not just at the labour market but also at the role of other institutions, such as the education system. A hypothesis such as the insider/outsider hypothesis described in this chapter, that is based simply on labour market regulation, may miss an important part of the story. This issue of how various institutional settings interact is a point to which we return in the concluding chapter.

This chapter also compares durations of unemployment for those who receive unemployment compensation and for those who do not. Our findings do not support the idea that durations of unemployment are longer for individuals receiving benefit in the German system than in the British system, contrary to Schmid and Reissert (1996).[36] However, we argue that this question requires a rather different sort of test from the one we were able to perform.

In any discussion of processes of social exclusion, we should bear in mind that these are the groups who are left behind in the competition for jobs. In both countries we find that it is older, not younger workers, who have the longest durations. In Germany, on average, women have longer durations, in Britain older men. In both countries those with the longest durations will have low qualifications, and will have had some breaks in their employment history. These are the unemployed most at risk of longer periods of unemployment.

Our results point to numerous issues that warrant further investigation. One such issue is working time preferences. Another is the kind of work that the unemployed find; some groups may exit quickly from unemployment, only to find themselves unemployed again in another six months. A few more months of unemployment may not be a negative outcome if it results in a better match between the skills and capabilities of a person on the one hand and the job requirements on the other. Estimates from a recent paper addressing this question for Britain suggests that the longer a person has been unemployed and searching for work, the less likely they are to quit or be laid off from their subsequent job (Boeheim and Taylor 2002). In addition, it would be very useful to know more about demand in local labour markets. The data we have – micro-level data on individuals – is not so suitable for this kind of analysis, limiting the attention we can give to the role of demand in labour markets.[37]

While this type of analysis would benefit from more information about the demand side of the labour market, and the kind of jobs that are available for the unemployed, an important finding relates to the supply side: that family situation is important in understanding unemployment, particularly for women. We pursue this link further in the next chapter, where we look at the link between welfare benefits and partners' employment.

## NOTES

1. East Germany is not included in this chapter. Important information on unemployment compensation on a monthly basis is only available until December 1993 in the German sample, so the analysis focuses on the 1980s and early 1990s. As discussed in Chapter 1, the scale of labour market intervention in East Germany in the early 1990s means it is problematic to include it in an analysis of transitions between unemployment and employment in this period.
2. Earnings dispersion measured here by first ranking employees according to their earnings, then taking the ratio of the lower earnings limit of the top decile (90 per cent of employees earn less than this) to the upper limit of the lowest decile (10 per cent of employees earn less than this) (OECD, 1996c).
3. Of course in many cases part-time work is low-skilled (O'Reilly and Bothfeld 2002).
4. See Chapter 3 Appendix, Table 3.1.A for details.
5. In this chapter we focus on continuous time models. Discrete time models are used in Chapter 6.
6. We use the Transitional Data Analysis (TDA 5.3) computer package developed for analysing event history models.
7. This assumption is not unproblematic. Though there are many reasons why the unemployed may leave the labour market, some may do so because they have been unable to find a job. In this case the transitions to employment and to non-participation are not independent. See Gangl (2003, Chapter 6) for further discussion.
8. See the Appendix at the end of the book for further details of both datasets.

9.  For Britain the calendar data is taken from the specially prepared work history files. See Halpin (1997) for further details.
10. The seasons are defined as: spring (January to March); summer (April to June); autumn (July to September); and winter (October to December). Spring is the reference category. An alternative strategy adopted by previous researchers (for example Hunt 1995; Fehlker and Purfield 1998) is to introduce a 'December dummy', which is coded one for spells ending in December, zero for those that do not. However, work by Kraus and Steiner (1998, p. 26) on modelling heaping effects in unemployment duration models concludes that 'in estimating proportional hazard models of unemployment durations derived from the calendar data for the GSOEP heaping effects may be ignored at relatively little cost, especially if the focus of interest is on the estimated coefficients of the explanatory variables'. We assume the effects would be similar with a piecewise constant model. In addition, if we were to introduce such a correction for Germany, we would also need to do so for Britain, and it is not clear why we should do this.
11. As it is not possible to distinguish those on active labour market programmes using the GSOEP data, the impact of active labour market programmes on exit from unemployment cannot be assessed in this chapter.
12. We count apprentices as employed because, if present, they would be counted as employed in the British data.
13. Further details of this manipulation of spells is given the final Appendix, Section A.2.1.
14. Problems of reporting unemployment in retrospective data are discussed in the final Appendix, Section A.2.1.
15. There are 1,978 spells from men and 1,160 spells from women.
16. Of German spells, 1,993 are from men, 1,592 from women.
17. For Britain, there are then 1,851 spells for men, 1,102 for women: for Germany, 1,343 male spells, 1,118 for women. In Germany this number also includes restricting observations to those ending in December 1993, because of missing data on receipt of benefits.
18. For Britain this information is recorded at a monthly level; for Germany information is only recorded yearly. However, this is not expected to substantially affect results, as we simply need to distinguish those who have spent all or most of their time employed, from those who have spent much less time employed.
19. On both surveys education is recorded at yearly intervals, at the time of survey, rather than monthly intervals. For those who record a change in educational qualification, we impute the month of change as June.
20. A problem for the German spells is that benefit calendars are only available until December 1994. Thereafter we only have a record of how many months in the year the respondent received benefits. Thus for analysis that includes benefit receipt for Germany spells are treated as censored after December 1994.
21. For details of measurement of these macroeconomic indicators see the final Appendix, Section A.2.2.
22. If we exclude this interaction term the difference between the countries for this age group is even larger.
23. An exception to this is secondary-level vocational training. In Germany this group has shorter durations of unemployment, in Britain they have longer durations of unemployment than the reference group, those with incomplete or lower secondary education.
24. For example, Gangl (2002) finds a negative effect on the receipt of unemployment compensation for displaced workers in Germany, though he takes any record of unemployment benefit in the spell, rather than the monthly measure used here. Kaiser and Siedler (2001) also find a negative effect of the receipt of unemployment compensation on the duration of unemployment for West German men. However, they examine a somewhat different period (1991–95), measure unemployment in a different way (using a modified version of these data sets), and presumably also measure receipt of unemployment benefit in a different way, as receipt of benefit is no longer recorded on the monthly calendars of the GSOEP after 1993.
25. When we include an alternative measure of labour market demand that measures regional unemployment, the results are very similar for both countries. However, there are a

substantial number of missing cases for the regional information so percentage change in overall employment is the preferred measure.

26. We do not include this variable in the main model presented in Table 5.1 because of the substantial number of missing cases.

27. Distinguishing the different destinations of those who leave the labour market is beyond the scope of this chapter.

28. The gender findings are also similar to those of Kaiser and Siedler (2001), though the model used is somewhat different.

29. When we tested to see if there is an additional effect of being a lone mother with a child under five, we found no difference between lone mothers and married mothers with small children in Britain, but somewhat longer durations of unemployment for German lone mothers. However, the finding is not significant due to the small number of cases and should therefore be treated with caution. In addition, the labour force participation rate of lone mothers is very different in the two countries (see Chapter 2), and this may influence which lone mothers are in the sample of the unemployed as well as their durations of unemployment.

30. We were unable to examine the working-time preferences of the unemployed in our sample.

31. However, some of this effect is picked up by controlling for the proportion of time employed.

32. Steiner (1997) investigating extended benefit entitlement periods for those aged 42–57 also finds very little effect for women.

33. We do not present estimates here, but findings are available from the author.

34. In the final Appendix, Section A.2.1, we compare these samples to the preferred ILO measure of unemployed. As we discuss there, it is not feasible to use the ILO definition of unemployment for work histories.

35. Looking at the distribution of independent variables at the beginning of the unemployment spells, we do indeed find a considerably smaller proportion of unemployment spells for women with children under five in Britain (13.4 per cent) than in Germany (22.7 per cent).

36. The exception to this is those unemployed aged over 58 who receive benefits.

37. See Atkinson and Micklewright (1985, pp. 241–2) for a discussion of the limitations of micro-level data in this regard.

# 6. The labour force participation of the wives of unemployed men*

In Chapter 4 we found that the risk of poverty among the unemployed is highest in so-called 'workless households', where no other adult is working. Key to understanding the experience of unemployment is an appreciation of the role of another earner in protecting the unemployed from poverty.

When one partner in a couple becomes unemployed, one might suppose that the other partner will find a job in order to supplement the household income. This is the so-called 'added-worker' effect predicted by the classical economic approach to labour supply. Theoretical models of family labour supply suggest that the unemployment of one spouse should increase the likelihood of employment of the other spouse (see, for instance, Ashenfelter 1980).[1] Table 6.1 however, indicates the opposite of the 'added-worker' effect in Britain. In Britain, the employment rate of the wives of unemployed men is considerably lower than the employment rate of the wives of employed men. The data presented are for 1991 but replicate a well-established trend in Britain (see Dex et al. 1995 for a discussion). In West Germany, by contrast, Table 6.1 indicates little difference in the employment rates of the wives of employed and unemployed men. It is the task of this chapter to investigate this difference between Britain and West Germany using longitudinal data.[2]

Table 6.1   Employment rates of married** women aged 18–55 in Britain and West Germany, 1991

|  | Husband Employed | Husband Unemployed | All married Women, 18–55 | No. of Cases |
|---|---|---|---|---|
| Country | (%) | (%) | (%) |  |
| West Germany | 62.1 | 64.6 | 62.6 | 2,094 |
| Britain | 75.1 | 33.9 | 70.7 | 2,264 |

Note:   ** Married also includes women who are cohabiting partners.

Source:   Own calculations from 1991 waves of the BHPS and the GSOEP, weighted.

Table 6.1 suggests that in Britain 'worklessness' may cluster around certain sorts of households, an issue that has been the subject of considerable policy interest in recent years in Britain. In their chapter entitled 'The rise of the workless household', Gregg et al. (1999) draw our attention to the increasing polarisation of employment. They show how, though aggregate employment remained unchanged, in 1990 there were twice as many households out of work as in 1975. There has been a simultaneous rise in both 'work-rich' and 'work-poor' households. The authors note how, as the distribution of work widens, so too does the distribution of income. In the analysis in this chapter we investigate how a certain type of workless household comes into being, one in which the man is unemployed and the woman is out of the labour market.

In Chapter 1 we pointed to the tendency of typologies of welfare regimes to draw distinctions according to the treatment of individuals, predicting which types of individuals will be prioritised in each type of regime. In Chapters 4 and 5 our analysis also focused on outcomes for unemployed individuals. In this chapter we shift our focus to consider the impact of unemployment benefit on the labour market participation of spouses. While some of the typologies we examine do emphasise the role of families (Lewis and Ostner 1994; Gallie and Paugam 2000), these typologies do not stress the importance of the degree to which the welfare system treats spouses as independent of each other. This may vary significantly between welfare states, as it does between Britain and Germany.

## 6.1   PREVIOUS FINDINGS

A number of studies have examined possible explanations for the absence of an added-worker effect in Britain. One explanation is that women married to unemployed men may be seeking paid work in labour markets that provide fewer opportunities than do the local labour markets of most married women. Alternatively there may be common characteristics (either observable or unobservable) that make it less likely that either partner will be employed, such as the level of education, as argued by Ultee et al. (1988), or what Doris (1999b) describes as the 'taste' for market work. Another explanation proposed by economists is that the leisure times of husbands and wives may be complements rather than substitutes, so the couple may prefer to spend time together, rather than the wife working when the man is unemployed (Doris 1999b). Yet Whelan and McGinnity (2000) point to a profound disutility caused by unemployment, which is exacerbated by income poverty, suggesting that leisure, on these terms, may not be complementary. Another possible explanation is that women may be reluctant to take over the role of the 'breadwinner'. According to McKee and Bell (1985), in interviews with couples in which the husband was unemployed, both husbands and wives mentioned how negatively they viewed the prospect of the woman becoming the breadwinner; many became emotional at the prospect.

But the explanation at the core of much of the literature on this issue has been unemployment compensation. Though unemployment insurance, which insures individuals against the loss of income when unemployed, may also reduce the added-worker effect, most of the debate has been about means-tested benefits. Unemployment benefits which are means-tested against family income may generate disincentives to work for the spouse of the unemployed person. The possibility that administrative rules governing the entitlement to benefit income may discourage women from entering the labour market to offset the loss of household income, or worse, may encourage working women to leave the labour market, is a cause for concern – particularly given the link previously noted between unemployment in work-poor households and poverty. If this is the case, comparing Britain and Germany, two countries with very different approaches to means-testing the unemployed, could prove fruitful.

Evidence from previous research on Britain has produced somewhat inconclusive findings. Cooke (1987), in his review, finds some evidence for many of the explanations proposed above. Davies et al. (1992) in their analyses of individual labour markets find some 'cross-couple state dependence' in employment status – enough to warrant investigation – but stress the finding that unemployed men are more likely to have wives with low levels of labour force attachment, and that this accounts for more of any participation difference than cross-couple state dependence. Ercolani and Jenkins (2000), using a conditional logit model applied to monthly BHPS data, find a negative effect of means-tested income support on the partner's participation and find mixed effects of unemployment benefit.

Of studies that attempt to measure the budget constraint more explicitly, Kell and Wright (1990) report significant and large negative effects of means-testing on the participation of wives. Doris (1999a) finds that households headed by an unemployed man entitled to either unemployment benefit or income support are strongly affected by means-testing.

In Germany, policy interest in the subject has been much more limited. In a study on Germany using GSOEP data, Giannelli and Micklewright (1995) find no clear impact of a married man being unemployed on his wife's labour force status. They do find a negative effect of unemployment assistance on the wife's employment in one of their models, but the finding is not robust. However, they point out that their results apply to one country alone, and that variation in institutional details of benefit regimes may affect the findings. This is an issue we pursue in this chapter.

There have been very few cross-national analyses of this topic. Ultee et al. (1988) in a comparison of Canada, the Netherlands and the US stress the importance of educational homogamy in understanding why unemployment/non-employment comes in couples. They also note the role of regional unemployment. In addition to these factors, De Graaf and Ultee (2000) observe in a comparison of several European countries that association between partners' labour market status is also high in countries in which female employment rates are high. They suggest that regulations governing eligibility to unemployment benefits contribute to the explanation of inter-country differences, in particular in explaining the British case, though they do not investigate this explicitly. The cross-national study of most relevance to this chapter was carried out by Dex et al. (1995), who focus explicitly on unemployment benefit regimes. They compare the relationship between women's participation and their husband's labour force status in a range of benefit regimes (Britain, Denmark, Ireland, Sweden and the US). In countries where unemployment benefit is a wholly individual benefit, the wives of unemployed men do not appear to experience effects on labour market participation. Where unemployment benefits take a wife's earnings into account, there is always a significant negative effect on those wives' labour force participation. However, Dex et al. (1995) note the limitations of cross-sectional research and recommend a longitudinal perspective.

Finally, from a different perspective, a recent paper by DiPrete and McManus (2000) compares the income mobility effects of certain 'trigger' events such as employment changes in the household and changes in household composition, in Germany and the US. A salient finding for our purposes is that, following their male partner's employment exit, German women tend to increase their labour supply, suggesting an added-worker effect.

Since the various explanations of this phenomenon deal in part with the social policy regime, one route to exploring the issue is to conduct cross-national comparisons. As Dex et al. (1995) argue, 'cross-national comparisons are an ideal method for exploring the effects of country-specific differences such as the differences in policy regimes and the incentives they set up'. In this chapter we compare the labour force participation of wives in two countries with different policy regimes. In particular, Britain and Germany differ considerably in the extent of means-testing of the unemployed. They also differ, as we see in Table 6.1, in the gap in the employment rate of the wives of unemployed men.

We attempt to address this issue by looking at a group of married or cohabiting women's labour force transitions.[3] We first briefly review features of the benefit systems in Britain and Germany that might be expected to affect labour force transitions, and formulate some hypotheses. In the following section we discuss the data used and review preliminary evidence on the association between husbands' and wives' labour force states. We then discuss approaches to modelling this process, and explain and introduce the choice of model. We use event history modelling to examine women's transitions in and out of paid employment. After a discussion of the results, we draw some conclusions about similarities and differences between Britain and Germany. While there have been cross-national (Dex et al. 1995) and longitudinal (De Graaf and Ultee 1991; Giannelli and Micklewright 1995) analyses of this issue, this is the first piece of work that is both comparative and longitudinal.

## 6.2   UNEMPLOYMENT BENEFIT REGIMES AND INCENTIVES FOR WIVES TO WORK

As a prelude to comparing the labour market transitions of women, we first review the 'unemployment benefit regimes' in Britain and Germany, and how they might affect incentives for wives to work.

Similarities and differences between unemployment compensation in Britain and Germany were the subject of Chapter 3 and were summarised in Table 3.1. The particular aspect of unemployment compensation that concerns this chapter is whether a husband's unemployment-related benefits are linked to his wife's earnings. A link can arise if the man's benefit is means-tested on the basis of family income, or if any part of the benefit is withdrawn when the woman is working or earning. We would expect that withdrawal of benefits would create a disincentive for the wife to work, the scale of which would be likely to depend on the rate of withdrawal of the benefit and its amount. Our particular focus will therefore be the extent and nature of means-testing, whether there is extra money paid for a dependent spouse, and whether there are earnings disregards.

As we saw in Chapter 3, there are means-tested and non-means-tested benefits paid to the unemployed in both Britain and Germany, but there is a significant difference in the proportion of the unemployed receiving each. The majority of the unemployed in Germany receive insurance benefit, while in Britain the majority receive means-tested benefit. Indeed, in Chapter 3 we characterised Germany as an 'insurance system with means-tested elements' and Britain as a 'means-tested system with insurance elements'.

Insurance-based benefit is normally paid on the basis of an individual's past contributions and is not means-tested on family income. In Germany, the unemployed receive a slightly higher rate of *Arbeitslosengeld* if they have children, but there is no extra allowance paid for partners. In this case we would expect no significant effect of a man's unemployment on his wife's participation rate. With British insurance benefit a dependant's allowance is added on to the main unemployment benefit where a man has a non-employed wife. In 1996, this extra allowance was 76 per cent of the amount payable to the claimant (Child Poverty Action Group 1997). This allowance is withdrawn if the wife earns more than this amount. In the case of British unemployment insurance benefit then we would expect that wives of unemployed men would experience a small disincentive effect to participate in the labour market.

In both countries there are means-tested benefits for those who are either not eligible to insurance benefit, or are no longer eligible to insurance benefit because their unemployment has persisted. These schemes are means-tested on family income and thus create a disincentive for the wife to work. There are important earnings disregards in the application of means-testing. In the British scheme the earnings disregard for the spouse is low, £5 per week for most of those on income support in the early 1990s. We expect this to act as a strong disincentive for wives to work. If the wife does work she will be more likely to work full-time than part-time. There are two means-tested benefits in Germany: *Arbeitslosenhilfe* (unemployment assistance) and *Sozialhilfe* (social assistance). For those receiving *Arbeitslosenhilfe* the earnings disregard in 1993 was higher than in Britain at DM150 or around £50, with a DM70 addition for children. There is no adult dependant's allowance for *Arbeitslosenhilfe*. Receipt of *Arbeitslosenhilfe* is expected to create a disincentive for wives to work, though we expect the disincentive to be lower than in Britain, as the earnings disregard is higher and there is no dependant's allowance, and there may be an incentive for wives to work short hours part-time (below the threshold). *Sozialhilfe*, the final safety net for the unemployed in Germany, carried a (variable) earnings disregard of around DM30–60 per week in the mid-1990s. The allowance paid for the dependent spouse is usually around 80 per cent of that for the claimant. Though relatively few of the unemployed receive this benefit, we would expect there to be some disincentive effect on the wife's participation with this benefit too. A further relevant point concerns the differences between *Arbeitslosengeld* and *Arbeitslosenhilfe*. Both are earnings linked but the compensation rate is lower for the means-tested *Arbeitslosenhilfe*. Most of the unemployed move from *Arbeitslosengeld* to *Arbeitslosenhilfe* after 12 months,[4] providing they satisfy the means test. In Britain the difference in the amount paid by the two benefits is negligible.

The chapter assesses the evidence for these disincentives by modelling women's exits from and entries into employment in Britain and Germany, controlling for the women's characteristics and labour market characteristics. We now describe the data used, and then present some initial evidence on the labour force status of husbands and wives.

## 6.3   GERMAN AND BRITISH PANEL DATA AND THE LABOUR FORCE STATUS OF SPOUSES

As in other chapters, the analysis for Germany is based on data from the German Socio-economic Panel (GSOEP); the analysis for Britain is based on data from the British Household Panel Study (BHPS). The Appendix at the end of the book contains details of the datasets.

We select a sample of continuously married (or cohabiting) women throughout a 70-month period and analyse their transitions in and out of the labour market using monthly calendars.[5] As male unemployment may have an impact on marriage itself (Lampard 1994), there may be an indirect influence of male unemployment on female labour market participation. By excluding persons not continuously married we are conditioning on the stability of marriage. For this reason we need to ensure that the length of the period in both countries is identical (70 months). The period chosen is from December 1991 until September 1997 (inclusive) for Britain, and March 1988 until December 1993 for Germany. Information on unemployment compensation is only available until December 1993 in the German sample, and there were some important changes to the earnings disregard calculation for *Arbeitslosenhilfe* in January 1994. In Britain the BHPS only started in 1991, and the relevant calendar data are only available for the period 1991–97.

We use information about the annual regional unemployment rate to account for temporal and regional variation in the demand for labour. For this analysis we select only West German households; foreigners and later extensions of the survey are excluded. For Britain we select only non-ethnic minority households.[6] The women are all between 18 and 55 (inclusive) in the month the observation window starts. This generates a sample of 1,279 couples for Britain and 1,199 couples for West Germany.

### 6.3.1   Measuring Labour Force Status

In the first part of the analysis women's labour force statuses as recorded in the monthly calendar are aggregated from detailed categories into the following possibilities:

1. employment;
2. non-participation.

For most categories, labour force status is self-defined. 'Employment' includes full-time, part-time and temporary employment. The 'non-participation' category comprises the retired, those in full-time education and training, those in home duties, and 'others'.[7] Our focus is on women's moves between employment and non-participation; moves to unemployment are censored.[8]

In the second part of the analysis we distinguish part-time work from full-time work. Some authors have argued that women enter part-time work on rather different terms to full-time work (Blossfeld and Hakim 1997; O'Reilly and Fagan 1998). We saw in Chapter 2 that the rate of part-time work among women is much higher in Britain than in Germany. In addition, earlier in this chapter we noted how some benefit disincentives discourage wives from working part-time, while some encourage wives to work short-hours part-time work as opposed to full-time work. In the second part of the analysis we therefore distinguish women's labour market statuses into the following possibilities:

1. full-time employment;
2. part-time employment ;
3. non-participation.

The distinction between part-time and full-time work is made by the respondent in the monthly spell data. We have no details on hours worked. If we have no information on whether a spell of employment is part-time or full-time the spell is excluded from this analysis.[9]

In this chapter we treat the husband's labour force status as exogenous to his wife's and as a time-varying covariate in the model. For each individual we match the monthly calendar of the husband to that of his wife. As we are particularly interested in spells of unemployment for the husband, the husband's labour force status is categorised as one of:

1. employment;
2. unemployment;
3. non-participation.

In Table 6.2 we compare wives' participation for different labour force states of their husbands in Britain and Germany, using the data described above. This table using monthly data is broadly consistent with the cross-sectional statistics presented in Table 6.1. We see that, though for Germany there is a relatively small difference between the participation rate of the wives of employed and unemployed men, in Britain there is a large difference.[10] And while in West Germany the participation rate of the wives of unemployed men is actually somewhat higher than for wives of employed men, in Britain the opposite is the case. These results are almost identical to the cross-tabulations presented by Ercolani and Jenkins (2000) using the same data (BHPS) for Britain. They are somewhat different to those of

*Table 6.2    Comparing labour force status of working-age partners of employed and unemployed men in Britain (1991–97) and West Germany (1988–93)*

| | Wife/Partner's Labour Force Status | | | | | |
| --- | --- | --- | --- | --- | --- | --- |
| | Britain | | | Germany | | |
| Husband/Partner | Emp (%) | UE (%) | Out of lab force (%) | Emp (%) | UE (%) | Out of lab force (%) |
| Employed | 75.8 | 1.1 | 23.0 | 59.9 | 2.1 | 37.9 |
| Unemployed | 44.5 | 3.1 | 52.4 | 61.6 | 3.8 | 34.6 |
| Out of labour force | 47.4 | 2.3 | 50.2 | 56.2 | 1.7 | 42.0 |
| No. (of months) | 63,721 | 1,225 | 24,402 | 49,000 | 1,757 | 31,489 |

*Note*:    The unit of analysis is a month – we have pooled all months for all couples and then cross-tabulated the status of partners. Working age is defined as between 18 and 55 (inclusive) at the start of the observation period.

*Source*:    Own estimates from the GSOEP and BHPS monthly calendar data, unweighted.

Giannelli and Micklewright's (1995) estimates for Germany. In particular we report a higher proportion of women in employment for all states of the husband. This may be because we look at a later time period.[11]

Given that the differences between Britain and Germany may be due to a number of factors, we need to examine these differences, controlling for the wife's personal and labour market characteristics. The model we use is the subject of the next section.

## 6.4    MODELLING WOMEN'S LABOUR FORCE TRANSITIONS

We are primarily concerned with the decision of the woman to be employed or not, given that her husband is unemployed. In practice, this may not be an individual decision, but a joint decision with the husband. In this chapter the simpler assumption is made that it is an individual decision, i.e. that the husband's labour force status is exogenous.

Most of the econometric work to date that has looked at this problem has done so from a cross-sectional perspective. Davies et al. (1992) estimate a cross-sectional logistic regression model of a wife's participation in six labour markets in 1986, including a correction for heterogeneity. Dex et al.

(1995), in their cross-national comparison, use a logit or probit to model the dichotomous participation decision, including an instrumented wage for the woman's potential wage and a linearised budget constraint to account for differences in the tax systems. Garcia (1991) constructs a discrete choice model, which uses the detailed potential net income of the household for alternative labour supply decisions of the wife.

Using a different approach, Ercolani and Jenkins (2000) and Giannelli and Micklewright (1995) use panel data, but estimate a static model – the conditional logistic regression model. No account of the woman's potential wage or the budget constraint is included in these papers.

While it can correct for unobservables, this static approach by definition assumes independence of participation status over time. Using an event history modelling approach we can relax this assumption. We can ask the question 'What is the probability that a woman leaves the labour force when her husband becomes unemployed?' rather than 'What is the probability that a woman is out of the labour force, given that her husband is unemployed?' Equally, focusing on the opposite transition, we can ask 'What is a probability that a woman will move to employment when her husband becomes unemployed?' It is plausible that these are different processes, and that a woman's previous employment status will have a strong influence on her behaviour when her husband becomes unemployed. This is similar to the approach adopted by Giannelli and Micklewright (1995) in the second part of their paper. A limitation of this modelling strategy is that we do not know the woman's potential wage. It was not practicable to calculate a potential net wage for the wife given the monthly data used in this chapter, as the kind of information required is not available on these datasets.[12]

The form of event history modelling used in this chapter to analyse women's labour force transitions is discrete-time event history modelling (Allison 1982, 1984). Discrete-time models are particularly suited to our analysis because of the relatively short observation period and the fact that our response variable is already in a discrete monthly format. The model also allows easy and direct handling of time-varying covariates. The general approach is to model the conditional probability of a transition, given that the transition has not occurred. In the first part of the analysis we focus on transitions from employment to non-participation and from non-participation to employment. How does this hazard rate (or conditional probability) depend on the covariates? The most popular choice for discrete-time modelling is the logit link (Cox 1972; Allison 1982). Assuming duration dependence in the hazard, the logit link specifies the relationship between the hazard rate and the covariates thus:

$$\log[p_{it}/(1 - p_{it})] = \alpha_t + \beta_t x_{it}$$

where $\alpha_t$ is a set of constants $(t = 1...T)$ – the baseline hazard – when $x = 0$, and $\beta_t$ allows the effect of the covariates $(x_{it})$ to vary with time. The model is estimated using maximum likelihood estimation. If we assume no duration dependence in the hazard, the logit link is simply:

$$\log[p_i/(1 - p_i)] = \alpha + \beta x_i$$

Our reasons for presenting findings on the latter model, which assumes no duration dependence, are outlined in the discussion on censoring below.

In the second part of the analysis, which distinguishes part-time work, we use discrete-time models to analyse the hazard rates of transitions between part-time employment, full-time employment and non-participation, using a competing risks model (Allison 1982). Using the logit link described above, this results in a multinomial logistic regression.

One common problem of duration data of this kind is censoring. Censoring exists when incomplete information is available about the spell because of a limited observation period (in our case 70 months). The two main forms of censoring of concern for us are right censoring and left censoring.[13] Right censoring occurs when the period of observation ends before a person has made the transition, and is well handled by the model we use (Allison 1984). Left censoring is when a spell begins before the observation period and we do not know when it begins. Provided we assume that there is no duration dependence in the hazard, it may easily be shown that left censoring is of little practical importance (Giannelli and Micklewright 1995). If we wish to allow for duration dependence in the hazard rate, we need to exclude left-censored spells. However, this would exclude many transitions out of longer spells of employment and inactivity: while 70 months is quite a long period for looking at unemployment, it is a relatively short period if we are looking at employment or inactivity. We would then be selecting only those with 'shorter' spells of employment or inactivity, and this might also bias the findings.

While most of the analysis assumes no duration dependence in the hazard, and includes left-censored spells, we re-ran all the models to check if our results are sensitive to this assumption. These results are reported in the text. In addition, we include a number of variables that measure some aspects of the work history prior to the spell. Including a measure of the woman's previous labour market history, and the husband's duration of unemployment, allows us to 'control', to some extent, the history prior to the spell. After the models were estimated, a significance of difference test was applied comparing each coefficient for Britain and for Germany (see Chapter 4, endnote 28 for more details of this test).

One key covariate of interest in this model is the husband's monthly labour force status, which we described above. Another is the unemployment benefit received by the husband. For receipt of benefits, both surveys record the type of benefit in monthly calendars in a similar way to labour force status. This information is matched to information about unemployment spells, and dummy variables constructed, indicating the husband's receipt of unemployment-related benefits. For Germany, social assistance (*Sozialhilfe*) is not reported in the monthly calendars for this period. This is clearly a problem, as those who we classify as receiving no benefit may actually be receiving social assistance. However, as only a small proportion of German unemployed receive social assistance (see Table 3.1 in Chapter 3), we do not expect this to substantially affect our findings.

As labour force participation is expected to vary by age and generation we include the age of both partners at the start of the spell. Other control variables in the models are time-varying. Given the limited state provision of childcare in Britain and Germany, we expect the presence and age of children to affect women's labour force participation. Educational qualifications are also expected to affect women's participation, as highly educated women are more likely to be employed. Educational qualifications are coded according to a variant of the 'casmin' schema (see König et al. 1988).[14] We represent the effects of fluctuations in the macroeconomic cycle by using annual data on regional unemployment from national sources.[15]

Finally, we include a longer-term measure of labour force experience. 'Proportion of time previously employed' is measured as the proportion of time employed since entering the labour market and before the woman's spell began, using data from the long-term work histories on the surveys. Information about a woman's previous employment history could be proxy information for a number of factors. We expect it to have a strong effect on women's transitions.

## 6.5   EMPIRICAL FINDINGS

In this section we present the results of our models. As previously noted, our primary focus is on the husband's labour force status, particularly unemployment, and the benefits he receives. For this reason only the results pertaining to the husband's labour force status are presented in the main text. The detailed results for the first model in each table are presented in the corresponding Appendix table at the end of this chapter. The results of a significance of difference test are given in the last column of each table.

Women's transitions from labour force inactivity to employment are presented in Table 6.3, and their transitions from employment to inactivity are presented in Table 6.4. For each of these transitions we present three models for each country. In model 1 we simply distinguish the husband's labour force status, with the employed husband as the reference category, focusing on the effect of the husband's unemployment on the woman's probability of changing labour force status. However, for a number of reasons there may be a delay in a wife's change in status when her husband becomes unemployed. Firstly, a woman may initially believe that her husband's unemployment will not last long enough to justify the transaction costs associated with finding a job, only to give it up again when he returns to work. Equally, she may not give up her job immediately if she believes her husband's unemployment will not last. Secondly, it may take the woman time to find a job, particularly if it is also necessary to find alternative childcare arrangements. So in model 2 we distinguish spells of the husband's unemployment into very short term (one to six months), medium term (seven to 12 months) and long term (greater than or equal to 13 months). Finally, in model 3, given our interest in the effect of benefit receipt on the wife's employment, we distinguish the husband's unemployment by benefit status. For each of these models we include the other covariates described above, details of which are given in the notes to each table and in the Appendix.

The first set of models focuses on the wife's transition from labour force inactivity to employment (Table 6.3). The most important finding from model 1 is that while in Britain the wives of unemployed men are less likely to move to employment than the wives of employed men, in Germany the opposite is the case. This difference is significant using the significance of difference test – column (7). In fact the findings for Germany are consistent with what we described earlier as an 'added-worker' effect, that the wives of unemployed men tend to take up a job to compensate for the lost earnings of their husbands. The findings are also consistent with DiPrete and McManus (2000), who find that German women increase their labour supply to offset declines in labour earnings by the male breadwinner. The effect in Britain is consistent with previous findings and with Tables 6.1 and 6.2. For both countries the findings are significant at the 0.05 level.

When we distinguish the husband's unemployment spell by different durations of unemployment (model 2), we find the strongest effect, as expected, for long-term unemployment. In Britain the negative effect of the husband's unemployment increases in a stepwise fashion with increasing duration of unemployment. In Germany, there is actually a slight negative effect on the transition for the husband's unemployment spells of seven to 12 months, but a strong positive effect for the husband's unemployment spells of 13 months and over. The difference between the coefficients for long-term unemployed husbands is significant – see column (7). So German women only become 'added workers' when their husbands have been unemployed for one year or more. There are a number of possible factors that may influence this, either singly or in combination. As noted above, these women

*Table 6.3   Estimates of parameters of hazard rates: transition from labour force inactivity to employment*

| Husband's Status | Britain | | | Germany | | | T-stat. of Diff. |
|---|---|---|---|---|---|---|---|
| | Coeff. | s.e. | p-value | Coeff. | s.e. | p-value | |
| | (1) | (2) | (3) | (4) | (5) | (6) | (7) |
| (1) Model 1 | | | | | | | |
| *Ref: husband employed* | | | | | | | |
| Unemployed | −0.534 | 0.228 | 0.019 | +0.658 | 0.284 | 0.021 | −3.27 |
| Out of labour force | −0.767 | 0.198 | 0.000 | −0.065 | 0.207 | 0.752 | −2.45 |
| (2) Model 2 | | | | | | | |
| *Ref: husband employed* | | | | | | | |
| Unemployed 1–6 mths | −0.323 | 0.363 | 0.374 | +0.468 | 0.462 | 0.311 | −1.35 |
| Unemployed 7–12 mths | −0.545 | 0.508 | 0.283 | −0.142 | 1.012 | 0.889 | −0.36 |
| Unemployed 13 + mths | −0.675 | 0.329 | 0.040 | +0.992 | 0.375 | 0.008 | −3.34 |
| Out of labour force | −0.766 | 0.198 | 0.000 | −0.063 | 0.207 | 0.760 | −2.45 |
| (3) Model 3 | | | | | | | |
| *Ref: husband employed* | | | | | | | |
| Receiving insurance | −0.003 | 1.012 | 0.998 | +0.092 | 0.422 | 0.828 | −0.09 |
| Receiving assistance | −0.738 | 0.291 | 0.011 | +1.261 | 0.427 | 0.003 | −3.87 |
| No benefit recorded | −0.173 | 0.363 | 0.634 | +2.591 | 0.800 | 0.001 | −3.14 |
| Out of labour force | −0.764 | 0.198 | 0.000 | −0.074 | 0.207 | 0.721 | −2.41 |
| No. of cases (months) | 23,920 | | | 30,248 | | | |

*Notes*:
Women are aged 18–55 (inclusive) at the beginning of the observation period.
Other covariates included in all the models are: wife's age at start of spell; husband's age at start of spell; wife's education level (casmin); husband's education level (casmin); number of children aged 0–3, 3–5, 5–16; employment rate in the region of residence; and proportion of wife's time in employment since leaving education.
For full results of model 1 for each country see Appendix Table 6.1.A at the end of this chapter.
A 'model chi-square' statistic is calculated for each of the models, by taking the difference between the initial −2 log-likelihood of the model (i.e. without any covariates) and the final −2 log-likelihood for the full model. The model chi-square for the models are the following: Britain – 127.7, 128.3, 128.5; Germany – 289.11, 290.23, 291.05.

*Source*:   Own estimates from the GSOEP and BHPS monthly calendar data.

may be initially unsure of the duration of their husbands' unemployment or it may take them some time to find a job. Another factor is that after 12 months of unemployment the amount of benefit falls by around 12–15 per cent for most unemployed German men, as they move from *Arbeitslosengeld* to *Arbeitslosenhilfe*, which may encourage the wife to work to compensate for the fall in income.

In model 3 we look at the effect of the husband's benefit receipt on his wife's transition from labour force inactivity to employment. In Britain we find quite a difference between the effects of means-tested and insurance-based benefits. For women whose unemployed husbands receive insurance-based benefits, their probability of transition is rather similar to the wives of employed men. The wives of unemployed men receiving (means-tested) assistance benefit in Britain are much less likely to move to employment, and this difference is significant. We noted in Table 3.1 in Chapter 3 that the majority of the unemployed in Britain receive (means-tested) assistance benefits, and our finding is consistent with the much-discussed disincentive effect of means-tested benefits in Britain. In Germany, the wives of unemployed men receiving assistance benefit and of those receiving no benefit are much *more* likely to enter employment than the wives of employed men, and this difference is significant compared to Britain for both these groups – see column (7). It is for these wives that the added-worker effect operates. The probability of the wives of unemployed men who receive insurance-based benefits (the majority) entering employment is not significantly different from that of the wives of employed men, the reference category.

We should add that in both Britain and Germany there is a strong correlation between those receiving assistance benefit and the long-term unemployed. So for Germany the most plausible explanation of our findings seems to be that the added-worker effect is strongest for the wives of long-term unemployed men, and that this outweighs any disincentive effect of assistance benefit. In Britain it seems that any added-worker effect is outweighed by other effects, one of which could certainly be a disincentive effect of assistance benefit. At this point we should reiterate our earlier comment that the assistance benefits in Britain and Germany reported in this table are of a rather different nature. In Germany, unemployment assistance is earnings-linked, has no dependant's allowance and has a significantly higher earnings disregard than in Britain (see Table 3.1, Chapter 3). In Britain the assistance benefit is flat-rate, with a generous dependant's allowance and a very low earnings disregard.

Turning to wives whose husbands are out of the labour force, there is also a difference in findings between Britain and Germany. However, some of this difference may depend on the reasons why the husband is out of the labour force, and investigating these is beyond the scope of this chapter. From Appendix Table 6.1.A at the end of the chapter, we can see that the effects of the other covariates in the models are largely as expected. Wives with young children (under three-years-old) in Britain are less likely to move to employment, while in Germany the effect of having children of any age is small and statistically not significant. In both countries more educated women are more likely to move to employment. Finally, a strong predictor of whether a woman will move to employment in either country is her previous employment history, measured as the proportion of time since leaving school spent in employment.

In Table 6.4 we turn to examine women's transitions from employment to inactivity. As in Table 6.3, we present the results of three models for each country along with the significance of difference test. The results of the full model, including all covariates, are in Appendix Table 6.2.A at the end of the

*Table 6.4    Estimates of parameters of hazard rates: transition from employment to labour force inactivity*

| | Britain | | | Germany | | | T-stat. of Diff. |
|---|---|---|---|---|---|---|---|
| | Coeff. | s.e. | p-value | Coeff. | s.e. | p-value | |
| Husband's Status | (1) | (2) | (3) | (4) | (5) | (6) | (7) |
| **(1) Model 4** | | | | | | | |
| *Ref: husband employed* | | | | | | | |
| Unemployed | –0.318 | 0.342 | 0.352 | –0.638 | 0.422 | 0.130 | 0.59 |
| Out of labour force | +0.699 | 0.166 | 0.000 | +0.067 | 0.191 | 0.727 | 2.55 |
| **(2) Model 5** | | | | | | | |
| *Ref: husband employed* | | | | | | | |
| Unemployed 1–6 mths | –0.024 | 0.454 | 0.957 | –1.284 | 1.006 | 0.202 | 1.14 |
| Unemployed 7–12 mths | –4.087 | 5.028 | 0.416 | –0.946 | 1.021 | 0.354 | –0.61 |
| Unemployed 13+ mths | –0.200 | 0.510 | 0.695 | –0.255 | 0.515 | 0.620 | 0.08 |
| Out of labour force | +0.699 | 0.166 | 0.000 | +0.070 | 0.191 | 0.715 | 2.49 |
| **(3) Model 6** | | | | | | | |
| *Ref: husband employed* | | | | | | | |
| Receiving insurance | –0.670 | 1.002 | 0.503 | –0.308 | 0.510 | 0.545 | –0.32 |
| Receiving assistance | –0.069 | 0.512 | 0.894 | –0.795 | 0.737 | 0.280 | 0.81 |
| No benefit recorded | –0.421 | 0.506 | 0.405 | –3.331 | 4.284 | 0.437 | 0.67 |
| Out of labour force | +0.700 | 0.166 | 0.000 | +0.069 | 0.191 | 0.718 | 2.49 |
| No. of cases (months) | 63,611 | | | 47,909 | | | |

*Notes*:
Women are aged 18–55 (inclusive) at the beginning of the observation period.
Other covariates included in all the models are: wife's age at start of spell; husband's age at start of spell; wife's education level (casmin); husband's education level (casmin); number of children aged 0–3, 3–5, 5–16; employment rate in the region of residence; and proportion of wife's time in employment since leaving education.
For full results of model 4 for each country see Appendix Table 6.2.A. Model chi-square for the models, as described in the notes to Table 6.3, are the following: Britain – 172.0, 175.8, 172.5; Germany – 277.7, 279.5, 285.6.

*Source*:    Own estimates from the GSOEP and BHPS monthly calendar data.

chapter. For each of the models 4, 5, and 6, it should be noted that none of the coefficients for the husband's unemployment are significant in either country. So while model 4 indicates that the wives of unemployed men are less likely to move to inactivity from employment in both countries, this effect is not significant. Investigating the issue further in model 5, the coefficients suggest that in Germany it is the wives of short-term unemployed men who are least likely to leave employment – though again the findings are not statistically significant. Turning to the effect of the benefit that the husband receives, we find some cross-country differences, though these effects are not robust to the significance of difference test, as the standard errors of the coefficients are large. In summary, the results of the analysis of this transition suggest that the wives of unemployed men do not have a greater tendency to leave employment in either country.

The results of other covariates are presented in this chapter's Appendix. In general, those with higher education are less likely to leave employment, although the effect is weakened by the addition of the measure of employment history to the model. In both countries women with children are more likely to leave the labour market than those without. As expected, the younger the child, the larger the effect. Finally, in both Britain and Germany, the largest effect on withdrawal from the labour market is previous labour market history – women who have more employment experience are more likely to stay in employment.

We tested our findings using a sample that excludes all left-censored spells, i.e. includes only those spells that began after the start date.[16] These models include a simple form of duration dependence in the hazard. For Germany the findings for the transition from inactivity to employment are similar, except that in this model the wives of short-term unemployed men are also more likely to move to employment than the wives of employed men. For Britain, the findings for the transition from inactivity to employment are somewhat different. With this sample the negative effect of the husband's unemployment on this transition only remains for wives of husbands who are long-term unemployed or who are receiving income support. For the transition from employment to inactivity the findings for the husband's employment status are similar. For the reasons discussed above, we prefer to present the findings of models that include left-censored spells.

## 6.6   PART-TIME FINDINGS

As an extension of the previous models we now distinguish women's transitions to employment between full-time and part-time work.[17] In Table 6.5 we present the effects of the husband's labour force status alone on the six

*Table 6.5*   *Estimates of hazard rates for transitions between full-time work, part-time work and non-participation*

| Husband's Status | Britain | Germany | | Britain | Germany | |
|---|---|---|---|---|---|---|
| | (1) | (2) | (3) | (4) | (5) | (6) |
| (Model 7) | Non-participation to full-time | | T-stat. of of diff. | Non-participation to part-time | | T-stat. of diff. |
| *Ref: husband employed* | | | | | | |
| Unemployed | 0.133 | +0.981 | −1.11 | −0.735 | 0.122 | −1.82 |
| | *(p = 0.77)* | *(p = 0.11)* | | *(p = 0.00)* | *(p = 0.76)* | |
| Out of labour force | +0.174 | +0.016 | +0.26 | −1.151 | −0.330 | −2.33 |
| | *(p = 0.61)* | *(p = 0.97)* | | *(p = 0.00)* | *(p = 0.18)* | |
| (Model 8) | Full-time to non-participation | | T-stat. of diff. | Full-time to part-time | | T-stat. of diff. |
| *Ref: husband employed* | | | | | | |
| Unemployed | +0.201 | +0.146 | 0.07 | −0.090 | Infinity | − |
| | *(p = 0.7)* | *(p = 0.81)* | | *(p = 0.86)* | | |
| Out of labour force | +0.682 | +0.403 | +0.60 | −0.259 | −1.839 | +1.45 |
| | *(p = 0.02)* | *(p = 0.26)* | | *(p = 0.49)* | *(p = 0.07)* | |
| (Model 9) | Part-time to non-participation | | T-stat. of diff. | Part-time to full-time | | T-stat. of diff. |
| *Ref: husband employed* | | | | | | |
| Unemployed | −0.236 | −0.557 | +0.44 | +0.039 | −0.325 | +0.33 |
| | *(p = 0.58)* | *(p = 0.35)* | | *(p = 0.93)* | *(p = 0.75)* | |
| Out of labour force | +0.517 | +0.230 | +0.82 | −0.867 | −1.630 | +0.66 |
| | *(p = 0.04)* | *(p = 0.35)* | | *(p = 0.1)* | *(p = 0.11)* | |

*Notes:*
Women are aged 18–55 (inclusive) at the beginning of the observation period.
Other covariates included in all the models are: wife's age at start of spell; husband's age at start of spell; wife's education level (casmin); husband's education level (casmin); number of children aged 0–3, 3–5, 5–16; employment rate in the region of residence; and proportion of wife's time in employment since leaving education.
Model chi-square for the models are the following: Britain – 161.2, 159.2, 164.8; Germany – 272.0, 99.9, 151.2.

*Source:*   Own estimates from the GSOEP and BHPS monthly calendar data.

possible transitions between three statuses for women. As discussed above, these six transitions are modelled as three multinomial models – inactivity to full-time work and to part-time work; full-time work to inactivity and to part-time work; part-time work to inactivity and to full-time work.

The main effects of note for us are for the transitions from inactivity in model 7. Here we discover that in Germany the wives of unemployed men are somewhat more likely to move into full-time employment than the wives of employed men. In Table 6.5 the effect is marginally significant – further modelling shows this effect to be significant for the long-term unemployed, as in Table 6.3. In summary, the added worker effect in Germany operates in the following way: women find work after their husband has been unemployed for some time, and they find full-time work.[18]

Further to our finding in Table 6.3 that British women married to unemployed men are less likely to move to employment, here we find that the effect is large and statistically significant only for part-time work (see Table 6.5).[19] Further modelling shows this effect to be present only when the husband is in receipt of means-tested income support. From this we can conclude that women whose husbands receive income support are less likely to work part-time. The wives of unemployed men who may wish to supplement the low benefit income of their husband by working part-time do not do so. If the earnings disregard to income support is only £5 per week and if there is a relatively generous supplement to income support for dependants, it may be difficult for the woman to earn more than this amount working part-time. Which couples is this most likely to affect? In Chapter 2 we argued that mothers with children of school-going age are more likely work part-time than women without children, so we might expect the former to be particularly affected. In Chapter 4 we found that households with children are more vulnerable to income poverty than those without. Thus the disincentive effect of income support is likely to be strongest for the families who need the extra money most.

## 6.7	CONCLUSIONS

What have we learned from our analysis of the labour force transitions of wives? The significant findings relate to women's transitions into employment. In Germany, when a man becomes unemployed, his wife is more likely to enter employment than if he were employed. In Britain, when a man becomes unemployed, his wife is less likely to enter employment than if he were employed – in particular she is less likely to enter part-time employment. Both of these mechanisms come into effect when the husband has been unemployed for 13 months or more and is normally receiving means-tested benefit (or no benefit in Germany). In Germany, those receiving means-tested benefits are the minority – most of the unemployed in Germany receive insurance benefit, and our findings suggest that the labour market behaviour of their wives is no different from that of the wives of employed men. So, in beginning to understand the differences in participation rates we noted at the beginning of this chapter, we have discovered that when men become unemployed in Germany women move into employment, while in Britain they do not.

Why is this the case? This question is more difficult. In Germany there certainly seems to be evidence of an 'added-worker' effect: any disincentive effect of benefits we might have expected is outweighed by this. When we turn to Britain, the question is more complex. As regards some of the explanations proposed at the beginning of this chapter, we have ruled out an added-worker effect. The argument about local labour markets is more difficult to test, though we do control for regional unemployment rates. The explanation about the labour force attachment of women we do include in our model and find it to have resonance. The wives of unemployed men have, on average, spent less of their post-education life in the labour market, and this affects their propensity to enter employment. However, we find an effect of the husband's current labour force status – specifically unemployment – even after controlling for this. While there may be some effect of the wife being a reluctant breadwinner, we have no reason to suspect that this effect would be much larger in Britain than in Germany. Instead, we are left with the strong suspicion that there is a disincentive effect of means-tested benefit in Britain, which partly explains why the wives of unemployed men are less likely to enter employment than others.

Conversely, we find no significant effects for the transition of the wives of unemployed men out of employment. Other covariates in the model, like women's previous labour market history and the presence of young children, have a much greater influence on women's transitions out of the labour force than their husbands' current unemployment.

From a methodological point of view, we have discovered some positive effects of using a dynamic perspective to address this issue. We can relax the assumption that the wife's current status is independent of her status immediately previous to her current status, which is very much in keeping with the idea that the past conditions the present. Using cross-sectional data, as in Table 6.1, we observe what proportion of the wives of unemployed men are employed at any given time. Using longitudinal data we can distinguish those women who were working when their husbands became unemployed from those who were out of the labour force at the time. We can therefore look at two separate processes that embody cross-couple dependence in labour force status: on the one hand, a move from employment to labour force inactivity and on the other, a move from inactivity to employment. Our findings illustrate how useful it can be to view these as two separate processes, which is only possible using longitudinal data.

There are limitations to our analysis. We cannot include information on the husband's receipt of *Sozialhilfe* in Germany for this period. It is also not possible to include a potential wage for the wife. In addition, we treat the husband's labour force status as strictly exogenous to the wife's – household decision-making may be more complex than presented!

Notwithstanding the limitations, we argue that we can still draw some conclusions about the polarisation of employment and worklessness and its implications for income poverty. As noted in Chapter 4, means-tested income support in 1990s Britain was not enough to protect many individuals covered by it from poverty. The finding that means-tested benefits in Britain tend to discourage a second earner implies that the unemployment benefit system itself may be contributing, in part, to the 'rise of the workless household' noted in the at the beginning of this chapter. And the rise of workless households in Britain is surely of concern for the issue of social exclusion: not just individuals but whole households are lacking both employment and very often sufficient resources to participate in society. In Germany we find that women tend to enter employment when their husbands are unemployed. So not only do German unemployed men tend to receive more generous insurance benefits than unemployed men in Britain, they also become, in the course of their unemployment, more likely to live in a household where their wives are working.

As noted in the introduction to this chapter, typologies of welfare pay little or no attention to spouses and to the degree to which spouses are treated as independent of each other in the welfare system. This chapter serves as a timely reminder that unemployment compensation may affect the participation of the partners of the unemployed, and that this effect should be considered when comparing unemployment welfare regimes. Together with De Graaf and Ultee (2000), we argue that future research should incorporate the dimension of 'spousal autonomy': the degree to which spouses are treated as dependent or independent by social security systems. This is point to which we return in our concluding chapter.

## NOTES

\*     An earlier version of this chapter was first published as McGinnity, F. (2002), 'The labour force participation of the wives of unemployed men. Comparing Britain and West Germany using longitudinal data', *European Sociological Review*, **18** (4), 473–88. Reproduced by permission of Oxford University Press.

1.     For the origins of the concept of an 'added-worker effect' and early empirical estimates of its magnitude in the US, see Humphrey (1940).

2.     As in Chapter 5, East Germany is not included in this chapter. Once again the analysis focuses on the 1980s and early 1990s in Germany, and as discussed in Chapter 1, the scale of labour market intervention in East Germany in the early 1990s means it is problematic

to include it in an analysis of unemployment in this period. In any case in Table 2.6 in Chapter 2, we see that there are very few couples in East Germany where the husband is unemployed and his partner inactive: a more relevant question here might be to examine couples where both partners are unemployed.

3.  Throughout this chapter, where reference is made to 'wives' or 'husbands' these terms also include cohabiting couples.

4.  Following changes in the mid-1980s, older unemployed people with long contribution records are eligible for longer periods of *Arbeitslosengeld* than the standard 12 months. See Chapter 3 for details.

5.  At each wave in both surveys respondents were asked to indicate their labour force status for the preceding 12 months. In Britain, the period refers to the 12 months prior to the survey, in Germany, to the preceding calendar year.

6.  For this size of sample the numbers of non-white households in the BHPS is small, and in both Britain and Germany female labour force participation patterns are significantly different between white and ethnic minority households.

7.  For Germany there are some months where individuals report multiple statuses. For this analysis we take any record of employment as a spell of employment. For example, if a woman reports both part-time work and home duties in one month we take her status that month to be part-time employment.

8.  An alternative strategy would be to model the exit to unemployment as part of a multinomial model with unemployment and non-participation as the two possible 'choices'. A technical problem with this approach is that there is only a very small number of cases in the sample who make the transition to unemployment. A conceptual problem is the notion of 'choosing to become unemployed' for those women who are in employment. We are interested in the impact of the husband's labour force status on the labour supply of the wife, and our analysis assumes that the husband's status is exogenous to the wife's. If we assume that unemployment is not voluntary (and there are benefit penalties in both countries for voluntary unemployment, see Chapter 3), it is difficult to conceive of a woman's transition to unemployment as a reaction to her husband's unemployment.

9.  Those spells excluded in this way include a small number of spells of self-employment in Britain. For Germany, self-employed spells are included, as self-employed spells are not distinguished from spells of dependent employment in the German data.

10. This is the case even though the employment rate of the wives of unemployed men in Britain is somewhat higher than in Table 6.1. Table 6.1 is based on data from 1991, at the beginning of the British period of observation in Table 6.2.

11. In addition, our findings may be slightly affected by our spell 'cleaning' routine, where we take any reported employment in a month to be evidence of employment. Giannelli and Micklewright (1995) do not provide details of how they deal with multiple reported states.

12. This means that we cannot explicitly distinguish wives with a high earning potential from those with a low earning potential, aside from using covariates like education and labour force experience. If a wife's earning potential is not adequately captured by these covariates, we may possibly overestimate the effect of her husband's unemployment on her labour market transitions, as wives of unemployed men will tend to have lower earning potential than wives of employed men, and this may mean that they are less likely to enter the labour market, regardless of their husband's status.

13. For a thorough treatment of censoring see Allison (1984).

14. As on both surveys education is recorded at yearly intervals, at the time of the survey we imputed the month of change as being June.

15. For further details of the measurement of both educational qualifications and macro-economic indicators see the Appendix at the end of the book.

16. The results are not presented for reasons of space, but are available from the author on request.

17. Ideally, we would have data on the number of hours the women worked, but we believe that even the rough distinction between full- and part-time is more informative than a simple focus on all employment.

18.  They might also find short-hours part-time work, but the effect may be masked as we cannot distinguish short-hours part-time work from longer-hours part-time work with our data.
19.  For other transitions presented in Table 6.5, the results tend to be not statistically significant, partly because of the low number of cases making certain transitions.

# APPENDIX

*Table 6.1.A*  *Estimates of parameters of hazard rates – transition from labour force inactivity to employment, Britain and Germany, model 1*

|  | Britain | | Germany | |
|---|---|---|---|---|
|  | Coefficient | p-value | Coefficient | p-value |
| Wife's age | −0.003 | 0.008 | −0.006 | 0.000 |
| *Wife's education* | | | | |
| *Ref: incomplete or* | | | | |
| *lower secondary* (1ab) | | | | |
| Basic vocational (1c) | +0.048 | 0.811 | −0.351 | 0.018 |
| Secondary voc. (2ac) | −0.119 | 0.444 | +0.668 | 0.007 |
| Secondary gen. (2bc) | −0.111 | 0.495 | −0.293 | 0.094 |
| Tertiary (3ab) | +0.421 | 0.007 | +0.231 | 0.316 |
| *Ref: husband employed* | | | | |
| Husband unemployed | −0.534 | 0.019 | +0.658 | 0.021 |
| Husband out of the labour force | −0.767 | 0.000 | −0.065 | 0.752 |
| Husband's age | +0.001 | 0.304 | +0.003 | 0.001 |
| *Husband's education* | | | | |
| *Ref: incomplete or lower* | | | | |
| *secondary* (1ab) | | | | |
| Basic vocational (1c) | +0.074 | 0.740 | +0.627 | 0.005 |
| Secondary voc. (2ac) | +0.009 | 0.956 | +1.167 | 0.007 |
| Secondary gen. (2bc) | −0.182 | 0.233 | +0.356 | 0.153 |
| Tertiary (3ab) | −0.275 | 0.056 | +0.483 | 0.071 |
| *Ref: no. of children* | | | | |
| No. of children aged 5–16 | +0.300 | 0.000 | +0.076 | 0.149 |
| No. of children aged 3–5 | −0.059 | 0.635 | −0.017 | 0.877 |
| No. of children under 3 | −0.251 | 0.037 | +0.057 | 0.568 |
| Regional unemployment rate | +0.026 | 0.386 | −0.021 | 0.303 |
| Proportion of time employed | +1.167 | 0.000 | +1.823 | 0.000 |
| Constant | −4.157 | 0.000 | −3.980 | 0.000 |
| −2 log-likelihood | 3,848.396 | | 5,172.313 | |

*Table 6.2.A   Estimates of parameters of hazard rates – transition from employment to labour force inactivity, Britain and Germany, model 4*

|  | Britain | | Germany | |
|---|---|---|---|---|
|  | Coefficient | p-value | Coefficient | p-value |
| Wife's age | 0.000 | 0.718 | 0.000 | 0.704 |
| *Wife's education* | | | | |
| *Ref: incomplete or* | | | | |
| *lower secondary* (1ab) | | | | |
| Basic vocational (1c) | −0.507 | 0.026 | +0.057 | 0.719 |
| Secondary voc. (2ac) | −0.045 | 0.769 | +0.139 | 0.614 |
| Secondary gen. (2bc) | +0.092 | 0.535 | −0.519 | 0.010 |
| Tertiary (3ab) | −0.208 | 0.169 | −0.426 | 0.087 |
| *Ref: husband employed* | | | | |
| Husband unemployed | −0.318 | 0.352 | −0.638 | 0.130 |
| Husband out of the labour force | +0.699 | 0.000 | +0.067 | 0.727 |
| Husband's age | 0.000 | 0.732 | +0.001 | 0.098 |
| *Husband's education* | | | | |
| *Ref: incomplete or lower* | | | | |
| *secondary* (1ab) | | | | |
| Basic vocational (1c) | −0.252 | 0.228 | +0.228 | 0.314 |
| Secondary voc. (2ac) | +0.077 | 0.638 | +0.253 | 0.565 |
| Secondary gen. (2bc) | −0.320 | 0.049 | +0.365 | 0.161 |
| Tertiary (3ab) | +0.074 | 0.591 | +1.093 | 0.000 |
| *Ref: no. of children* | | | | |
| No. of children aged 5–16 | +0.082 | 0.165 | +0.115 | 0.035 |
| No. of children aged 3–5 | +0.365 | 0.017 | +0.579 | 0.000 |
| No. of children under 3 | +0.741 | 0.000 | +0.991 | 0.000 |
| Regional unemployment rate | +0.028 | 0.337 | +0.006 | 0.772 |
| Proportion of time employed | −2.191 | 0.000 | −1.372 | 0.000 |
| Constant | −4.280 | 0.000 | −4.802 | 0.000 |
| −2 log-likelihood | 4,589.366 | | 5,231.66 | |

# 7.   Conclusions

In this final chapter we seek first of all to summarise our most important findings. We then reflect on these findings in the light of the typologies we discussed in Chapter 1, assessing how much the findings support, qualify or undermine these approaches. Previously, we have discussed these typologies in the light of individual chapters: here we summon all the available evidence from the different chapters. In keeping with the focus on institutions and policies, we then discuss some policy implications of the findings. We also discuss some methodological issues and reflect on some insights we have gained into both comparative and longitudinal research. Finally, we give the reader a sense of how research of this kind might proceed, as we outline some strategies for future research.

## 7.1   COMPARING UNEMPLOYED MEN AND WOMEN IN BRITAIN AND GERMANY

In the context of different state responses to the challenge of unemployment, it was the task of this book to investigate outcomes for individual unemployed men and women in Britain and Germany. What have we found?

### 7.1.1   Comparing Unemployment and Poverty

Our first area of analysis (Chapter 4) was the financial consequences of unemployment. We measured whether the household income of unemployed individuals, adjusted for household composition, was below various proportions of the average income in their country. We thereby measured relative financial deprivation, often considered a guide to whether or not people have the material resources to participate in the normal activities of their society. Overall, we find that the British unemployed are much more at risk of income poverty than the German unemployed. This is the case for a range of income poverty measures and equivalence scales.

With regard to type of benefit, in Germany there are clear advantages to having worked and contributed to the unemployment insurance fund. In Britain, the difference in income poverty rates between those unemployed receiving contribution-based benefits and those receiving means-tested benefits is smaller than in Germany. There is not such a clear advantage, in terms of income poverty at least, in receiving insurance-based benefit in Britain.

There are major differences in the income experience of unemployment across different household types. In both countries there is a 'cushioning' effect of a second earner. Unemployment hits income hardest when the breadwinner becomes unemployed in a single breadwinner household or when a single person becomes unemployed. However, the cushioning effect is most apparent in Britain, where single people are over 16 times more likely to be income poor than those living in a household with another earner; in Germany, single people are only five times more likely to be poor. The exception to this finding is unemployed lone mothers living independently. Lone mothers living independently are at much greater risk of income poverty in Germany than in Britain.[1]

In terms of gender differences, in both countries we find unemployed women less likely to be poor than unemployed men. Our interpretation is that the cushioning effect of the partner's income would seem to outweigh any disadvantage women suffer relative to men in receipt of benefit.[2] This is not to say that women do not suffer any consequences of unemployment, nor that all unemployed women are less vulnerable to poverty than men. In addition, this finding assumes that households share resources. We discuss the implications below.

In addition to cross-sectional analysis, we subjected our hypotheses about income poverty to further scrutiny using panel data. In particular, we responded to the criticism that with cross-sectional analysis it is difficult to distinguish between association and causation, that the explanation of our findings may simply be that the unemployed are disproportionately drawn from the ranks of the poor in Britain. However, looking at those who are employed one year and unemployed the next, we find that there is indeed a greater fall in income in Britain than in Germany, consistent with our hypothesis and previous findings.

A limited number of cases means we cannot always distinguish East Germany, which in the mid-1990s had the same benefit system as West Germany but a rather different labour market.[3] Where we do distinguish East and West Germany, we discover that, overall, the financial impact of unemployment in East Germany is not as great as in either West Germany or Britain. Our interpretation is that the combination in East Germany of more extensive insurance benefits, because of longer and more continuous work histories, and of more prevalent dual-earner households means that the economic consequences of unemployment are not so great. However, the very small number of 'marginal' unemployed in East Germany – those receiving social assistance and unemployed lone mothers – are even more disadvantaged relative to other unemployed people than in West Germany.

### 7.1.2 Comparing Durations of Unemployment

In Chapter 5 we compared the process of escape from unemployment using event history modelling in Britain and West Germany. In many of our typologies the German system is characterised as one that favours 'insiders' – those with continuous employment records. We widen the idea of the institutional regulation of unemployment beyond the benefit system to include employment regulation, the education system and the family. We identified a number of weaker labour market groups – women, the low-skilled and the young – and compared their durations of unemployment. We explored the argument that the German system may leave these weaker labour market groups at greater risk of remaining unemployed.

The most notable finding of the chapter is that gender differences in the duration of unemployment are much greater in Germany than in Britain. In particular, being married with children under five-years-old has a strong effect on German women's unemployment durations, and not such a marked effect for British women. Women in Britain may more easily find jobs that do not conflict with family responsibilities: this seems particularly relevant for mothers of children of school-going age, who we find to have shorter durations of unemployment than women with no children. We argue that the greater availability of part-time work in Britain may be one of the factors explaining this cross-national difference. We conclude that women in Germany are indeed one 'weaker' labour market group that is at greater risk of remaining unemployed. Though we might expect family situation to have certain effects on women's unemployment, these findings are a strong reminder that we cannot generalise from the experience of one country to all countries.

Comparing the unemployment durations of the young unemployed (under 25s) with the prime-age unemployed, however, we find no evidence to support the hypothesis that the young unemployed are disadvantaged in Germany. Though the German labour market may be more regulated, our findings instead support the argument that the German system of education and training plays a crucial role in transitions for most young people. The young unemployed in Britain also escape unemployment more quickly than the older unemployed. In terms of unemployment duration, then, young people are not disadvantaged in either country.

Using education as a proxy for skill level, we examined the effect of education on escape from unemployment. We found that education has a strong impact on the duration of unemployment in both countries. Those with lower qualifications have longer durations of unemployment than those with higher qualifications.

Finally we compared the durations of unemployment of those who received unemployment compensation with those who did not. Our findings do not support the idea that durations are longer for those receiving benefit in the insurance system, as Schmid and Reissert (1996) propose. Compared to those who do not receive benefit, it is in Britain that those who receive unemployment compensation have longer durations of unemployment, not in Germany. The exception to this is those aged over 57 in Germany: here durations are longer for those who receive benefits than those who do not. However, limitations of the data and method lead us to be cautious in our conclusions about the effect of unemployment compensation on the duration of unemployment.

### 7.1.3   Comparing Partners' Employment

Given that we find household employment to have such a strong influence on poverty among the unemployed, it seemed highly relevant to investigate how benefits might affect household employment. In the debate on means-tested and insurance benefits, discussed in Chapter 1, it is argued that means-testing can lead to a particularly high disincentive for partners of the unemployed to work, a disincentive that does not apply for insurance benefits. Is the greater reliance on means-testing in the British system contributing to the growth of workless households there?

Here we find important differences between Britain and Germany. In Britain, women are less likely to move into employment when their husband becomes unemployed than when the husband is employed. In Germany, the opposite is the case: women are more likely to move into employment when their partner becomes unemployed. We interpret these findings as providing evidence of an added-worker effect in Germany and a disincentive effect of benefits in Britain. For low-income couples in Britain, when the husband becomes unemployed there is a penalty attached to the couple supplementing the – already low – household income by the wife working part-time. This finding has implications for the polarisation of worklessness and income poverty, which we discuss in Section 7.3.1 below. However, the effect of a husband's unemployment and the benefits he receives depends on whether or not the woman already has a job. In cases where a woman is already employed, we find that she is no more likely to leave her job if her husband is unemployed than if he is employed. This is true in both countries.

## 7.2 THEORETICAL REFLECTIONS ON WELFARE PROVISION FOR THE UNEMPLOYED

What are the implications of these findings for the different approaches to comparing welfare states and unemployment discussed in Chapter 1? In Chapter 1 we noted two common features of the different approaches. The first is that welfare states differ – institutions matter. In Chapter 3 we argued that British and German welfare provision for the unemployed do indeed differ fundamentally in approach. In Germany, compensation for unemployment is dominated by insurance provision; unemployment is seen as a risk that individuals themselves insure themselves against, with some support from employers and the state. In Britain, means-tested benefits now dominate welfare provision for the unemployed. The unemployed are seen as a group who, in the absence of their own resources, need to be protected from poverty by the state. However, we also note that means-tested benefits are the only option for some of the unemployed in Germany. Likewise, some of the British unemployed receive insurance benefits.

The second common feature of the different approaches is the idea that principles of welfare provision stratify outcomes for the unemployed. Our detailed analysis of outcomes has shown that different approaches to welfare provision for the unemployed do indeed translate into different outcomes. However, the picture is not always straightforward; in particular, an important finding is that other institutions also matter, especially the family and the market.[4] We discuss this point in more depth in Section 7.2.2 below.

### 7.2.1 Exploring Typologies

We now turn to consider the implications of our findings for individual typologies of welfare. It is important to note that our aim was not to test these typologies in any systematic way, but rather to use insights from them to provide a framework for our comparison. In any case, the focus of this book is welfare provision for the unemployed, and the scope of some of the typologies is much broader than this. Our conclusions are of necessity limited to those aspects of the typologies that we investigated empirically.

Esping-Andersen characterises Germany as having a more stratified, status-based system of welfare provision than Britain. Probing a bit more deeply into how the different systems operate in practice, in Chapter 3 we noted that in Germany the amount of benefit the unemployed receive depends to a large extent on their previous employment. In Britain, benefits are, as Esping-Andersen suggests, more likely to be based on need. When we look at poverty risk among the unemployed, we find that poverty risk in Germany is linked to past work history, much more than in Britain. However, in the

British system, a substantial minority do receive benefits based on their past work record, while in Germany there is a residual assistance scheme, which does not perform well in replacing market income.

In Gallie and Paugam's (2000) typology of unemployment welfare regimes, the liberal welfare system (Britain) puts an emphasis on poverty alleviation but the German employment-centred system is expected to protect the income of the unemployed better. The findings of Chapter 4 confirm Gallie and Paugam's predictions; ironically the British system is less effective at preventing poverty than the German system, at each level of income poverty considered, despite the stated aim of poverty alleviation. We also find that employment history is more rewarded in the German system, with a residual group without any contributions (those receiving social assistance) suffering particularly high levels of poverty. This corresponds to Gallie and Paugam's characterisation of the scheme as one of insiders and outsiders. This insider–outsider theme is echoed in Chapter 5. Here we find that in Germany one group of labour market outsiders – women – have particularly long durations of unemployment. By contrast another group of potential outsiders, young people, have shorter durations of unemployment in Germany. The low-skilled have longer durations of unemployment – but for the most part to no greater extent than in Britain.

With regard to gender-sensitive approaches to welfare states, in Chapter 3 we noted that both welfare systems favour unemployed men. In both countries women are disadvantaged in entitlement to insurance benefits, as more of them have discontinuous work histories or work part-time. In Britain, the system of means-testing means that married women who become unemployed typically have to rely on their partner's income.

Nevertheless, we find that in both countries, unemployed women, though disadvantaged in terms of entitlement, are less vulnerable to poverty overall than unemployed men. However, this finding is based on the assumption that household income is shared equally. If this assumption does not hold, it may well be that women, when they lose their own source of income from employment, are worse off than we estimate, as discussed in Section 7.4.2 below. There is no indication of a substantial difference between Britain and Germany in this regard, as Daly (1996) might have predicted. However, in support of Daly's analysis (2000), we find that unemployed lone mothers living independently in Germany are much more at risk of poverty than in Britain, though the number of cases is small.

Our findings in Chapter 4 do not support the hypothesis that single breadwinner households are favoured in the British and German welfare systems (Lewis and Ostner 1994) – at least they are not well protected when that single breadwinner becomes unemployed. In both systems single breadwinner households fare very badly if the breadwinner becomes unemployed.

Those who fare best are dual-earner households. However the compensation systems may be organised in principle, dual breadwinner households are much better protected from the income risk of unemployment, especially in Britain.

Consistent with the expectations derived from the gender-sensitive typologies of welfare, in Chapter 5 we find that family situation is particularly salient for women's unemployment. Women with young children have longer durations of unemployment than women with no children. The fact that this is particularly true of Germany supports Daly's (1996) argument. However, we also note that the age of children is important; unemployed mothers in Britain whose children are over five actually have shorter durations of unemployment than women without children.

Finally, we should reiterate at this point that the main thrust of the gender typologies is to integrate the private, unpaid sector into the analysis of welfare. While the insights of the gender-sensitive typologies were very useful for an analysis of gender and unemployment, investigating unemployment only gives a very partial empirical assessment of these typologies.

Schmid and Reissert (1996) contrast means-tested and insurance systems, and argue that Britain and Germany are examples. We argue in Chapter 3 that, while true for the majority of the unemployed, this characterisation should be somewhat qualified, as both countries combine elements of both means-testing and insurance benefits. Regarding poverty outcomes, our findings provide evidence that the German, insurance-based system is better at protecting incomes for the unemployed overall than the British means-tested system, as Schmid and Reissert suggest. However, those receiving means-tested benefit in Germany are not so well protected, and the level of means-tested benefit is also important. As Nolan et al. (2000) point out, Ireland is an example of a means-tested system where poverty rates are substantially lower than in Britain, largely because the benefits are set at a higher rate. Contrary to Schmid and Reissert, it is not only the institutional features of the benefit system that matter, but also the level of benefits, and the level of benefits may change within the existing institutional structure. Variation within institutional structures over time is important for outcomes, and tends to be underemphasised by comparative typologies. Here our discussion in Chapter 3 of changes in the last decades to the British benefit system is important, and we return to this point later in this chapter.

Regarding Schmid and Reissert's argument that means-tested systems reduce moral hazard, our evidence is limited by the data. With the evidence available to us we find, contrary to Schmid and Reissert, a limited effect of receipt of benefit on the duration of unemployment in Britain, and no such effect in Germany. In addition, Schmid and Reissert make the point that it is in situations of 'almost indeterminate' benefit duration that we should expect the greatest moral hazard. Comparing Britain and Germany, in practice it is means-tested benefits, not insurance-based benefits, that are in almost all cases of unlimited duration.

An important aspect of the comparison between welfare-based and insurance-based systems – not included in Schmid and Reissert's typology – is the disincentive that means-tested benefits create for a partner's employment. In Chapter 6 we show that in Britain women are less likely to move into part-time work when the husband is receiving means-tested benefits. This problem does not arise with insurance benefits, as they are paid on an individual basis.

The final typology we discuss contrasts rigid and flexible labour markets, highlighting the role of labour market regulation in understanding unemployment. We tested a particular hypothesis emerging from this approach, that labour market regulation affects the structure of unemployment. The hypothesis is that weaker labour market groups – women, the young and the low-skilled – have longer durations of unemployment in more regulated labour markets like Germany than in more flexible labour markets like Britain (Esping-Andersen 1998). We find that for unemployed women in Germany this is indeed the case – their unemployment durations are longer than unemployed men – in contrast to Britain. However, for other groups the hypothesis is not supported. We find that the young unemployed have shorter durations of unemployment in Germany than the prime-age group (aged 25–39), while in relative terms those with lower educational qualifications do not have longer unemployment durations in Germany than they do in Britain. In explaining unemployment durations, we argue that it is important to consider not just the state regulation of employment and unemployment, but also other institutional factors, in this case the education and training system.

### 7.2.2   Limitations of Typologising

One important conclusion of this book for the typologies considered is that for a comparative analysis of unemployment, it is important to consider the interaction of multiple institutions – the labour market, education system, family and welfare state. In terms of evaluating outcomes for the unemployed, any typology solely based on unemployment compensation, for example, will be lacking.

The need to take into account patterns of family employment and support becomes clear in the analysis of poverty among the unemployed in Chapter 4, where family situation is crucial, in durations of unemployment for women with young children in Chapter 5, and in the analysis of the effect of unemployment on the labour market participation of partners (Chapter 6). While gender-sensitive typologies of welfare do highlight the role of the family, as do Gallie and Paugam's (2000) and indeed Esping-Andersen's (1999) more recent typology, albeit to a lesser extent, the issue of entitlement to benefits and how welfare interacts with family structures has far from fully been incorporated into welfare typologies. In particular, as noted in Chapter 6, an additional dimension to welfare typologies should be the degree of 'spousal autonomy', i.e. the degree to which spouses are treated as dependent or independent by social security systems.

Gender typologies of welfare states, to be applicable to unemployment, need to be sensitive to market differences and how these affect women's employment and unemployment, as highlighted in Chapter 5 on women's unemployment durations. Equally, theories of the labour market and its regulation need to account for other institutions, such as the system of education and training, as illustrated by youth unemployment durations in Chapter 5. However, this is not to advocate a typology where institutions interact so closely that, almost by definition, a type of welfare state is wedded to a type of labour market. Esping-Andersen (1990), for example, couples welfare states closely with labour market structures.[5] Given that different combinations of institutions may produce different outcomes, in the comparative analysis of unemployment it would seem useful to allow different institutions – such as the labour market, the education system, the family and the welfare state – to vary independently, and to investigate the interaction between them.

A second important limitation of typologising is that typologies tend to be static and seek to 'fix' the characteristics of welfare regimes (see also Daly 1997). Most do not even attempt to consider regime change. Even where scholars do attempt to incorporate 'trajectories of change' into their typology (as, for example, in Esping-Andersen 1990), there is still a sense in which these paths are predetermined by the logic of the typology. There is a temptation in comparative research not to muddy the water: clear differences that persist over time are easier to conceptualise. The idea of specifying diverse paths of reform and how these emerge is not usually high on the agenda of comparative research. A dynamic approach to comparative research using longitudinal data may force us to be more rigorous in our typologising and to overcome some of the problems of static comparison. Chapter 3 showed that welfare provision can change quite rapidly, and a comparison of Britain and Germany 10 years after the analysis in this book might yield rather different results. Unfortunately the span of available data in Britain was not sufficient to incorporate these major policy shifts, but the point here is that it is only with a longitudinal perspective that we open up the possibility. Incorporating a dynamic approach remains a task for future research.

Nevertheless our use of typologies to generate hypotheses in this book was well-rewarded. They proved a rich source of hypotheses, highlighting different axes of variation and bringing coherence to the policies and outcomes analysed. However, each one alone provides a somewhat incomplete picture. Their simplicity is both a strength – and a limitation.

## 7.3   POLICY IMPLICATIONS

While much of this book has been concerned with the comparison of two social policy regimes, in general it has not highlighted the implications of findings for current or future policy. In this section we reflect on some of the implications. In particular we discuss our findings in the light of the criteria or rhetoric of the systems themselves. We consider the different approaches to welfare for the unemployed – means-testing in Britain and social insurance in Germany – and reflect on how they meet, or fail to meet, their aims.

### 7.3.1   The British Approach – Means-testing the Unemployed

Our findings in Britain suggest that, although means-tested benefits require the unemployed to have no other income source, the benefits are not enough to protect the unemployed from income poverty. The rhetoric often used to defend means-tested benefits suggests that their chief purpose is poverty alleviation, but on the criteria we use they fail to achieve this aim. These findings are of particular concern given the growing extent of means-testing of the unemployed in recent years in Britain. In Chapter 3 we noted the dramatic rise in the proportion of the British unemployed reliant on means-tested benefits. In addition, the 1996 reform reduced insurance payments from 12 months to six months, further reducing the proportion of the unemployed receiving insurance benefits. There are no indications that the current Labour government is planning either to reverse these changes or to introduce substantial increases in benefit rates paid to the unemployed, relative to average earnings.

The targeting of means-tested benefits imposes strict conditions on those who receive them. We find the presence of an employed adult in the household to have a significant impact on the well-being of the unemployed and their families – it reduces the likelihood that the family will be income poor. However, the conditions under which means-tested benefits are given require that there be no income from other sources – or rather if there is, then the benefit will be reduced accordingly.

We noted in Chapter 6 that a large proportion of the British unemployed live in households where there is no work. We also showed that the wives of British unemployed men are less likely to move into employment, particularly part-time employment, when their husband becomes unemployed. We interpreted this as a disincentive effect of the benefit. Part-time employment, as noted in Chapter 2, is an area of rapid job growth, especially for women. Many low-income households with small children supplement their income through a second earner, usually the wife, working part-time. This option is strongly discouraged by the means-tested benefit system as it operated in Britain in the period analysed.

There is some evidence in Britain of a recognition of the problems of a benefit system that discourages participation when nobody in the household is working. There have been some measures to increase in-work benefits like tax credits, and benefit withdrawal rates have been reduced in some cases. If the aim is to share resources and employment more evenly, and in particular to promote 'welfare to work' (the strategy espoused by the Labour government), in the context of increased means-testing, the unintended consequences of means-testing should be carefully considered.

### 7.3.2   The German Approach – Insurance Benefits

While insurance benefits avoid some of the problems of means-testing, they must confront the question of who doesn't receive the benefits (Webb 1994).[6] What is available for those who do not qualify for insurance benefit, and under what conditions? Our analysis for Germany suggests that those for whom the social insurance system fails do not fare well at all.

Social assistance (*Sozialhilfe*) is a residual, stigmatised benefit in Germany, which very much falls between the lines of most accounts of welfare for the unemployed in Germany. The results in Chapter 4 show extremely high rates of poverty among those receiving social assistance in Germany. The benefit is received by a minority of the unemployed there, up to approximately 8 per cent in unified Germany, a higher proportion when we take West Germany alone. Indeed, when we compare overall rates of poverty among the unemployed, we find lower rates of poverty in Germany than in Britain. However, were we to compare the poverty outcomes of social assistance recipients alone, we might find the British–German comparison looked somewhat different. The people who rely on social assistance are those with insufficient contributions, who are at the margins of the German labour market – those in temporary jobs and lone mothers. We find a situation where the insurance benefit system rewards those with continuous labour market histories, but not those without.

From the mid-1990s there have been calls to reform social assistance as it is paid to the unemployed in Germany, by merging the two assistance benefits, unemployment assistance and social assistance, into one centrally administered, needs-based benefit for the unemployed (Reissert, forthcoming). It remains to be seen if and under what conditions this reform would be realised. Centralising payments would certainly have the advantage of taking the pressure off local authorities in areas of high unemployment, increasing the redistribution effect of unemployment compensation between federal states.[7] However, if the benefit rate and means-testing criteria of this new benefit were set close to that of social assistance, one might expect a rise in income poverty among the unemployed, given the high rates of poverty found among social assistance recipients in Chapter 4. This may not be true if additional payments are introduced to up social assistance under specific circumstances, or if general benefit levels are set much higher than existing social assistance payments.

Another reform option is to widen the coverage of insurance-based benefits. This approach is particularly appealing, as the changing nature of employment means that the number of those working part-time or with unstable work patterns is likely to increase at the expense of lengthy, continuous careers. Some moves in this direction have recently been made in Germany. In 1999, the coverage of unemployment insurance was extended to part-time workers who work 15 hours a week or earn DM630 or more, though hours or earnings lower than these thresholds are still excluded (O'Reilly and Bothfeld 2002). 'Part-time unemployment benefit' was also introduced in 1999, which replaces benefit for a part-time job that was lost, even if the individual continues working in another part-time job (Reissert forthcoming). Social insurance has recently been widened to cover periods of care like childrearing.[8] These measures could be extended further to cover other periods of work and care. However, as Clasen (1997) notes, there are limits to how coverage could be widened while still receiving the support of the main contributors, whose contributions are deducted from their wages. Such measures may test the solidarity of the social insurance system.

### 7.3.3   Eligibility and Conditions for Benefit

In the late 1990s both public debate and legislation in Germany on the conditionality attached to benefits and job search behaviour seemed to be heading very much in the direction of British policy. As noted in Chapter 3, British policy in the early 1990s had been to sharpen work tests, tighten eligibility and enhance job search activities, and this approach has continued with the introduction of the Jobseekers Allowance in 1996, which has tightened checks on jobseekers and required jobseekers to accept jobs in other occupations after only three months. The New Deal programmes have in general increased the conditionality attached to benefit receipt, and in particular they have intensified job search behaviour.

The debate on work incentives had been delayed in Germany until the mid-1990s, due to a number of factors such as the political inappropriateness of such a debate following reunification and the collapse of the East German economy (Reissert, forthcoming). However, the introduction of a new law in 1998 saw a marked shift in the underlying philosophy of labour market policy towards more British-style regulations (Reissert, forthcoming). In a break with previous German tradition, this law abolished the protection of previous qualifications and defined the suitability of job offers in purely monetary terms. After six months a benefit recipient is required to accept a job offer if the net earnings are higher than unemployment benefit (Sell 1998).[9]

While it is not clear how strictly these regulations are being applied in practice,[10] it may be potentially problematic applying British-style regulations in Germany regarding what is a 'reasonable job' (*Zumutbarkeit* in Germany). Such regulations may be easier to apply in Britain, where credentials are not so fixed. In Germany, where the vocational training system contributes to a labour market organised around occupations, as discussed in Section 2.4, Chapter 2, forcing the unemployed to accept a job outside their occupation is a larger, potentially more problematic step. This is an example of the importance of considering how policy changes in one area – such as welfare policy – may be affected by other institutions, such as the education system.

## 7.4 COMPARATIVE RESEARCH ON UNEMPLOYMENT: METHODOLOGICAL REFLECTIONS AND DIRECTIONS FOR FURTHER RESEARCH

The observation that social science is a compromise between the desirable and the possible is particularly true of comparative research. We are very fortunate that there are fewer problems with data availability than there were some years ago, and while national published data sources may compile rather different sets of national statistics, the surveys used in this book gather information on very similar issues in similar ways. However, even comparisons with reliable, similar datasets face problems of comparability. The more detailed the comparison, the clearer the differences. In the following section we discuss the measurement of unemployment with future research in mind. We then consider some of the benefits and limitations of the comparative and longitudinal perspective we adopted, pointing to avenues for future research.

### 7.4.1 Measuring Unemployment

In Chapter 2 we argued that the internationally defined ILO measure of unemployment was superior for comparative research, and it was a slightly amended version of this we used in Chapter 4. However, the ILO definition has its drawbacks. For example, discouraged workers, particularly older workers, who have not been seeking work actively in the past four weeks are excluded, as is anyone who has done a few hours' casual work in the past week.

For our purposes, a particular problem of the ILO measure is that it is not available for work history data, an issue noted in the Appendix at the back of this book (Section A.2.1). This is not just a problem of the two surveys we use, but has to do with the ILO definition itself. When asking people about their monthly labour force status, as is done in work history surveys, it is unrealistic to expect people to answer questions about their search activity and availability for each month in the past year. This is even truer of longer-term work histories. Recall of past labour force status, in particular unemployment, is itself prone to error, but it seems more unreasonable to expect that people will be able to give information about job search and availability for periods in the past. Thus, if we are to carry out longitudinal analysis of unemployment and labour force transitions, we need to use the definitions of labour force status as they appear in surveys. We can modify the work history data somewhat to make it more comparable, as we did in Chapters 5 and 6, but we cannot construct an ILO definition of unemployment with it. In the compromise between the desirable and the possible, we need to use the information we have in the surveys for analysing labour market transitions, while noting the limitations of the measures from a comparative perspective. If dynamic, innovative modelling of labour market transitions is to develop, this seems the most realistic path available.

### 7.4.2   Intra-household Sharing

Throughout the analysis of income poverty in this book we have assumed that household income is shared equally within households. We argued that while this may be a somewhat crude assumption to make, the assumption of no sharing within the household seems more unrealistic. However, given the strong finding that the income of another earner in the household protects unemployed individuals from the worst consequences of unemployment, equal sharing is an important assumption. If the assumption is wrong in some households, it may mean for example that we underestimate the income poverty of unemployed women, as women are more often dependent on another earner than men. Previous research has argued that women's access to an independent income is crucial for their well-being (Davis and Joshi 1994). If this is the case, those women who move from employment to being unemployed and not even receiving unemployment benefit undergo a particularly striking change.[11]

There are a number of ways in which research on this topic could proceed. One strategy would be to apply a different range of sharing assumptions within households, so that at least if we could not pinpoint how much sharing went on, we could estimate the upper and lower boundaries of individual resources. This is the approach adopted by Davis and Joshi (1994), Sutherland (1997) and Rake (1998), though their studies do not focus specifically on the welfare of the unemployed. A different approach would be to incorporate a focus on sharing into qualitative research on unemployment and poverty, asking more open questions about how resources are shared, and if and how sharing changes as a result of unemployment. Through such research we could obtain a more complete picture of how the financial consequences of unemployment differ for men and women. However, research of this type is particularly difficult to carry out.

### 7.4.3    Incorporating a Rational Choice Perspective

Another fruitful area for further research would be to combine large-scale longitudinal data analysis, such as that in Chapters 5 and 6, with models of individual behaviour using a rational choice framework, as suggested by Blossfeld (1998). How are the patterns we have observed generated at the level of individual processes? A rational choice approach would allow us to incorporate the role of individuals, acting within specific constraints. For example an extension of Chapter 6 would be to model the decision of the wife of an unemployed man whether or not to work, attempting to disentangle the effects of: preferences, including the effect of previous work history and norms of behaviour; available job opportunities; and the potential incentives and disincentives created by the social welfare system. The power of longitudinal analysis in this respect is that we can model the behaviour of individuals as a series of processes, each dependent on past choices.

## NOTES

1.  This finding should be qualified by the fact that for both countries the samples include a low number of cases of lone mothers living independently.
2.  The disadvantage unemployed women suffer in entitlement to benefit is considered in Chapter 3. It is also discussed later in this chapter, when we discuss gender typologies of welfare.
3.  See Chapters 2 and 3 for discussions of the labour markets and benefit systems respectively.
4.  We have not looked in any depth at community support or voluntary groups.
5.  In fact in Chapter 1 we deliberately gave only a partial description of this typology, focusing on welfare for the unemployed.
6.  The following discussion is limited to insurance benefits in Germany. As we have noted elsewhere in the book, insurance benefits in Britain are rather different from those in Germany. Insurance benefits in Britain are much closer to means-tested benefits, particularly in terms of the amount people receive.

7. The Federal Labour Office would pay this benefit, taking financial pressure off the municipalities, who currently pay *Sozialhilfe*.
8. Since 1998, parents returning to the labour market after parental leave (*Elternzeit*) have their entitlement to unemployment insurance (*Arbeitslosengeld*) calculated on the basis of the period prior to the birth of the baby. The period of parental leave is not included (Arbeitskammer des Saarlandes 2002).
9. The new law also requires benefit claimants to prove active job search to remain eligible for benefits.
10. As seen in Table 3.2 in Chapter 3, sanctions in Germany were relatively low, but there has been no research on the effect of recent changes.
11. This would happen in cases where the woman either worked part-time under the earnings or hours threshold, or had intermittent employment, so that she does not qualify for insurance benefit. If her husband has income from employment or benefits she will most likely not qualify for means-tested benefit.

# Appendix

## A.1 DATA SOURCES

The data sources used in this book are the British Household Panel Survey (BHPS) and the German Socio-economic Panel (GSOEP). Both these surveys are nationally representative panel studies: details of these surveys are given below.[1]

### A.1.1 The German Socio-economic Panel

The GSOEP has collected data since 1984 for West Germany and since 1990 for East Germany. There are four different samples in the GSOEP:[2] one of West Germans (A), one of foreigners living in West Germany (B), one of East Germans (C), and one of immigrants to West Germany since 1994 (D). Foreigners, East Germans and immigrants are over-sampled, in order to give large enough samples to analyse these groups separately. Of the four samples, the West German sample A covers persons in private households with a household head who does not belong to the main foreigner group of 'guest workers'. In 1984 it covered 4,528 households. Sample B covers persons in private households with a Turkish, Greek, Yugoslavian, Spanish or Italian household head, and in 1984 had 1,393 households. Sample C covers persons in private households where the household head is an East German citizen. In 1990, at the first wave, the sample size was 2,179 households. Sample D, the immigrant sample, started in 1994/1995 in two different samples. The first sample had 236 households and in 1995 the second sample had 295 households. This sample consists of households in which at least one household member is an 'ethnic' German who moved from Eastern Europe to West Germany after 1984. The analysis in this book was carried out on this 95 per cent sample, the version of the GSOEP made available for researchers outside Germany.

All samples in the GSOEP are multi-stage random samples, which are regionally clustered. While all of the samples were generated using probability sampling, the sampling frames were drawn from somewhat different sources due to the differing nature of the samples. For sample A a list of West German households, based on an electoral list, was the basis for generating the sample. Sample B was generated using immigrant registration records; the East German sample C was generated by creating a sample frame of private addresses drawn from the central residents' database. Sample D was more complex to create, as ethnic German immigrants do not need to register with the government as immigrants, and there is no official census of the population of immigrants.[3]

The interviewer tries to obtain a face-to-face interview with all members in a survey household aged 16 and over. In addition, one person is asked to answer a household-related questionnaire, which covers information on housing and household income, and on children in the household under 16. In principle, all persons who took part in the first wave, as well as their children, whenever born, are to be surveyed in the following years. In the case of residential mobility, the person is then followed within the Federal Republic of Germany, including into institutions (hospitals, nursing homes, etc.). Persons moving into an existing household are surveyed, or followed up if they subsequently leave. Persons moving away from the initial households who split off into new households are followed under a different household identifier; others in this new household are also surveyed. Temporary drop-outs, i.e. persons and households that could not be successfully interviewed in a given year, are followed until there are two consecutive drop-outs or a final refusal. In the GSOEP considerable effort is made to maintain the panel, for example by keeping interviewers consistent. Respondents also receive a lottery ticket.

### A.1.2   The British Household Panel Survey

The BHPS, which began in 1991, is a longitudinal survey of private households in Great Britain. Unlike the German Survey, there is only one sample. The initial selection of households for inclusion in the panel survey was made using a two-stage stratified systematic method. This sample design is an approximately 'equal probability of selection method' (epsem) design. The frame used for the selection of sample units was the small users Postcode Address File (PAF) for Great Britain – England, Wales and Scotland (south of the Caledonian Canal) – excluding Northern Ireland.

In a similar way to the GSOEP, once household membership is determined, interviews are sought with all resident household members aged 16 or over. In addition, proxy interviews with another household member, or telephone interviews, are carried out for eligible members who are either too ill or too busy to be interviewed. As there are no proxy interviews carried out in the GSOEP, information from proxy interviews is not used for analysis using the BHPS.

The follow-up procedure in the British survey is almost identical to the German survey. The sample for each wave thus consists of all adult original sample members plus their natural descendants plus other adult members of their households.[4] If households refuse to be interviewed in one year they are recontacted the following year, if it is thought that the refusal is likely to be for one year only. In the BHPS considerable effort is also made to maintain the sample, including sending a gift voucher after the survey.

### A.1.3 Topics Covered by the Surveys

The core topics in each survey are rather similar, and covered by a stable set of questions each year. The core topics include: population and demography, education and training, labour market and occupational dynamics, earnings, income and social security, housing, health, domestic labour, basic attitudes to life, and life satisfaction. In addition to the core topics in each of the surveys there are also special topics that are covered every couple of years, or in one wave only. For example, in both BHPS and GSOEP in the early waves a detailed employment biography and family biography was collected.

Both surveys then are excellent sources of information for a variety of issues surrounding unemployment and financial resources. They are specifically designed to analyse social change. Below we sketch the main information common to both surveys that is used in this study:

*Data for individuals*:
- gender, age and marital status;
- education and training qualifications;
- health problems;
- monthly calendars or records of labour force activity in the previous year;[5]
- monthly records of social security benefits (especially unemployment compensation);
- long-term labour force participation history since leaving school.

*Data for households*:
- details on other household members, and relationships within the household;
- information about children and their ages;
- region of residence;
- total household income.

Analysis can be conducted both at household and individual level. Information can easily be matched from individuals to households and across years.

### A.1.4    Sample Representativeness and Attrition

While the sampling procedure described above is designed to be as representative as possible, for a variety of reasons the final product may not be entirely representative of the populations in question. In the GSOEP the initial response rates (wave one) were estimated to be between 60 per cent (sample A) and 70 per cent (sample C). In the BHPS the response rate was estimated at 65 per cent of the target population.[6] An additional difficulty for these particular surveys is that they attempt to collect information from the same people year after year. In Table A.1.1 we look at the sample sizes of both surveys and their development over time. We are particularly interested in what proportion of the sample remains in the sample at each wave. For each wave we present the number of respondents in each sample as a proportion of the previous year.[7]

It can be seen from Table A.1.1 that in both surveys much of the drop-out occurs between the first two waves, and those who have stayed until the

*Table A.1.1*    *Development of sample sizes of individuals in the GSOEP (1984–96) and BHPS (1991–96)[8]*

|  | Sample Size (Individuals) | | | Sample Size as a % of Previous Year | | |
|---|---|---|---|---|---|---|
| Year | BHPS | GSOEP samples A & B | GSOEP sample C | BHPS | GSOEP samples A & B | GSOEP sample C |
| 1984 |  | 12,245 |  |  |  |  |
| 1985 |  | 11,090 |  |  | 90.57 |  |
| 1986 |  | 10,646 |  |  | 96.00 |  |
| 1987 |  | 10,516 |  |  | 98.78 |  |
| 1988 |  | 10,023 |  |  | 95.31 |  |
| 1989 |  | 9,710 |  |  | 96.88 |  |
| 1990 |  | 9,519 | 4,453 |  | 98.03 |  |
| 1991 | 9,912 | 9,467 | 4,202 |  | 99.45 | 94.36 |
| 1992 | 8,568 | 9,305 | 4,092 | 86.44 | 98.29 | 97.38 |
| 1993 | 7,839 | 9,206 | 3,973 | 91.49 | 98.94 | 97.09 |
| 1994 | 7,577 | 9,001 | 3,945 | 96.66 | 97.77 | 99.30 |
| 1995 | 7,183 | 8,798 | 3,892 | 94.80 | 97.74 | 98.66 |
| 1996 | 7,132 | 8,606 | 3,882 | 99.29 | 97.82 | 99.74 |

*Sources*:   GSOEP (100 per cent sample) and BHPS.

second wave tend to remain in the sample (Rendtel 1990). This is typical of panel surveys.

Another way of considering the sample size is to look at the last wave sample size as a proportion of the first wave sample size. Here we find that for Britain the 1996 wave sample size was 72.5 per cent of the first wave, while in West Germany the 1996 wave sample size is 70.3 per cent of the first wave sample size (1984). In 1996 the East German (sample C) was 87 per cent of its size in the first wave (1990).

Some types of attrition, such as death, do not necessarily make the samples unrepresentative. Other types of attrition are more problematic. Pischner and Rendtel (1993) in their investigations on the GSOEP conclude that in general it is people who find themselves in stressful life situations who are not as likely to continue to participate – for example, following marriage break-up. Some factors associated with refusal that may be salient for us are low household income and expected loss of job. Rendtel and Büchel (1994), in an article in which they test the effect of attrition on wages estimates, find that there are small if any attrition effects on income equations. The implications of attrition for samples of the unemployed and for poverty estimates are discussed in more detail below.

### A.1.5 Weighting

Given the sample attrition discussed above, and non-response at the first wave, the samples may become unrepresentative. If we wish to draw any conclusions from our samples about the population referred to, we need to weight the sample cases. In the following section our primary focus is on cross-sectional weighting of each wave, which is the weighting used for the poverty analysis in Chapter 4. For the most part, these surveys follow a rather similar procedure for weighting the data. There are two main steps.

In the first step, wave one is weighted to be representative. The first adjustment is for sample design, as it may not be fully representative. For example, in the German survey, foreigners and East Germans are heavily over-sampled relative to the other samples, as discussed in Section A.1.1. Secondly, weights are derived for non-response. This includes non-response at the household level, and non-response of individuals within responding households. In the British case, the weights are rescaled to the raw sample size. A final step for both surveys is to adjust the weights so that they correspond to larger national data sources for the first wave for a certain number of key characteristics.[9] In most cases this means little adjustment to the weights.

In the second step, for each subsequent wave these weights are adjusted according to the probability of the household staying in the sample (the inverse of the drop-out rates for each group), and the probability of non-response at that wave. Thus, for example, in deriving weights for wave two, we take the wave one weights and add an adjustment for the drop-out between wave one and wave two, and then for non-response (e.g. within the household) (see Haisken-De New and Frick 1998 for further details). The result for both surveys are a large number of weights, which are chosen and applied depending on the year in question, the type of analysis and the unit of analysis.

### A.1.6   Choice of Datasets and Reliability of Findings

The main factor driving the choice of datasets was the fact that most of the analysis we wished to carry out in this book is longitudinal. The BHPS and GSOEP are the only sources of longitudinal data of this kind available in Britain and Germany. For this reason there are no comparable data sources with which we can replicate the analysis for the longitudinal analysis in Chapters 5 and 6.

However, much of the analysis of poverty in Chapter 4 is from a cross-sectional perspective. For Germany, the GSOEP has clear advantages over other data sources for analysing poverty: the Microcensus only reports income in banded intervals, and the German expenditure survey, the EVS (Einkommens und Verbrauchstichprobe), is a rather select sample. For Britain, the Family Expenditure Survey (FES) is more commonly used for analysing poverty. However, when we compare estimates from the BHPS using the methodology used in Chapter 4 with those from the FES using the same methodology, we find very little difference in poverty estimates – if anything, a slight underestimation of poverty using the BHPS (see McGinnity 2001 for further details). In addition, in a detailed comparison of poverty estimates using the BHPS and the FES, Jarvis and Jenkins (1995) make a strong case that the BHPS income data is a reliable measure of poverty in Britain.

## A.2   MEASUREMENT ISSUES

### A.2.1   Measuring Unemployment

In this section we discuss the measurement of unemployment in the empirical analysis in some detail. The discussion partly draws on information from the discussion of unemployment definitions in Chapter 2, Section 2.2.1. We compare samples of the unemployed from the two surveys using different definitions of unemployment, and to other equivalent samples from other sources, for example the European Labour Force Survey and the German official statistics on registered unemployment. First we discuss the measure of unemployment used for the analysis of poverty among the unemployed in Chapter 4, and then from the work history files in Chapters 5 and 6.

The ILO definition of unemployment is discussed and used in Chapter 2. We argue that the core of the ILO definition is the idea that the unemployed should be actively seeking work. The measure used in Chapter 4 is a version of the ILO definition that incorporates this idea of actively seeking work. It does not include the availability criterion for either country, as availability was not measured on the British survey in 1993. The advantage of omitting the 'availability for work' requirement usually present in the ILO definition is

*Table A.1.2   Comparing samples of the unemployed in the GSOEP, 1996*

| | ELFS ILO | ILO1 (GSOEP) | ILO2 (GSOEP) | Registered* (GSOEP) | Registered (Official Statistics) |
|---|---|---|---|---|---|
| | (1) | (2) | (3) | (4) | (5) |
| Share of total (%) | 5.0 | 3.6 | 4.0 | 6.9 | |
| Share of labour force** (%) | 8.8 | 6.5 | 7.2 | 11.2 | 10.4 |
| | | (6.3) | (7.0) | (10.8) | |
| Sex: Men (%) | 53.1 | 46.2 | 46.0 | 47.8 | 51.9 |
| Women (%) | 46.9 | 53.8 | 54.0 | 52.2 | 48.1 |
| Age: Under 25 (%) | 12.1 | 16.3 | 20.2 | 11.7 | 12.6 |
| 25–40 (%) | 38.3 | 42.4 | 42.0 | 36.4 | 36.6 |
| 40–55 (%) | 31.0 | 35.0 | 32.1 | 29.1 | 30.2 |
| 55–65 (%) | 18.4 | 6.3 | 5.6 | 22.7 | 20.6 |
| Proportion of sample under the 50% median income poverty line (%) | N/A | 21.0 | 19.8 | 21.0 | N/A |
| Sample size (GSOEP, unweighted) | N/A | 588 | 663 | 1038 | N/A |

*Notes*:
*Registered = registered unemployed.
**Labour force does not include apprentices in the European Labour Force Survey.
Figures in brackets are estimates where apprentices are included in the labour force, as is normally the case in Germany.
All GSOEP analysis is weighted by the cross-sectional individual weight unless otherwise stated. ILO1 = no work last week, job search (three months only) and availability.
ILO2 = no work last week, job search without availability (used in Chapter 4).

*Sources*:   European Labour Force Survey, 1996 (Eurostat, 1997); *Statistisches Jahrbuch*, 1996; *Amtliche Nachrichten der Bundesanstalt für Arbeit* (ANBA) & GSOEP, 1996.

that those who need to make more complex arrangements to take up work, for example, women with small children, will be included among the unemployed.[10] Our modified ILO measure includes: those who (1) have actively sought work in a specified period (one month for Britain; three months for Germany) and (2) have not been in employment (in Britain, during the last week; in Germany, the principal economic status is used).

When we compare the German ILO sample to published European Labour Force Survey (ELFS) estimates, we find that a smaller proportion of the labour force is unemployed in the GSOEP than in the ELFS, despite the fact that we use a somewhat broader definition of unemployment in the GSOEP. One possible reason for this is sample attrition, i.e. that after 12 years there are fewer of the unemployed in the sample than at the beginning of the survey. As discussed above, those with low incomes and in stressful life situations are more likely to drop out of the panel (Pischner and Rendtel 1993). It is difficult to assess how this overall lower unemployment rate would affect our results. We can also see that the sample without the availability criterion, which we use in Chapter 4, contains a greater proportion of women, young people, and fewer of the unemployed in receipt of benefit than the strict ILO definition, as reported in the European Labour Force Survey or in the GSOEP itself.

Looking at Table A.1.3, we see that for Britain, like in Germany, the sample used in Chapter 4 also makes up a smaller proportion of the labour force than the official ILO definition reported in the European Labour Force Survey 1993 (Eurostat, 1995), despite the fact that the definition is somewhat wider. The sample used also has a greater proportion of men than the ELFS sample and has a greater proportion of under 25s. So, while the German survey has a greater proportion of women than the ELFS, the British survey has a greater proportion of men. In both surveys the samples tend to be younger.

For this book, a particular problem of the ILO measure of unemployment is that it is not available in work history data. This is to do with the way the ILO definition is constructed. When asking people about their monthly labour force status it is not feasible to expect people to answer questions about their search activity and availability for each month in the past year. This is even more problematic when applied to longer-term work histories. Thus as we carry out longitudinal analysis of unemployment and labour force transitions, we need to work with the definitions of labour force status as they appear on our surveys: registered unemployed in Germany, self-defined unemployed in Britain. The following discussion compares the samples used in Chapters 5 and 6 to the various ILO definitions, in 1993 (Britain) and 1996 (Germany).[11]

In the German survey, the sample of registered unemployed excludes those seeking unemployment under their own initiative, particularly the 'silent

*Table A.1.3   Comparing samples of the unemployed in the BHPS, 1993*

|  | ELFS ILO 1993 | ILO2 (Without Availability, BHPS) | Self-defined (BHPS) |
|---|---|---|---|
|  | (1) | (2) | (3) |
| Share of total (%) | 5.0 | 5.1 | 5.4 |
| Share of labour force (%) | 10.3 | 8.3 | 9.1 |
| Sex: Men (%) | 67.3 | 60.2 | 69.0 |
| Women (%) | 32.7 | 39.8 | 31.0 |
| Age: Under 25 (%) | 29.6 | 37.4 | 30.0 |
| 25–40 (%) | 36.6 | 33.0 | 31.7 |
| 40–55 (%) | 22.9 | 22.1 | 27.4 |
| 55+ (%) | 10.6 | 7.4 | 10.9 |
| Proportion of sample under the 50% median income poverty line (%) | N/A | 33.6 | 36.0 |
| Sample size, BHPS (unweighted) | N/A | 529 | 551 |

*Notes*:   All analysis is weighted by the cross-sectional individual weight unless otherwise stated. ILO2 = no work last week, job search without availability information (used in Chapter 4). Information on availability for work is not available for 1993.

*Source*:   European Labour Force Survey, 1993 (Eurostat, 1995) & BHPS, 1993.

reserve' (see Section 2.2.1 in Chapter 2). Comparing samples of the unemployed in 1996, we find that there are more women in the registered definition on the GSOEP than on the European Labour Force Survey (Table A.1.2, columns (1) and (4). The age distribution of these two samples is rather similar, with somewhat more registered unemployed in the 55 to 65 category. Comparing the different samples from the GSOEP, we find that while the gender distribution is similar, there is a greater proportion of the unemployed in the older age categories in the sample of registered unemployed than in either ILO sample from the GSOEP – Table A.1.2, columns (2), (3) and (4). The German sample of registered unemployed on the GSOEP is much larger than either of the ILO samples (see Table A.1.2).

In Britain, the definition of unemployment is self-defined. We discuss some of the drawbacks of self-defined unemployment in Chapter 2. In particular, women tend to be under-represented by this definition. Women are less likely to define themselves as unemployed because they are less likely to be receiving benefit, more likely to be seeking part-time work and also, because of domestic responsibilities, less likely to see themselves as 'without work'. If we compare the British sample of self-defined unemployed with the ELFS ILO estimates the samples actually look rather similar – see Table A.1.3, columns (1) and (3). There is a somewhat smaller proportion of women in the self-defined sample and they tend to be older, but otherwise similar. Compared to the ILO sample for Britain we use in Chapter 4, the self-defined sample is older, and has a much smaller proportion of women – see Table A.1.3, columns (2) and (3).

Clearly these samples are picking up somewhat different groups of the unemployed. For example, if we use the European Labour Force Survey ILO measure as a benchmark then in Chapters 5 and 6 we will have more women in the German sample and somewhat fewer women in the British sample. Given the limitations of the survey data, there is little we can do to modify the samples. However, we did make one modification to the German sample. With the registered definition of unemployment, respondents may be working short hours or in training at the same time. In order to make the definitions more compatible, considerable effort was made to modify the German spells to record unemployment only in those cases where unemployed respondents reported neither parallel paid employment nor parallel participation in formal education and training in the period. A similar strategy is employed by Gangl (forthcoming) in his comparison of West German and American unemployment spells. So for the analysis in Chapters 5 and 6 we use a modified version of registered unemployment for Germany, and self-defined unemployment for Britain.

This example of defining unemployment is linked to a wider issue in the German data, which is that individuals may report multiple statuses in any given month, while for our analysis it is necessary to have one status per month. For the analysis in Chapters 5 and 6 we set the following priorities: employment, education, unemployment and other. Information about parallel statuses is then ignored. For example, if a woman reports part-time work and home duties in any month we take her status to be part-time employment. This strategy may lead to an overestimation of employment and an underestimation of other states, but it is judged to be most compatible with the British data.

A final problem with the measurement of unemployment is how it is reported in retrospective data of the type used in Chapters 5 and 6. Some work has been carried out on the reliability of retrospective data. Elias (1997) finds significant under-reporting of unemployment in the BHPS. He concludes that unemployment data collected by recall methods and relating to periods more than three years earlier are unreliable. Paull (1997) similarly finds significant under-reporting of unemployment spells, particularly of short duration. However 'inter-wave accounts', i.e. the monthly calendars describing the individual's labour market status between waves, are considered much more reliable (Halpin 1997). These are what we use for both Britain and Germany. By using inter-wave accounts, respondents are never asked to recall unemployment more than two years before the date of interview, and in the majority of cases only 12 months before. We might expect some under-reporting of very short spells of unemployment to remain, but do not expect this to substantially affect the cross-national comparison.

### A.2.2 Measuring Education and Macroeconomic Fluctuations in Chapters 5 and 6

In the following section we describe the measurement of two important covariates used in both Chapters 5 and 6, namely educational qualifications and macroeconomic fluctuations.

Educational qualifications are coded according to a variant of the 'casmin' schema (König, Lüttinger and Müller 1988). This schema was initially developed to investigate social mobility from a comparative perspective, but has been widely used to research the effect of education on labour market outcomes (see for examples chapters in Shavit and Müller 1998; Brauns, Gangl and Scherer 1999). Indeed it is particularly well-suited to comparative research. The schema distinguishes educational credentials according to hierarchical level (length, quality and value of education) on the one hand, and general versus vocational orientation on the other. For most of our analyses, we employ a five-category version: (1ab) incomplete and lower secondary; (1c) basic vocational qualification; (2acvoc) secondary vocational qualification; (2bc) intermediate and higher general secondary; (3ab) tertiary (third level). The category 1ab is the reference category. The vocational–academic distinction offered by this schema is particularly useful for a British–German comparison, given that vocational training is much more prevalent and significant in Germany.

As we expect macroeconomic fluctuations to affect the transition to employment in Chapters 5 and 6, we introduce two measures of macroeconomic labour demand. In general, total employment follows developments in the macroeconomy, and can be seen as a crude indicator of the relative difficulty of finding a job.[12] In Chapter 2 we discuss changes in total employment: Figure 2.7 shows the percentage change in total employment in Britain and Germany for the period 1985–96. In both countries we see considerable fluctuations in total employment throughout the period, suggesting that we need to consider these changes in our models of labour market transitions. Our primary measure of macroeconomic labour market demand is simply percentage change in total employment in the year the unemployment spell started.

However, we also expect to find variation in the difficulty in finding a job in different regions of each country. It is indeed the case in Britain and Germany that unemployment rate varies by region.[13] To account for this, we combine spatial and temporal variation in the demand for labour by introducing regional unemployment rates for each region for each year. We use this as an alternative measure of labour market demand.[14] Data are taken for Britain from Labour Market Trends, and for West Germany from the *Statistisches Jahrbuch*. Hannan, Schömann and Blossfeld (1990) use a similar method of introducing changes in macroeconomic circumstances when examining sex and sector differences in the dynamics of wage growth. This is an example of what Blossfeld describes as a 'parallel process at the macro level' (Blossfeld 1998, p. 237).

## NOTES

1.  Much of the information below describing the surveys draws on the survey documentation, e.g. Haisken-De New and Frick (1998) and Taylor et al. (1999).
2.  Since 1998 additional samples have been added to the GSOEP. As they are outside the scope of this study, they are not discussed here.
3.  To locate immigrant households, address screening was carried out, firstly by a random walk method and then snowball sampling to increase sample size. Details of this process are found in Burkhauser et al. (1997).
4.  In the BHPS these new members, for the most part, are not followed up if they move house, unlike in Germany. They will only be reinterviewed if they are still co-resident with original sample members.
5.  In the GSOEP respondents are asked to fill out a calendar documenting their labour force status in the previous calendar year. In the BHPS they are asked to give the specific dates of labour force status changes.
6.  The 65 per cent figure for the BHPS refers to completed household interviews.
7.  Note that each new wave will include some new respondents, drawn into the sample in ways described in Sections A.1.1 and A.1.2, though these are a tiny proportion of the overall sample.
8.  Individuals with successful (full) interviews.
9.  In the GSOEP the marginal distributions of the first wave were matched to information on the sex, age and nationality of the head of household; the household size; the sex, age, marital status and nationality of the resident population of individuals; the sex and type of school of school children; and the sex, age and employment of those gainfully employed. In the BHPS marginal distributions for household tenure, household size and number of cars were corrected to the population marginals at the household and individual level. The same variables were used to make adjustments at the individual level (i.e. the population aged 16 or over were adjusted by tenure, household size, number of cars, age and sex).
10. See Russell (1996), Chapter 2, for a discussion of this issue.
11. It should be borne in mind that these two cross-sections will be a small part of the total period in these chapters (e.g. in Chapter 5, 1984–93 in Germany and 1991–96 in Britain).
12. It is, though, not unproblematic, as there could also be changes in, say, labour market participation rates, which mean that, although employment is growing, so too is the labour force, with the result that competition for jobs is still tough. However, as we are only interested in comparisons across time, as long as the labour market participation does not change considerably, changes in total employment should give us some indication of macroeconomic fluctuation as it affects the labour market.

13. In Britain, unemployment was particularly high in Northern England and Scotland in the 1980s, though in the recession of the 1990s this was not so much the case, and unemployment was consistently high all over the country (*Employment Gazette*, various years). In 1996 the Northern region showed higher unemployment than the South, though regional disparities were not as great as in the early 1980s. In West Germany, broadly speaking, unemployment is consistently lower in the southern federal states of Bavaria and Baden-Württemberg, and higher in Bremen, Hamburg, Niedersachsen and also Saarland (Statistisches Bundesamt 1998)

14. For Germany, the regions are based on Bundesländer: Baden-Württemberg; Bavaria; Bremen; Schleswig/Holstein; Hamburg; Lower Saxony; North Rhine Westphalia; Hessen; Rheinland-Saarland; West Berlin; Former GDR. Baden-Württemberg is used as the reference category. For Britain the regions are: Anglia, South East & London; North; Midlands; South West; Wales; Scotland; moved outside Britain. Anglia, South East and London is the reference category. As was the case with education, location is only measured at time of interview. Moving date is imputed to be six months before the interview.

# References

Allison, P. (1982), 'Discrete-time methods for the analysis of event histories' in S. Leinhardt (ed.), *Sociological Methodology*, San Francisco: Jossey-Bass.

Allison, P. (1984), *Event History Analysis*, Newbury Park, CA: Sage.

Allmendinger, J. (1989), 'Educational systems and labour market outcomes', *European Sociological Review*, **5** (3).

Andress, H.J. (1995), 'Analysen zum unteren Einkommensbereich – Auf und Abstiege, Ereignisse, Reaktionen und subjektives Wohlbefinden' in W. Zapf, J. Schupp and R. Habich (eds), *Lebenslagen im Wandel: Sozialberichterstattung im Laengschnitt*, Frankfurt: Campus Verlag.

Appelbaum, E. and R. Schettkat (1990), 'The impacts of structural and technological change: an overview', in E. Appelbaum and R. Schettkat (eds), *Labor Market Adjustments to Structural and Technological Progress*, New York: Praeger.

Arbeitskammer des Saarlandes (2002), *Mutterschutz. Erziehungsgeld. Elternzeit*, Saarbrücken: Arbeitskammer des Saarlandes.

Ashenfelter, O. (1980), 'Unemployment as disequilibrium in a model of aggregate labor supply', *Econometrica*, **48** (3).

Atkinson, A.B. (1987), 'On the measurement of poverty', *Econometrica*, **55** (4).

Atkinson, A.B. (1989), *Poverty and Social Security*, Hemel Hampstead: Harvester Wheatsheaf.

Atkinson, A.B. (1995), *Incomes and the Welfare State: Essays on Britain and Europe*, Cambridge: Cambridge University Press.

Atkinson, A.B. (1998), *Poverty in Europe*, Oxford: Blackwell Publishers.

Atkinson, A.B. (1999), *The Economic Consequences of Rolling Back the Welfare State*, Munich Lectures in Economics, Cambridge, MA: MIT Press.

Atkinson, A.B. and J. Micklewright (1985), 'Unemployment benefits and unemployment duration: a study of men in the United Kingdom in the 1970s', Suntory-Toyota International Centre for Economics and Related Disciplines (STICERD) Working Paper No. 6., London: LSE.

Atkinson, A.B. and J. Micklewright (1989), 'Turning the screw: benefits for the unemployed, 1979–1988', in A.B. Atkinson, *Poverty and Social Security*, London: Harvester Wheatsheaf.

Atkinson, A.B. and J. Micklewright (1991), 'Unemployment compensation and labour market transitions: a critical review', *Journal of Economic Literature*, **29** (4), December.

Atkinson, A.B., K. Gardiner, V. Lechene and H. Sutherland (1993), 'Comparing poverty rates across countries: a case study of France and the United Kingdom', in S. Jenkins, A. Kapteyn and B. van Praag (eds), *The Distribution of Welfare and Household Production*, Cambridge: Cambridge University Press.

Bäcker, G. (1991), 'Sozialpolitik im vereinigten Deutschland' in *Aus Politik und Zeitgeschichte*, vol. **3–4**.

Baldwin, P. (1990), *The Politics of Social Solidarity: Class Bases in the European Welfare State, 1875–1975*, Cambridge: Cambridge University Press.

Becker, G.S. (1993), *Human Capital: A Theoretical and Empirical Analysis with Special Reference to Education*, Chicago: University of Chicago Press.

Behrendt, C. (2000), 'Do means-tested benefits alleviate poverty? Evidence on Germany, Sweden and the United Kingdom from the Luxembourg Income Study', *Journal of European Social Policy*, **10** (1).

Bentolila, S. and G. Bertola (1990), 'Firing costs and labour demand: how bad is Eurosclerosis?' *Review of Economic Studies*, **57** (3).

Berger, H. (1999), 'Erwerbssituation der Haushalte', in H. Berger, W. Hinrichs, E. Priller and A. Schultz, *Privathaushalte im Vereinigungsprozeß: Ihre soziale Lage in Ost- und Westdeutschland*, Frankfurt: Campus.

Bernardi, F., R. Layte, A. Schizzerotto and S. Jacobs (2000), 'Who exits unemployment? Institutional features, individual characteristics and chances of getting a job. A comparison of Britain and Italy', in D. Gallie and S. Paugam (eds), *Welfare Regimes and the Experience of Unemployment*, Oxford: Oxford University Press.

Bloendal, S. and M. Pearson (1995), 'Unemployment and other non-employment benefits', *Oxford Review of Economic Policy*, vol. **11** (1).

Bloendal, S. and S. Scarpetta (1997), 'Early retirement in OECD countries: the role of social security systems', *OECD Economic Studies*, **29**.

Blossfeld, H.P. (1989), *Kohortendifferenzierung und Karriereprozeß: Eine Längsschnittstudie über die Veränderung der Bildungs- und Berufschancen im Lebenslauf*, Frankfurt: Campus.

Blossfeld, H.P. (1998), 'A dynamic integration of micro-and macro-perspectives using longitudinal data and event history models', in H.P. Blossfeld and G. Prein, *Rational Choice Theory and Large-scale Data Analysis*, Boulder, Colorado: Westview Press.

Blossfeld, H.P. and C. Hakim (eds) (1997), *Between Equalization and Marginalization: Women Working Part-time in Europe and America*, Oxford: Oxford University Press.

Blossfeld, H.P. and G. Rohwer (1995), *Techniques of Event History Modelling: New Approaches to Causal Analysis*, Mahwah, NJ: Lawrence Erlbaum.

Blossfeld, H.P., G. Giannelli and K.U. Mayer (1993), 'Is there a new service proletariat? The tertiary sector and social inequality in Germany', in G. Esping-Andersen (ed.), *Changing Classes: Stratification and Mobility in Post-industrial Societies*, London: Sage.

Blossfeld, H.P., A. Hammerle and K.U. Mayer (1989), *Event History Analysis*, Hillsdale, New Jersey: Lawrence Erlbaum Associates.

Boeheim, R. and M. Taylor (2000), 'The search for success: do the unemployed find stable employment?', Working Paper of the ESRC Research Centre on Micro-social change 2000–05, Colchester: University of Essex.

Bosch, G. and M. Knuth (1993), 'The labour market in East Germany', *Cambridge Journal of Economics*, **17** (3).

Brauns, H., M. Gangl and S. Scherer (1999), 'Education and unemployment: patterns of labour market entry in France, the United Kingdom and West Germany', MZES Working Paper No. 6, Mannheim: MZES.

Brown, J. (1990), *Victims or Villains? Social Security Benefits in Unemployment*, York: Joseph Rowntree Memorial Trust.

Brühl, A. (1996), *Mein Recht auf Sozialhilfe*, Munich: Deutscher Taschenbuch Verlag.

Büchel, F., M. Diewald, P. Krause, A. Mertens and H. Solga (2000), *Zwischen drinnen und draussen*, Opladen: Leske und Budrich.

Büchtemann, C. (1993), *Employment Security and Labor Market Behavior*, Ithaca, New York: Cornell University.

Büchtemann, C. and U. Walwei (1996), 'Employment security and dismissal protection', in G. Schmid, J. O'Reilly and K. Schoemann (eds), *International Handbook of Labour Market Policy Evaluation*, Aldershot, UK and Brookfield, USA: Edward Elgar.

Buhmann, B., L. Rainwater, G. Schmaus and T. Smeeding (1988), 'Equivalence scales, well-being inequality, and poverty: sensitivity estimates across ten countries using the Luxembourg Income Study Database', *Review of Income and Wealth*, **34** (2).

Bundesanstalt für Arbeit (various years), *Amtliche Nachrichten der Bundesanstalt für Arbeit*, Nuremberg.

Bundesministerium für Arbeit und Sozialordnung (2000), *Statistisches Taschenbuch 2000*, Bonn: Bundesministerium für Arbeit und Sozialordnung.

Burkhauser, R., M. Kreyenfeld and G. Wagner (1997), 'The German Socio-Economic Panel: a representative sample of reunited Germany and its parts', in T. Dunn and J. Schwarze (eds), Proceedings of the 1996 Second International Conference of the German Socio-Economic Panel Study Users, DIW Vierteljahresheft, 1/97, Berlin: DIW.

Burkhauser, R., T. Smeeding and J. Merz (1996), 'Relative inequality and poverty in Germany and the United States using alternative equivalence scales', *Review of Income and Wealth*, **42** (4).

Cantillon, S. and B. Nolan (1998), 'Are married women more deprived than their husbands?', *Journal of Social Policy*, **27** (2).

Casey, B. (1996), 'Exit options from the labour force', in G. Schmid, J. O'Reilly and K. Schömann (eds), *International Handbook of Labour Market Policy Evaluation*, Cheltenham, UK and Brookfield, US: Edward Elgar.

Castles, F. and D. Mitchell (1993), 'Worlds of welfare and families of nations' in F. Castles (ed.), *Families of Nations*, Dartmouth: Aldershot.

Chamberlayne, P. (1994), 'Women and social policy', in J. Clasen and R. Freeman (eds), *Social Policy in Germany*, London: Harvester Wheatsheaf.

Child Poverty Action Group (1996), *Rights Guide to Non-means-tested Benefits*, London: CPAG.

Child Poverty Action Group (1997), *Rights Guide to Non-means-tested Benefits*, London: CPAG.

Clasen, J. (1994a), *Paying the Jobless: a Comparison of Unemployment Benefit Policies in Great Britain and Germany*, Aldershot: Avebury.

Clasen, J. (1994b), 'Social security', in J. Clasen and R. Freeman (eds), *Social Policy in Germany*, London: Harvester Wheatsheaf.

Clasen, J. (1997), 'Social insurance in Germany: dismantling or reconstruction?' in J. Clasen (ed.), *Social Insurance in Europe*, Bristol: Policy Press.

Coleman, J. (1990), *Foundations of Social Theory*, Cambridge, MA: Harvard University Press.

Cooke, K. (1987) 'The withdrawal from paid work of the wives of unemployed men: a review of research', *Journal of Social Policy*, **16**.

Connelly, R. (1992), 'The effect of child care costs on married women's labor force participation', *Review of Economics and Statistics*, **74** (1).

Coulter, F., F. Cowell and S. Jenkins (1992), 'Equivalence scale relativites and the extent of inequality and poverty', *The Economic Journal*, **102** (414).

Cox, D. (1972), 'Regression models and life tables', *Journal of the Royal Statistical Society*, B34.

Crompton, R. (1997), *Women and Work in Modern Britain*, Oxford: Oxford University Press.

Daly, M. (1994), 'Gender in British income maintenance', *Sociology*, **28** (3).

Daly, M. (1996), *Social Security, Gender and Equality in the European Union*, Brussels: European Commission.

Daly, M. (1997), 'Welfare states under pressure: cash benefits in European welfare states over the last ten years', *Journal of European Social Policy*, **7** (2).

Daly, M. (2000), *The Gender Division of Welfare: The Impact of the British and German Welfare States*, Cambridge: Cambridge University Press.

Davies, R. (1994), 'From cross-sectional to longitudinal analysis', in A. Dale and R. Davies (eds), *Analyzing Social and Political Change*, London: Sage.

Davies, R., P. Elias and R. Penn (1992), 'The relationship between a husband's unemployment and his wife's participation in the labour force', *Oxford Bulletin of Economics and Statistics*, **54** (2).

Davis, H. and H. Joshi (1994), 'Sex, sharing and the distribution of income', *Journal of Social Policy*, **23** (3).

De Graaf, P. and W.C. Ultee (1991), 'Labour market transitions of husbands and wives in the Netherlands between 1980 and 1986, a contribution to the debate on the new underclass', *The Netherlands' Journal of Social Sciences*, **27**.

De Graaf, P.M. and W.C. Ultee (2000), 'United in employment, united in unemployment? Employment and unemployment of couples in the European union in 1994', in D. Gallie and S. Paugam (eds), *Welfare Regimes and the Experience of Unemployment in Europe*, Oxford: OUP.

Department of Social Security (various years), *Social Security Statistics*, London: HMSO.

Department of Social Security (1995), *Households Below Average Income 1979–1992/93*, London: HMSO.

Dex, S., S. Gustafsson, N. Smith and T. Callan (1995), 'Cross-national comparisons of the labour force participation of women married to unemployed men', *Oxford Economic Papers*, **47** (4).

DiPrete, T. and P. McManus (2000), 'Family change, employment transitions, and the welfare state: household income dynamics in the United States and Germany', *American Sociological Review*, **65** (June).

DiPrete, T., P. de Graaf, R. Luijkx, M. Tahlin and H.P. Blossfeld (1997), 'Collectivist versus individualist mobility regimes? Structural change and job mobility in four countries', *American Journal of Sociology*, **103** (2).

Disney, R. (1999), 'Why have older men stopped working?', in P. Gregg and J. Wadsworth (eds), *The State of Working Britain*, Manchester: Manchester University Press.

Disney, R. and S. Webb (1991), 'Why are there so many long-term sick in Britain?' *Economic Journal*, **101** (405).

Dolado, J., F. Kramarz, S. Machin, A. Manning, D. Margolis and C. Teulings (1996), 'The economic impact of minimum wages in Europe', *Economic Policy*, **11** (23).

Doris, A. (1999a), 'The effect of the means testing of benefits on household income and the incentives to work of the wives of unemployed men', Maynooth University Working Paper, March 1999. Dublin: Maynooth University.

Doris, A. (1999b), 'Means testing disincentives and the labour supply of the wives of unemployed men: results from a fixed effects model', Maynooth University Working Paper. Dublin: Maynooth University.

Düll, N. and K. Vogler-Ludwig (1998), 'Germany', in *SYSDEM Trends*, **30**.

Eardley, T., J. Bradshaw, J. Ditch, I. Gough and P. Whiteford (1996), 'Social assistance in OECD countries, Volume II: Country Reports', Department of Social Security Research Report No. 47, London: HMSO.

Elias, P. (1997), 'Who forgot they were unemployed?', Working Paper of the ESRC Research Centre on Micro-social change 97–19, Colchester: University of Essex.

Ercolani, M. and S. Jenkins (2000), 'The labour force participation of women married to unemployed men. Is there an added worker effect?', Unpublished paper, Institute for Labour Research, University of Essex.

Erikson, R. and J. Goldthorpe (1993), *The Constant Flux*, Oxford: Clarendon Press.

Esping-Andersen, G. (1990), *The Three Worlds of Welfare Capitalism*, London: Polity Press.

Esping-Andersen, G. (1998), 'The effects of regulation on unemployment levels and structure: the evidence from comparative research', Unpublished paper, Department of Sociology and Social Research, University of Trento.

Esping-Andersen, G. (1999), *Social Foundations of Postindustrial Economies*, Oxford: Oxford University Press.

European Commission (1994), 'Growth, competitiveness, employment: the challenges and ways forward into the 21st century', White Paper, Luxembourg: European Commission.

European Commission (1995), *Social Protection in Europe*, Luxembourg: European Commission.

European Commission (1997), *Employment in Europe*, Luxembourg: European Commission.

European Commission (1999), *Employment in Europe*, Luxembourg: European Commission.

Eurostat (1998), *ECHP Longitudinal Users Database Waves 1 and 2 Manual*, Luxembourg: Eurostat.

Eurostat (various years), *Labour Force Survey*, Brussels: European Commission.

Evans, M. (1996), 'Means-testing the unemployed in Britain, France and Germany', STICERD Welfare State Programme Discussion Paper WSP/117, London: London School of Economics.

Evans, M., D. Piachaud and H. Sutherland (1994), 'Designed for the poor – poorer by design?' STICERD Welfare State Programme Discussion Paper WSP/105, London: London School of Economics

Fawcett, H. and T. Papodopoulus (1997), 'Social exclusion, social citizenship and de-commodification: an evaluation of the adequacy of support for the unemployed in the European Union', *West European Politics*, **20** (3).

Fehlker, C. and C. Purfield (1998), 'A tale of two countries. A comparison of UK and German unemployment spells', Paper presented to the Third German Socio-economic Panel Users Conference, Berlin, July 1998.

Ferrera, M. (1996), 'The southern model of welfare in social Europe', *Journal of European Social Policy*, **6** (1).

Gallie, D. and S. Paugam (2000), *Welfare Regimes and the Experience of Unemployment in Europe*, Oxford: Oxford University Press.

Gallie, D., S. Jacobs and S. Paugam (2000), 'Poverty and financial hardship among the unemployed', in D. Gallie and S. Paugam, *Welfare Regimes and the Experience of Unemployment in Europe*, Oxford: Oxford University Press.

Gallie, D., C. Marsh and C. Vogler (1994), *Social Change and the Experience of Unemployment*, Oxford: Oxford University Press.

Gangl, M. (2002), 'Welfare state stabilization of employment careers: unemployment benefits and job histories in the United States and West Germany', Discussion Paper FS I 02–207 WZB für Sozialforschung.

Gangl, M. (2003), *Unemployment Dynamics in the United States and West Germany: Economic Restructuring, Institutions, and Labor Market Processes*, Heidelberg: Physica/Springer.

Garcia, J. (1991), 'A participation model with non-convex budget sets: the case of the wives of the unemployed in Great Britain', *Applied Economics*, **23** (8).

Gauthier, A. (1996), *The State and the Family. A Comparative Analysis of Family Policies in Industrialized Countries*, Oxford: OUP.

Giannelli, G. and J. Micklewright (1995), 'Why do women married to unemployed men have low participation rates?', *Oxford Bulletin of Economics and Statistics*, **57** (4).

Ginsburg, N. (1979), *Class, Capital and Society*, London: Macmillan.

Gornick, J., M. Meyers and K.E. Ross (1997), 'Supporting the employment of mothers', *Journal of European Social Policy*, **7** (1).

Gosling, A., P. Johnston, J. McCrae and G. Paull (1997), *The Dynamics of Low Pay and Unemployment in Early 1990s Britain*, London: Insitute for Fiscal Studies.

Green, F. (2000), 'Training in work', Paper presented to the seminar 'Employability and the Quality of Working Life", at Nuffield College Oxford, October 26.

Gregg, P., K. Hansen and J. Wadsworth (1999), 'The rise of the workless household', in P. Gregg and J. Wadsworth (eds), *The State of Working Britain*, Manchester: Manchester University Press.

Grimshaw, D. and J. Rubery (1997), 'Workforce heterogeneity and unemployment benefits: the need for policy reassessment in the European Union', *Journal of European Social Policy*, **7** (4).

Grubb, D. (2000), 'Eligibility criteria for unemployment benefits', *OECD Economic Studies*, **31**, Paris: OECD.

Grubb, D. and W. Wells (1993), 'Employment regulation and patterns of work in EC countries', *OECD Economic Studies*, **21**.

Hagenaars, A., K. de Vos and A. Zaidi (1994), *Poverty Statistics in the Late 1980s*, Luxembourg: Eurostat.

Hahn, T. and G. Schön (1996), 'Besonderheiten ostdeutscher Arbeitslosigkeit', in H.J. Andress (ed.), *Fünf Jahre Danach: Zur Entwicklung von Arbeitsmarkt und Sozialstruktur im vereinten Deutschland*, Berlin: de Gruyter.

Haisken-De New, J. and J. Frick (eds) (1998), *Desktop Companion to the German Socio-Economic Panel Study (GSOEP). Version 2.2*, Berlin: DIW.

Halpin, B. (1997), 'Unified BHPS work-life histories: combining multiple sources into a user-friendly format', Technical Papers of the ESRC Research Centre on Micro-social Change, Technical Paper 13, Colchester: University of Essex.

Halsey, A., H. Lauder, P. Brown and A. Wells (1997), *Education, Culture, Economy and Society*, Oxford: Oxford University Press.

Hanesch, W. (1996), 'Armut und Unterversorgung in Deutschland', in H.J. Andress (ed.), *Fünf Jahre Danach: Zur Entwicklung von Arbeitsmarkt und Sozialstruktur im vereinten Deutschland*, Berlin: de Gruyter.

Hannan, M., K. Schömann and H.P. Blossfeld (1990), 'Sex and sector differences in the dynamics of wage growth in the Federal Republic of Germany', *American Sociological Review*, **55** (5).

Hauser, R. (1995), 'Das empirische Bild der Armut in der Bundesrepublik Deutschland', *Aus Politik und Zeitgeschichte*, B31–32.

Hauser, R. (1997), 'Vergleichende Analyse der Einkommensverteilung und der Einkommensarmut in den alten und neuen Bundeslaendern, 1990 bis 1995', in I. Becker and R. Hauser (eds), *Einkommensverteilung und Armut. Deutschland auf dem Weg zur Vierfünftelgesellschaft?*, Frankfurt: Campus.

Hauser, R. and B. Nolan with K. Mörsdorf and W. Strengmann-Kuhn (2000), 'Unemployment and poverty: change over time', in D. Gallie and S. Paugam (eds), *Welfare Regimes and the Experience of Unemployment in Europe*, Oxford: Oxford University Press.

Hennock, E. (1987), *British Social Reform and German Precedents. The Case of Social Insurance 1880–1914*, Oxford: Clarendon Press.

Höllinger, F. (1991), 'Frauenerwerbstaetigkeit und Wandel der Geschlechtsrollen im internationalen Vergleich', *Kölner Zeitschrift für Soziologie und Sozialpsychologie*, **43** (4).

Holst, E. (2000), *Die Stille Reserve am Arbeitsmarkt: Grösse – Zusammensetzung – Verhalten*, Berlin: Sigma.

Holst, E. and J. Schupp (1995), 'Apekte der Arbeitsmarktentwicklung in Ostdeutschland', DIW Wochenbericht 23/95 Berlin: DIW.

Holst, E. and J. Schupp (1996), 'Erwerbstatigkeit von Frauen in Ost und Westdeutschland weiterhin von steigender Bedeutung', DIW Wochenbericht 28/96. Berlin: DIW.

Hujer, R. and H. Schneider (1995), 'Institutionelle und strukturelle Determinanten der Arbeitslosigkeit in Westdeutschland: Eine mikroökonomische Analyse mit Paneldaten', in B. Gahlen, H. Hesse and H.J. Ramser (eds), *Arbeistlosigkeit und die Möglichkeiten ihrer Überwindung*, Wirtschaftswissenschaftliches Seminar Ottobeuren, Band 25. Tübingen: Mohr.

Humphrey, D. (1940), 'Alleged "additional workers" in the measurement of female labor supply', *Review of Economic Studies*, **47**.

Hunt, J. (1995), 'The effect of unemployment compensation on unemployment duration in Germany', *Journal of Labour Economics*, **13** (1).

Hutton, S. (1994), 'Men's and women's incomes: evidence from survey data', *Journal of Social Policy*, **23** (1).

Jackman, R. and S. Savouri (1999), 'Has Britain solved the "regional problem?"', in P. Gregg and J. Wadsworth (eds), *The State of Working Britain*, Manchester: Manchester University Press.

Jahoda, M., P.F. Lazarsfeld and H. Zeisel (1933), *Die Arbeitslosen von Marienthal: Ein soziographischer Versuch über die Wirkungen langandauernder Arbeitslosigkeit*, reprinted in S. Hirzel (ed.) (1975), Frankfurt a.M.: Suhrkamp.

Jarvis, S. and S. Jenkins (1995), 'Do the poor stay poor? New evidence about income dynamics from the British Household Panel Survey', ESRC Occasional Paper 95-2, Colchester: University of Essex.

Jarvis, S. and S. Jenkins (1996), 'Changing places: income mobility and poverty dynamics in Britain', ESRC Working Paper 96–19, Colchester: University of Essex.

Jenkins, S. (1991), 'Poverty measurement and the within household distribution: agenda for action', *Journal of Social Policy*, **20** (4).

Jenkins, S. (2000), 'Modelling household income dynamics', *Journal of Population Economics*, **13** (4).

Jenkins, S. and F. Cowell (1994), 'Parametric equivalence scales and scale relativities', *The Economic Journal*, **104** (425).

Kaiser, L. and T. Siedler (2001), 'Die Dauer von Arbeitslosigkeit in Deutschland und Großbritannien: Ein internationaler Vergleich (1990–1995)', in IAB, Mitteilungen aus der Arbeitsmarkt- und Berufsforschung 4/2001.

Kangas, O. (1994), 'The politics of social security: on regressions, qualitative comparisons, and cluster analysis', in T. Janoski and A. Hicks (eds), *The*

*Comparative Political Economy of the Welfare State*, Cambridge: Cambridge University Press.

Kell, M. and J. Wright (1990), 'Benefits and the labour supply of women married to unemployed men', *Economic Journal* (supplement), **100** (400).

Kerr, C., J. Dunlop, F. Harbison and C. Myers (1960), *Industrialism and the Industrial Man: The Problems of Labor and Management in Economic Growth*, Cambridge, MA: Harvard University Press.

Klös, H-P. and K. Lichtbau (1998), 'Möglichkeiten und Grenzen internationaler Querschnittvergleiche', in J. Schupp, F. Büchel, M. Diewald and R. Habich, *Arbeitsmarktstatistik zwischen Realitaet und Fiktion*, Berlin: Sigma.

König, Lüttinger and Müller (1988), 'A comparative analysis of the development and structure of eductional systems: methodological foundations and the construction of a comparative educational scale', CASMIN Working Paper no. 12, Mannheim: University of Mannheim.

Kraus, F. and V. Steiner (1998), 'Modelling heaping effects in unemployment duration models – with an application to retrospective event data in the German Socio-economic Panel', *Jahrbücher für Nationalökonomie und Statistik*, **217** (5).

Krause, P. (1998), 'Low income dynamics in a unified Germany', in L. Leisering and R. Walker (eds), *The Dynamics of Modern Society*, Bristol: Policy Press.

Kronauer, M. (1998), 'Social exclusion and underclass new concepts for the analysis of poverty', in H.J. Andress (ed.), *Empirical Poverty Research in Comparative Perspective*, Aldershot: Ashgate.

Kruppe, T., K. Schömann and H. Oschmiansky (1999), 'Transitions to retirement', inforMISEP Policies, Edition no. 65, Spring.

Lampard, R. (1994), 'An examination of the relationship between marital dissolution and unemployment', in D. Gallie, C. Marsh and C. Vogler, *Social Change and the Experience of Unemployment*, Oxford: Oxford University Press.

Leibfried, S. and W. Voges (eds) (1992), 'Armut im Modernen Wohlfahrtstaat', *Sonderheft der Kölner Zeitschrift für Soziologie und Sozialpsychologie*, Köln: Westdeutscher Verlag.

Leisering, L. and S. Leibfried (1999), *Time and Poverty in Western Welfare States*, Cambridge: Cambridge University Press.

Lewis, J. (1992), 'Gender and the development of welfare regimes', *Journal of European Social Policy*, **2** (3).

Lewis, J. (1997), 'Lone mothers: the British case', in J. Lewis (ed.), *Lone Mothers in European Welfare Regimes*, London: J. Kingsley Publishers.

Lewis, J. with B. Hobson (1997), 'Introduction', in J. Lewis (ed.), *Lone Mothers in European Welfare Regimes*, London: J. Kingsley Publishers.

Lewis, J. and I. Ostner (1994), 'Gender and the evolution of European social policies', Zentrum für Sozialpolitik working paper 4/94. Bremen: Zentrum für Sozialpolitik.

Lieberson, S. (1985), *Making it Count*, Berkeley: University of California Press.

Littlewood, P., I. Glorieux, S. Herkommer and I. Jönsson (1999), *Social Exclusion in Europe. Problems and Paradigms*, Aldershot: Ashgate.

Martin, J. (1996), 'Measures of replacement rates for the purpose of international comparisons: a note', *OECD Economic Studies*, **26**, 1996/1.

Marx, K. (1864), *Capital, Volume One*, reprinted in R. Tucker (ed.) (1978), *The Marx-Engels Reader*, Second edn, New York: W.W. Norton and Company.

McGinnity, F. (2001), 'Who benefits? A comparison of welfare and outcomes for the unemployed in Britain and Germany', Unpublished doctoral thesis, Oxford: Nuffield College.

McKay, S. and K. Rowlingson (1999), *Social Security in Britain*, London: Macmillan.

McKee, L. and C. Bell (1985), 'Marital and Family Relations in Times of Male Unemployment', in B. Roberts, R. Finnegan and D. Gallie (eds), *New Approaches to Economic Life*, Manchester: Manchester University Press.

Menard, S. (1995), *Applied Logistic Regression Analysis*, London: Sage.

Meyer, T. (1997), *Ungleich besser? Die ökonomische Unabhaengigkeit von Frauen im Zeichen der Expansion sozialer Dienstleistungen*, Berlin: Sigma.

Mitchell, D. (1991), *Income Transfers in Ten Welfare States*, Aldershot: Avebury.

Morris, L. (1991), 'Social security provision for the unemployed', Social Security Advisory Committee, Research Paper 3, London: HMSO.

Mortensen, D. and C. Pissarides (1999), 'Unemployment responses to "skill-biased" technology shocks: the role of labour market policy', *Economic Journal*, **109** (455).

Müller, W. and Y. Shavit (1998), 'The institutional embeddedness of the stratification process: a comparative study of qualifications and occupations in thirteen countries', in Y. Shavit and W. Müller (eds), *From School to Work: A Comparative Study of Educational Qualifications and Occupational Destinations*, Oxford: Clarendon Press.

Müller, W., S. Steinmann and R. Ell (1998), 'Germany: education and market entry', in Y. Shavit and W. Müller (eds), *From School to Work. A Comparative Study of Qualification and Occupations in Thirteen Countries*, Oxford: Oxford University Press.

Murray, I. (1995), *Desperately seeking – a Job: A Critical Guide to the 1996 Jobseeker's Allowance*, London: Unemployment Unit.

Nickell, S. (1997), 'Unemployment and labour market rigidities: Europe versus North America', *Journal of Economic Perspectives*, **11** (3).

Nickell, S. (1999), 'Unemployment in Britain', in P. Gregg and J. Wadsworth (eds), *The State of Working Britain*, Manchester: Manchester University Press.

Nolan, B., R. Hauser and J.P. Zoyem (2000), 'The changing effects of social protection on poverty', in D. Gallie and S. Paugam (eds), *Welfare Regimes and the Experience of Unemployment in Europe*, Oxford: Oxford University Press.

O'Connor, J. (1973), *The Fiscal Crisis of the State*, New York: St. Martin's Press.

O'Connor, J. (1996), 'From women in the welfare states to gendering welfare regimes', *Current Sociology*, **44** (2).

OECD (1982), *Economic Surveys – Germany*, Paris: OECD.

OECD (1983), *Economic Surveys – Germany*, Paris: OECD.

OECD (1991), *Employment Outlook*, Paris: OECD.

OECD (1994), *OECD Jobs Study, Parts I and II*, Paris: OECD.

OECD (1995), *Economic Outlook*, Paris, no. 57, Paris: OECD.

OECD (1996a), *Economic Surveys – Germany*, Paris: OECD.

OECD (1996b), *Economic Surveys – United Kingdom*, Paris: OECD.

OECD (1996c), *Employment Outlook*, Paris: OECD.

OECD (1997a), *Economic Outlook*, December, No. 62, Paris: OECD.

OECD (1997b), *Employment Outlook*, Paris:OECD.

OECD (1997c), *Labour Force Statistics, 1976–1996*, Paris: OECD.

OECD (1998), 'Getting started, settling in: the transition from education to the labour market', in *Employment Outlook*, Paris: OECD.

OECD (1999), *Employment Outlook*, Paris: OECD.

OECD (2000), *Employment Outlook*, Paris: OECD.

Office for National Statistics (1985–1998), *Employment Gazette*, London: Office for National Statistics.

O'Reilly, J. and S. Bothfeld (2002), 'What happens after working part-time? Integration, maintenance or exclusionary transitions in Britain and Western Germany', *Cambridge Journal of Economics*, **26** (4).

O'Reilly, J. and C. Fagan (1998), *Part-time Prospects: International Comparisons of Part-time Work in Europe, North America and the Pacific Rim*, London: Routledge.

Orloff, A. (1993), 'Gender and the social rights of citizenship: the comparative analysis of gender relations and welfare states', *American Sociological Review*, **58** (3).

Ostner, I. (1993), 'Slow motion: women, work and the family in Germany', in J. Lewis (ed.), *Women and Social Policies in Europe*, Aldershot, UK and Brookfield, US: Edward Elgar.

Ostner, I. and J. Lewis (1995), 'Gender and the evolution of European social policies', in P. Pierson and S. Leibfried (eds), *Fragmented Social Policy*, Washington: Brookings Institute.

Paugam, S. (1996), *L'exclusion. L'état des Savoirs*, Paris: La Decouverte.

Paull, G. (1997), 'Dynamic labour market behaviour in the British Household Panel Survey: the effects of recall bias and panel attrition', Discussion Paper 10, Centre for Economic Performance, London: CEPR.

Pedersen, L., H. Weise, S. Jacobs and M. White (2000), 'Lone mothers' poverty and employment', in D. Gallie and S. Paugam (eds), *Welfare Regimes and the Experience of Unemployment in Europe*, Oxford: Oxford University Press.

Pfau-Effinger, B. (1998), 'Culture or structure as explanations for difference in part-time work in Germany, Finland and the Netherlands?', in J. O'Reilly and C. Fagan (eds), *Part-time Prospects: International Comparisons of Part-time Work in Europe, North America and the Pacific Rim*, London: Routledge.

Pierson, P. (1994), *Dismantling the Welfare State? Reagan, Thatcher and the Politics of Retrenchment*, Cambridge: Cambridge University Press.

Pischner, R and U. Rendtel (1993), 'Quer und Laengschnittgewichtung des Sozio-ökonomichen Panels', DIW Discussion paper No. 69. Berlin: DIW.

Pischner, R. and G. Wagner (1995), 'Bilanz der Erwerbschancen fünf Jahre nach der Wende in Ostdeutschland', DIW Wochenbericht 46/95. Berlin: DIW.

Przeworski, A. and H. Teune (1970), *The Logic of Comparative Social Inquiry*, New York: Wiley.

Ragin, C.C. (1987), *The Comparative Method*, Berkeley: University of California Press.

Rake, K. (1998), 'Ageing and inequality: older women and men in the British, French and German welfare states', Unpublished doctoral thesis, Oxford: Nuffield College.

Reissert, B. (forthcoming), 'Unemployment protection in Germany: the system and its changes in the 1990s', in J. Clasen, M. Ferrera and M. Rhodes (eds), *Welfare States and the Challenge of Unemployment: Reforming Policies and Institutions in the European Union*, London: Routledge.

Rendtel, U. (1990), 'Teilnahmebereitschaft in Panelstudien: Zwischen Beeinflussung, Vertrauen und Sozialer Selektion', *Kölner Zeitschrift für Soziologie*, 42.

Rendtel, U. and F. Büchel (1994), 'Tests for non-ignorable panel attrition and their application on wage estimates from the GSOEP', DIW Discussion paper No. 89. Berlin: DIW.

Rendtel, U., R. Langeheine and R. Bernsten (1998), 'The estimation of poverty-dynamics using different measurements of household income', *Review of Income and Wealth*, **44** (1).

Robinson, P. (1997), *Labour Market Studies: UK*, Luxembourg: Commission of the European Communities.

Room, G. (1995), *Beyond the Threshold. The Measurement and Analysis of Social Exclusion*, Bristol: The Polity Press.

Rosenhaft, E. (1994), 'The historical development of German Social Policy', in J. Clasen and R. Freeman (eds), *Social Policy in Germany*, London: Harvester Wheatsheaf.

Rothschild, K. (1993), 'Like a Lehrstück by Brecht: notes on the German reunification drama', *Cambridge Journal of Economics*, **17** (3).

Rubery, J., Smith, M., Fagan, C. and Grimshaw, D. (1998), *Women and European Employment*, London: Routledge.

Ruspini, E. (1998), 'Women and poverty dynamics in Germany and Britain', *Journal of European Social Policy*, **8** (4).

Russell, H. (1996), 'Women's experience of unemployment: a study of British women in the 1980s', Unpublished doctoral thesis, Oxford: Nuffield College.

Russell, H. and P. Barbieri (2000), 'Gender and the experience of unemployment', in D. Gallie and S. Paugam (eds), *Welfare Regimes and the Experience of Unemployment in Europe*, Oxford: OUP.

Sainsbury, D. (1994), *Gendering Welfare States*, London: Sage.

Saraceno, C. (1997), *Family Change, Family Policies and the Restructuring of Welfare*, Paris: OECD.

Schluter, C. (1995), 'Social security and social assistance in Germany', STICERD Welfare State Programme Research Note WSP/RN/29. London: LSE.

Schmid, G. and B. Reissert (1996), 'Unemployment compensation and labour market transitions', in G. Schmid, J. O'Reilly and K. Schömann (eds), *International Handbook of Labour Market Policy Evaluation*, Cheltenham, UK and Brookfield, US: Edward Elgar.

Schmid, G., B. Reissert and G. Bruche (1992), *Unemployment Insurance and Active Labour Market Policy: An International Comparison of Financing Systems*. Detroit: Wayne State University Press.

Schömann, K. (2002), 'Training transitions in the EU: different policies but similar effects?', in K. Schömann and P.J. O'Connell, *Education, Training and Employment Dynamics: Transitional Labour Markets in the European Union*. Cheltenham, UK and Northampton, MA, USA: Edward Elgar.

Sell, S. (1998), 'Entwicklung und Reform des Arbeitsförderungsgesetzes als Anpassung des Sozialrechts an flexible Erwerbsformen? Zur Zumutbarkeit von Arbeit und Eigenverantwortung von Arbeitnehmern', in IAB, Mitteilungen aus der Arbeitsmarkt- und Berufsforschung, **31** (3).

Shavit, Y. and W. Müller (1998), *From School to Work. A Comparative Study of Qualification and Occupations in Thirteen Countries*, Oxford: Oxford University Press.

Siebert, H. (1997), 'Labour Market Rigidities: At the Root of Unemployment in Europe', *Journal of Economic Perspectives*, **11** (3).

Smith, M., C. Fagan and J. Rubery (1998), 'Where and why is part-time work growing in Europe?', in J. O'Reilly and C. Fagan, *Part-time Prospects: International Comparisons of Part-time Work in Europe, North America and the Pacific Rim*, London: Routledge.

Spiezia, V. (2000), 'The effects of benefits on unemployment and wages: a comparison of unemployment compensation systems,' *International Labour Review*, **139** (1).

Statistisches Bundesamt (various years), *Statistisches Jahrbuch für die Bundesrepublik Deutschland*, Stuttgart: Metzer-Pöschel.

Statistisches Bundesamt (1998), *Sozialhilfe in Deutschland: Entwicklung und Strukturen*, Stuttgart: Metzer-Pöschel.

Statistisches Bundesamt (2001), *Überblick über die Verfügbarkeit EU-harmonisierter Erwerbstätigen- und Arbeitslosenzahlen sowie Arbeitslosenquoten*, Mimeo, Wiesbaden: Statistisches Bundesamt.

Steiner, V. (1997), 'Extended benefit entitlement periods and the duration of unemployment in West Germany', ZEW Discussion Paper, Mannheim: ZEW.

Sutherland, H. (1997), 'Women, men and the redistribution of income', *Fiscal Studies*, **18** (1).

Taylor, M. (ed.) with J. Brice, N. Buck and E. Prentice-Lane (1999), *British Household Panel Survey User Manual Volume A: Introduction, Technical Report and Appendices*, Colchester: University of Essex.

Trappe, H. (1995), *Emanzipation oder Zwang? Frauen in der DDR zwischen Beruf, Familie und Sozialpolitik*, Berlin: Akademie Verlag.

Ultee, W., J. Dessens and W. Jansen (1988), 'Why does unemployment come in couples? An analysis of (un)employment and (non)employment homogamy tables for Canada, the Netherlands and the United States in the 1980s', *European Sociological Review*, **4** (2).

van Kersbergen, K. (1995), *Social Capitalism: A Study of Christian Democracy and the Welfare State*, London: Routledge.

van Oorschot, W. (1991), 'Non-take-up of social security in Europe', *Journal of European Social Policy*, **1** (1).

Voges, W. and G. Rohwer (1992), 'Receiving social assistance in Germany: risk and duration', *Journal of European Social Policy*, **2** (3).

Wagner, G., R. Burkhauser and F. Behringer (1993), 'The English language public use file of the German Socio-Economic Panel', *Journal of Human Resources*, **28** (2).

Webb, S. (1994), 'Social insurance and poverty alleviation: an empirical analysis', in S. Baldwin and J. Falkingham (eds), *Social Security and Social Change*, Hemel Hempstead: Harvester Wheatsheaf.

Whelan, C.T. (1994), 'Social class, unemployment and psychological sistress', *European Sociological Review*, **10** (1).

Whelan, C.T. and F. McGinnity (2000), 'Unemployment and satisfaction: a European analysis', in D. Gallie and S. Paugam (eds), *Welfare Regimes and the Experience of Unemployment*, Oxford: Oxford University Press.

Wilensky, H. and C. Lebeaux (1965), *Industrial Society and Social Welfare*, New York: Free Press.

# Index